Case Studies in Counseling Older Adults

Larry B. Golden

The University of Texas at San Antonio

Merrill
is an imprint of

Upper Saddle River, New Jersey
Columbus, Ohio

Library of Congress Cataloging-in-Publication Data

Case studies in counseling older adults / [edited by] Larry B. Golden.—1st ed.
  p. ; cm.
 Includes bibliographical references and index.
 ISBN-13: 978-0-13-223262-3
 ISBN-10: 0-13-223262-6
 1. Older people--Counseling of--Case studies. I. Golden, Larry B.
 [DNLM: 1. Mental Disorders--therapy--Case Reports. 2. Aged. 3.
Middle Aged. 4. Psychotherapy--methods—Case Reports. WT 150 C337
2009]
 HV1451.C37 2009
 362.6'6–dc22

                                        2008021794

Vice President and Executive Publisher: Jeffery W. Johnston
Publisher: Kevin M. Davis
Acquisitions Editor: Meredith D. Fossel
Senior Managing Editor: Pamela D. Bennett
Senior Project Manager: Mary M. Irvin
Editorial Assistant: Maren Vigilante
Senior Art Director: Diane C. Lorenzo
Cover Design: Candace Rowley
Cover Image: SuperStock
Operations Specialist: Matt Ottenweller
Director of Marketing: Quinn Perkson
Marketing Coordinator: Brian Mounts

This book was set in ITC Garamond by Aptara®, Inc. It was printed and bound by King
Printing Co., Inc. The cover was printed by King Printing Co., Inc.

Pearson Education Ltd.   Pearson Education Australia Pty. Limited
Pearson Education Singapore Pte. Ltd.   Pearson Education North Asia Ltd.
Pearson Education Canada, Ltd.   Pearson Educación de Mexico, S.A. de C.V.
Pearson Education—Japan   Pearson Education Malaysia Pte. Ltd.

Merrill
is an imprint of

PEARSON

3 4 5 6 7 8 9 10 V0CR 16 15 14 13 12
ISBN 13: 978-0-13-223262-3
ISBN 10:   0-13-223262-6

In Memory of Chester Norwood

Chet's courage was an inspiration to all of us who were with him at the end of his life.

Foreword: An Interview with J. Jeffries McWhirter

This is an interview with my mentor, J. Jeffries McWhirter, Professor Emeritus, Arizona State University (ASU). I met Jeff about thirty years ago (or so), when I was a single, long-haired doc student and Jeff was a newly minted assistant professor at ASU, husband and father. The Vietnam War was raging violently, and the Peace Movement was sweetly humming. Jeff and his wife, Mary, befriended me, as they have many ASU students. Now I am 64, married, and a grandfather, while Jeff is 69, still happily married to Mary, and a grandpa many times over (fifteen, soon to be sixteen). Jeff retired from ASU three years ago.

LG: Jeff, why did you retire? I thought you loved your work.

JM: I didn't particularly want to retire, but the social engineers created a situation for ASU faculty that financially I was just about as well off not working at all. They gave me a year's salary spread over two years for doing nothing!

LG: So, what's it like just sitting in a rocking chair all day?

JM: Since retiring, I've arranged short-term teaching assignments at NYU, Vanderbilt, and the University of Southern Maine. This year, because of a shortage of regular faculty, I'm teaching two courses each semester at ASU. I spent a month as a Fulbright Senior Specialist at Hacettepe University in Ankara, Turkey, where twenty-nine years earlier I had held a traditional Fulbright professorship. I've helped some of my children who are also counselor educators write the fourth edition of *At-Risk Youth: A Comprehensive Response*. I've been a research assistant to my oldest son, who is writing a history book on constitutional law. I keep up a small private practice as a psychologist. I have chaired seven accreditation site visits to counseling psychology Ph.D. programs. Mary and I, along with her two brothers and sometimes some of our grandchildren, have visited Chile, Uruguay, Argentina, Bolivia, Ecuador, Cuba, Belize, Guatemala, and the Maritime Provinces of Canada.

LG: What do you miss about full-time academic life?

JM: Well, they took away my office and my phone, and losing both of them has been a real pain. I had been in my office for twenty years and I had the same phone number for thirty-four years, so I was really attached to them. Of course, it's not as much of a problem for me as for the poor sucker that got my phone. I wonder if people are still calling me at that number—must be driving him or her crazy. Seriously, I know it's a cliché, but I really do miss my students. But it's something more than just that—I have had contact with some really nice students in New York, Maine, and Tennessee. It's more that my ASU students and I somehow belonged to the same tribe, family, or clan, and I don't quite belong anymore. This was particularly obvious to me at last winter's graduation ceremony—the first one that I attended since I retired. We have a special hooding ceremony for our graduate students that our Master of Counseling students—who don't get much individual attention at the large university commencement—organized a few years ago. About a dozen MC students were hooded by faculty. I did not know a single one of them! And the doctoral students who were being graduated were in their first or second year of their program when I last saw them. What happened? How could this be?

I suppose what I'm really missing is the community of scholars that my ASU students have represented to me. I do know that I can go to almost any school, clinic, or agency in Phoenix and run into former students. That is one of my great satisfactions. It is a sense of connectedness with something that is bigger than me.

LG: What don't you miss?

JM: Faculty meetings, chairing committees, grading comprehensive examinations, completing my annual performance evaluation. There's probably more. . . .

LG: Jeff, would you mind rambling on a bit about your experience of growing old.

JM: This getting old is a kick. I'm one of those people who have to experience or live something before I really understand it. Inside every 69-year-old man (such as myself) is a 19-year-old kid who just can't believe what is happening. Several years ago, I attended my fiftieth grade school reunion. I couldn't understand where all those old people came from. When I catch my reflection in the glass of the building I am passing, I see an old man, and it is shocking.

I used to wonder why old people say outrageous things. Now I think I know: Nobody challenges us. When I started at ASU, I had a wonderful colleague who was then about my age now. He loved recreational arguing about anything. Before I knew him, he was the Vice President for Academic Affairs at ASU. Apparently, he used to find out when various departments held their meetings and he made a habit of dropping in, raising a controversial issue, and enjoying the ensuing argument. Faculty complained about getting home three hours late for dinner. In later life, he complained that everyone was so respectful because of his age that he couldn't get an argument started. I don't like to argue much, but I know what he means. Younger people treat me like I'm fragile or that I know a whole lot more than I do. Neither is true.

Since retiring, I've lost my audience, i.e., my students. For nearly fifty years, my dear Mary has previewed my jokes and quips. My long-suffering children have heard all of my lectures. So at the same time I lose my classroom, my family has heard about enough. Pity the poor stranger or acquaintance I happen to run into.

LG: Jeff, would you mind talking about the health problems you've faced?

JM: For years my model for living my life and thinking about the end of it has been a great poem by Oliver Wendell Holmes, "The Wonderful One Horse Shay." The shay in the poem, ". . . was built in such a wonderful way that it ran in a perfect way. . . until it turned 100 years and a day. . . ." And then in one day the entire buggy collapsed in a heap of parts. Well, I didn't make it to a hundred. When I turned 60 (and 60 is not old if you're a tree), stuff started to fall off—a carpal tunnel operation, microscopic surgery on my knee, dental problems with new fillings and caps and a tooth implant, prostate cancer and subsequent surgery, major complications with the surgery with a nicked bowel, a heart attack and triple bypass surgery. When I stand up, my knees sound like breakfast cereal—Snap, Crackle, and Pop. Besides the little brown spots that appear on my skin seemingly overnight, I also have harmless skin tags popping up (skin tags! Isn't that cute). But this old shay is still functioning, more or less, and plenty happy to be alive.

LG: There's nothing like a bout of cancer or a heart attack to raise some big questions.

JM: The fabled wisdom of the elderly grows from the acute awareness that we are not going to be here forever. I think more intensely about what comes next. I am a Catholic, and spirituality has always been important to me.

LG: I've heard people talk about their certainty of eternal life through Jesus Christ. This offers them great comfort as they confront death. Do you have that kind of certainty? I don't.

JM: I don't have any certainty at all, Larry. I don't think anyone really knows. In fact, I have really profound doubt that anything or anyone is out there. If I had absolute, 100 percent, gold-plated proof that there is a God and that there is a life after death, then there would be no need for faith. It is living your life "as if" there were a God. It is about making a faith commitment that something happens after we die. I have come up with perfectly good reasons—for me—that support my faith commitment. Beginning in my early teens, almost every year that I have lived has been better than the year that preceded it. So I assume that the trend will continue. Actually, I think the after-death experience is going to be a great, exciting, fabulous adventure. Besides, what if I am wrong? I won't ever know it.

There is always the possibility that my stance about my personal beliefs is a form of being cantankerous. I've developed this "I don't give a damn what anyone thinks" attitude. Jung discusses the shadow, that part of the personality that lays hidden. Jung suggests that as one gets older, that shadow emerges with more force. I vaguely remember reading about a study that was done with the elderly in a retirement community. The researchers collected interview data that gave them some ideas about the personality characteristics of the residents. A year later they came back for a follow-up of the study. All of the gentle, lovely, and sweet people had died; the cantankerous, obstinate, stubborn, cranky, and grouchy people were the only ones left to do the follow-up interview. That gives me hope.

LG: What do you want counselors to know about counseling with older adults?

JM: Because religion seems to be so important to people from virtually every ethnic tradition, I believe counselors and psychologists need to carefully examine their own belief system about the end times. The subject of religion and spirituality is more appropriate for discussion than it was when I was first trained. This is especially important in working with elderly clients. Obviously, helpers need to continue to avoid imposing their belief system on their clients. I never do what I call "God talk" with my clients unless they bring it up first. But having a better understanding of what you believe puts you in a better situation to help your clients define their belief systems.

Years ago, Albert Ellis demonstrated that antecedent events did not lead automatically to emotional consequences. He argued that our belief system or the way we interpreted or thought about the event led to our emotional reaction. Cognitive reframing is one of the great tools we can use to help both our elderly clients and ourselves. When my knees—or whatever—hurt, I reframe the experience:

- I consider the alternative; I could be outta here. At my age, if I didn't hurt, I would be numb or dead.
- Of course I hurt. I have used this body well—basketball, tennis, backpacking, hiking, and running 5 miles a day for thirty years. What did I think—it was going last forever?
- I'm just working off days in purgatory. (Sorry, we Catholics have the advantage of believing in purgatory, so we can work off here on earth some of the bad stuff we've done.)
- Okay, then, this is just the price I have to pay for still being around to play with my grandchildren, and it's worth it.
- I just assume that this ache is a message from God reminding me to get ready to come home.

There is a great passage in the Torah. The writer describes the valiant woman: "She laughs at the days to come." Laughter is one of the great tools to help us get through. And, if we use it correctly, humor can be a great tool for helping our clients face old age.

LG: Thank you, Jeff.

Preface

My major interest during my professional life has been counseling children and families. I became intensely curious about counseling older adults at about the same time that I could no longer deny that I was an older adult. I joined the Association for Adult Development and Aging (AADA) and volunteered to serve on the editorial board of their journal, *Adultspan*. My university gave me a wonderful gift, a Faculty Development Leave. I used the time for an internship in counseling with older adults at Jewish Family and Children's Service of San Antonio.

I secured a contract for this book from Pearson/Merrill, who, like me, sees a bright future in counseling with older adults. This market niche is growing, and counselors can expect plenty of business from aging Baby Boomers. Baby Boomers are the first generation that has been universally exposed to counseling. Who among us 50- or 60-somethings has *never* seen a therapist?

I asked J. Jeffries McWhirter, a dear mentor and esteemed counselor educator, to write a Foreword. Jeff has plenty of wisdom and humor to share about his experience with aging and retirement.

I wrote the Introduction, "A Perspective on Counseling with Older Adults," to create a context for the eighteen case studies. In selecting authors, I looked for therapists who have experience in counseling older adults. In some cases, I found them by word of mouth. A search of the professional literature turned up some on-target articles. Then I inquired whether the author was also a practitioner. The result for me has been the privilege of working closely with eighteen outstanding authors.

This was a hard book to organize because each case is idiosyncratic. The approaches used were diverse, and I couldn't devise a neat organizing principle. I eventually decided to order the cases by the client's age, and so the first case is about a 50-year-old and the last one is about an 87-year-old. This simple organization exposes an interesting developmental phenomenon. There are two kingdoms of aging: the "young old" and the "old old." An example of the former is Mary Finn Maples's case study of group counseling with high-functioning professionals exploring issues raised by pending retirement. On the other extreme, Bret Hendricks advocates for an 87-year-old nursing home resident.

The Summary of Cases is a table that offers at-a-glance comparisons. For example, the reader will see that Dorothy Breen uses cognitive behavioral therapy to help a 77-year-old woman living in a rural community cope with depression triggered by a health crisis. You will see the age of the counselor as well as the age of the client. In some cases, age matters when counseling an older person.

I have provided a short introduction to each case. The author's opening paragraphs describe the presenting problem and demographic information. The reader should know that in every case the identities of clients have been disguised.

Under the heading "Conceptualization," the author develops a rationale for diagnosis and therapeutic goals. The author explains the choice of a theoretical orientation or strategy and lets us in on the treatment plan.

Under "Process," the author provides a session-by-session account of what happened.

"Outcome" describes the results, for better or worse. I did not ask authors to present their most successful cases. I wanted them to choose a case that had meaning for them. I wanted to meet the clients that they wouldn't or couldn't forget.

For me, the most interesting section is "Reflections." Here, with the benefit of hindsight, authors explain what they might have done differently. In addition, authors talk about their own personal and professional growth. A benefit of working with older adults is that it leads us to examine our own feelings and attitudes about our own aging bodies, personalities, and spirits.

This book beats with the pulse of living psychotherapy, and I anticipate that readers will develop strong feelings about these cases. Authors have provided their e-mail addresses (see the biographical statements at the ends of the cases) and have assured me that they would love to hear from readers. Take them up on it and make contact.

As I have gotten older, I take less for granted. I gratefully acknowledge the help I received with proofreading from Chanté Cross, Lizette Salinas, and Taneem Chowdhury, who are graduate assistants in our counseling program, and expert assistance from Editor Meredith Fossel and Project Manager Mary Irvin at Pearson/Merrill, as well as copyeditor Lynne Lackenbach. Finally, I would like to thank the reviewers of my manuscript for their insights and comments: Mary Andre, University of Southern California; Joseph Bertinetti, University of Nebraska at Omaha; Leslie Brody, Boston University; Montserat Casado, University of Central Florida; and Joseph Cervantes, California State University, Fullerton.

Larry B. Golden, Ph.D.
Associate Professor
Department of Counseling
The University of Texas at San Antonio

Contents

Summary of Cases

Practitioner and Age	Client's Gender and Age	Salient Contextual Issues (Family; Economics; Health; Race/Ethnicity)	Presenting Problems in Counseling	Therapeutic Strategies
John M. Littrell, 62	Woman, early 50s	Late-life career change	Sleep disturbance	Solution-focused therapy, metaphoric storytelling
Thelma Duffey, 40	Woman, 55	4 divorces, no children; financially well fixed; life-threatening cystic fibrosis	Alcohol abuse, difficulty with intimacy	Relational-cultural theory, music therapy
Marijane Fall, 65	Woman, 57	Married; middle-class; psychosomatic complaints	Depression, panic disorder	Cognitive-behavioral therapy, physical exercise
Mary Finn Maples, 72	Men and women, median age 60	Well-educated professionals who volunteer for a group experience	Concerns about retirement	Small-group counseling
Collie W. Conoley, 56, and Jane Close Conoley, 59	Woman, 60, and her parents, 84 and 87	Sisters intervene to assist frail parents; upper middle-class	Aging parents resist limits placed on their independence, care-giving issues	Solution-focused therapy, multigenerational conjoint therapy
Beverly Snyder, 60	Woman, 60	Difficulty sustaining relationships or holding jobs; mental illness	Bipolar disorder, self-mutilation, suicidal ideation	Sandtray play therapy, cognitive-behavioral therapy
Susan A. Adams, 58	Couple, early 60s	Traditional marriage; recent death of parents; husband forced to retire, loses pension	Depression, marital dysfunction	Transactional Analysis, narrative therapy; conjoint therapy
Fred Stickle, mid-30s, and Jill D. Duba, mid-50s	Woman seen in therapy at ages 46, 62, and 64	Three life changes: empty nest, spouse dies, new dating relationship	Episodes of situational depression	Client-centered therapy, cognitive-behavioral therapy
Heather Trepal, 26	Woman, 64	African American grandmother raising the children of her incarcerated daughter; fearful of Child Protective Services; high blood pressure	Stress, adjustment to grandparenting responsibilities	Parenting skills training, advocacy for respite care
Montserrat Casado-Kehoe, mid-30s	Man, 65	Retired widower of murdered wife, struggling financially	Depression, complicated grief, existential crisis	Kübler-Ross's stages of grief, experiential counseling, letter writing, empty chair
Catherine Roland, 55	Woman, 66	Widow lives alone; highly educated, athletic, corporate position	Grieving, fear of aging and death, mysterious vision problems	Relational therapy, client-centered therapy
Mary Ballard, 44	Man, 70	Widower; psychosomatic complaints	Depression, grieving, alcohol abuse	Solution-focused therapy, consultation

Practitioner and Age	Client's Gender and Age	Salient Contextual Issues (Family; Economics; Health; Race/Ethnicity)	Presenting Problems in Counseling	Therapeutic Strategies
Ana Blancarte, 40s	Woman, 72	Mexican American widow; history of psychiatric problems	Bipolar disorder, depression, anxiety, grieving	Psychodynamic psychotherapy
Dorothy Breen, 56	Woman, 77	Married woman in rural community; health crisis forces adjustments	Depression, stress of caregiving	Cognitive-behavioral therapy
Barbara Herlihy, 56	Woman, 82	African American widow, activist resident of low-income public housing destroyed by Hurricane Katrina	Hospitalized for suicidal depression	Feminist and racial identity perspective, systemic therapy
Peggy Whiting, 53	Man, 84	Widower in assisted-living facility; cardiopulmonary disease	Grieving, alcoholism	Narrative reconstruction
Suzanne Degges-White, 41	Woman, 87	Widow lives with granddaughter; arthritis, heart problems	Reclusive, turning, away from social interests	*Gerotranscendence* as reframe, life review
Bret Hendricks, 38	Woman, 87	Widow in nursing home; mild strokes	Agitated depression, disruptive behavior	Cognitive therapy, music therapy and reminiscence, advocacy

Introduction: A Perspective on Counseling with Older Adults

Larry Golden

In Shakespeare's immortal soliloquy from *As You Like It,* the end game of the life span does not come off well, "Last scene of all, That ends this strange eventful history, Is second childishness and mere oblivion; Sans teeth, sans eyes, sans taste, sans everything." Writing about 1600 AD, the Bard describes the catastrophic losses of old age. Has this perspective changed? There are persistent and powerful myths that tap into our fears of growing old and that unnerve counselors who work with older adults. The prospect of counseling with old people is, therefore, depressing to the extent that our expectations of our own aging are depressing. I would prefer a twist on the story that is more to the liking of counselors, a peculiar species of professional who thrive on optimism but are famously subject to burnout.

Given what we know about human development, is old age a positive or a negative part of the life span? In his comprehensive book, *Psychotherapy with Older Adults,* Bob Knight (2004) says, "The loss-deficit model of aging, which portrays the normative course of later life as a series of losses and the typical response as depression, has been an integral part of the practitioner heritage" (p. 5). However, Knight maintains that while older adults are confronted by life's toughest challenges, such as chronic illness and grieving, they come armed with maturity and wisdom.

We owe much to Erik Erikson, who saw real possibilities in the latter part of the life span, a period when we reflect back on our lives, adapt to our triumphs and disappointments, and incorporate memories and experiences into meaningful beliefs about ourselves and the world (Glover, 1998). Out of such adaptation, or lack thereof, we achieve either *integrity* or *despair.*

Integrity permits the acceptance of responsibility for accomplishments and failures (Erikson, 1982). Erikson describes *despair* as representing a fear of death (Bee & Boyd, 2003). His concept of *despair* reminds me of eternal buyer's remorse: "If only I had. If only I hadn't. But now I've run out of time." On the other hand, I see *integrity* as: "I made mistakes and I learned from them. Overall, it was worth the journey." Erickson (as cited in Broderick & Blewitt, 2004, p. 496) assures us, "Healthy children will not fear life, if their elders have integrity enough not to fear death."

As a psychologist, I welcome any philosophy that holds out hope for growth. *Gerotranscendence* is an optimistic theory about the last stage of human development. In this paradigm, the last stage is marked by "closing in" and selectivity in activities. Although it may appear as symptoms of dementia, depression, or isolation, gerotranscendence, by contrast, is a healthy withdrawal that allows the old person to spend time preparing for the end of life (Tornstam, 1997).

Where possible, I use the case studies from this book as examples. Suzanne Degges-White uses gerotranscendence to conceptualize her case, "'Tired of Living' or 'All Packed and Ready to Go'?" Jane, 87, lived with her newly divorced oldest grandchild, Penny, and it was Penny who made the referral. She was worried that her grandmother was becoming withdrawn and antisocial. For Degges-White, depression, the obvious diagnosis, just didn't fit. She found it helpful, instead, to think of Jane's behavior as an appropriate response to the final life transition.

Dementia and Alzheimer's disease are the death knell for counseling, because our "talking cures" require clients to *think!* While the elderly are subject to some mild cognitive decline, dementia does not necessarily go with the territory. I like the way Bob Knight (2004) puts it: "To identify normal aging with dementia would be roughly analogous to identifying adolescence or young adulthood with schizophrenia" (p. 7). Neither schizophrenia nor dementia should define the age and stage in which it most often occurs. Even with the loss of cognitive function, there is always something that can be done. At the risk of sounding flip, which I certainly don't intend, if behavior modification can work with pigeons, why not with demented humans?

Older adults actually have some cognitive advantages. According to Paul Baltes and his colleagues in the Berlin Aging Study (as cited in Knight, 2004), we do, indeed, become wise with age if wisdom is defined as relativism of values and cognition of uncertainty. This means that older adults are better able to perceive two opposing viewpoints as both having elements of truth. Seniors also acquire expertise that trumps age-related deficits in cognitive processes. For example, their multigenerational experience makes the elderly expert in family dynamics.

I got my invitation to join the Older Adults Club from AARP when I turned 50. Now I have sixty-five years of accumulated wisdom and expertise. Shakespeare wouldn't be immortal if he didn't speak truth about the human condition. I would like to think that I can gracefully accept that truth at the same time that I aspire to more than *sans everything!* And I ask: Can counseling help us finish well?

■ Counseling Interventions with Older Adults

Sigmund Freud was unenthusiastic about psychotherapy with people over 50 years of age because he believed that personality is formed by early adolescence. As we age, the character of a person becomes rigid, was Freud's take on the old saw, "You can't teach an old dog new tricks." Carl Jung, on the other hand, recognized that our choices in our younger years are constricted by rigid roles and, consequently, the focus is outward and social. In later life, if we are lucky and wise, we can make some space to explore the person we really are, looking inward to examine the Self. This final stage in Jungian individuation brings maturation and wisdom.

Happily, there is evidence that supports the effectiveness of counseling with older adults (Gatz et al., 1998; Knight, 2004; Myers & Harper, 2004; Zalaquett & Stens, 2006). In his review of the literature, Knight (2004) concludes that psychological interventions with older adults are just as effective as with younger adults. Psychosocial treatments are effective for depression in older adults (Zalaquett & Stens, 2006). In their 2004 article, "Evidence-Based Effective Practices with Older Adults," Myers and Harper (2004) found support for a wide range of useful interventions for various mental health problems in older adults, including reminiscence therapy, behavioral therapy, cognitive therapy, brief psychodynamic therapy, bibliotherapy, and group counseling.

I think it is fair to conclude that the counseling interventions we learned about in our training programs should work with older adults, albeit with adaptations for slowed mental processing speed. So, rather than try to identify counseling theories that work well with an aging population—because they *all* do—let's examine some overarching mental health concerns for seniors, as well as interventions to address those concerns.

Existential Issues. When I took "Counseling Theories" at Arizona State many years ago, our professor punctuated his lecture about Viktor Frankl by asking us to write our own obituaries. This exercise encouraged a perspective that isn't easily accessible to the young. We all know that we'll die someday, but I kept my mind off this unpleasant idea for decades by worrying about other things such as defending my dissertation, saving my marriage, keeping my kid off drugs, and getting tenure. The older I get, the more I smell Death's foul breath. It doesn't help that I'm not convinced that there's an afterlife.

In her case study for this book, Montserrat Casado-Kehoe ("Existential Crisis and the Loss of a Spouse") met a 65-year-old man who was grieving for his murdered wife. Profound existential fault lines were exposed that many of us will face when losing a spouse. How do I manage day by day? Who am I? What is my purpose on earth? And then, why would anyone intentionally take another's life?

In their case study, "The Existential Issues of Freedom and Responsibility: Every Year It Is Getting Harder to Deny Them!," Collie and Jane Conoley learn that when a person can no longer drive a car, something philosophically profound is lost, beyond losing one's wheels. The disabled elderly lose their freedom through no fault of their own, and they can't earn it back.

While few people are propelled into counseling by existential issues per se, the human need for meaning may lurk behind their presenting symptoms. "Life review" (sometimes called "structured reminiscence therapy") is a technique that helps elderly clients talk about the meaning of their lives. Older adults normally reminisce and, with the benefit of a curious counselor, life review can be therapeutic (Bee & Boyd, 2003). By asking clarifying questions, the counselor helps the client recreate a well-rounded life story. I like to use a timeline and ask the client to write about positive experiences above the line and negative ones below.

Bret Hendricks ("The Music of Memory") played recorded music to help 87-year-old Brenda remember past events. In her case, Suzanne Degges-White uses "life review" as a way of allowing her 87-year-old client to search for meaning in how she lived and to prepare for death. Degges-White suggests that, rather than routinely ask, "How do you feel today?" it is more beneficial to encourage your client to "Tell me about your life."

Retirement. Retirement is rife with stressful change. Retirees may struggle with living on a reduced income, finding a second career, crafting a leisure lifestyle, creating a meaningful new identity, and shifting roles between spouses (Myers & Harper, 2004). On the downside (the side that might elicit an appointment with a counselor), without the buffers of career and children, retired couples may spend far too much time together in their empty nest, depending only on each other for companionship (Hansen, 2007). The presenting problem is likely to be escalating marital conflict. Other retired couples may find their troubled adult children clambering back into the nest, relying on their aging parents for money, food, and shelter. This brings to mind a lesson from the world of nature—parent eagles promptly destroy their nest after the last eaglet takes flight.

Some retirees who seek the kind of idealistic second careers that enable them to "give back" are enrolling in counseling, psychology, and social work graduate programs (Lowe, 2005; Paterson, 2008). Older counselors report that young clients perceive their "gray hair" as indicative of wisdom and trustworthiness (Paterson, 2008). The bad news could be that because retirees can afford to work for less, they may exert downward pressure on a pay scale that is already depressed.

In his case study ("Like a Stab in the Back"), John M. Littrell helps a woman in her early 50s embark on a new career as a counselor. Finally, she lands a counseling position, but then her clients present such nightmarish problems that she develops a sleep disturbance.

Mary Finn Maples ("The 'Transition' Experience: Group Counseling for Baby Boomers") brings together six professionals ranging in age from 56 to 78. Maples says, "My goal was to relieve the mystery, apprehension, and fear about retirement among professionals who valued their work as their meaning in life. . . . It almost appeared to me that they had seen the idea of retirement as some sort of death or disabling experience."

As for those, such as myself, who may think that planning for every eventuality in retirement is the answer, we would do well to consider the Jewish adage: "If you want to make God laugh, make plans."

Grandparenting. There before your eyes are your beautiful grandchildren, comforting assurance of life's continuity. Grandma and Grandpa savor the magic of childhood and then, when the grandchildren get tiresome, hand them over to Mom and Dad! But there's another scenario that's less magical. As a result of circumstances such as parental unemployment, substance abuse, and parental incompetence, grandparents wind up *raising* their grandchildren (Kelch-Oliver, 2008).

In "The Second Time Around," Heather Trepal tells the story of Ginny, 64, who takes on the full-time care of three grandchildren when her daughter is sent to prison for prostitution and drug dealing. Trepal helps Ginny improve her parenting skills and encourages her to join a support group and seek respite care. A confounding complication is that Ginny avoids any involvement whatsoever with "the system," fearing that Child Protective Services will take the children away.

Caregiving. While caregiving for a frail parent or disabled spouse can be deeply rewarding, it can also be a familial "lion's den," where the pitfalls are easily underestimated, including sheer exhaustion, unresolved parent–child conflict, and sibling rivalries. Family therapy is the straightforward treatment of choice but may be impractical in this age of widely dispersed family members. If scheduling family sessions is workable, communicating about the impairments of the person being cared for can be very helpful. You want everyone on the same page, with an accurate diagnosis and prognosis. Above all, family members must recognize the caregiver's hard work and negotiate how the burden can be shared.

In her article, "Refeathering the Nest: From Dutiful Daughter to Self-Aware Caregiver" (2007, p. 31), Katy Butler offers tips for caregivers:

- Find somewhere to vent. Express negative feelings, usually anger and guilt, to a friend, partner, electronic bulletin board, or support group.
- Acknowledge past wounds. Taking care of your parent may be a last chance to get resolution and do things differently this time around.
- Assemble a support team. Caregivers, especially women, should be assertive and not let siblings off the hook too easily.
- Pay attention to inequities of work, money, and power. The caregiver should be in charge and control the money. The primary caregiver should be paid for time and lost wages, either via a regular paycheck or a bigger share of the inheritance.
- Consult a lawyer. A power-of-attorney document gives offspring the right to manage a parent's financial affairs. A durable power of attorney is crucial when it's time to shift from lifesaving medicine that extends life to a hospice approach that eases pain. In addition, there may be a legal way to reduce taxes that will be due on the estate.

In "Catherine's Story: Challenges of Aging in a Rural Community," Dorothy Breen's 77-year-old client winds up in the emergency room with a possible heart attack. But her chest pain is the result of the stress of caregiving for her frail husband. Breen uses cognitive behavioral therapy to help Catherine set reasonable limits on her caregiving. Based on my reading of this case, Breen is kind and supportive to Catherine. Kindness goes a long way.

Grieving. Recently, my university gave me a Faculty Development Leave so that I could get supervised practice in counseling with older adults at Jewish Family and Children's Service of San Antonio. I was impressed by the fact that symptoms related to grieving were presenting problems for nearly all of my older clients. This is also true for the preponderance of the eighteen case studies in this book. If we live long enough, we accumulate losses. Unless both spouses die simultaneously (from my point of view, an exit to be wished for), one partner is destined to be left alone.

Depressive symptoms are a natural result of grief, but counselors (and third-party payers) want to distinguish between normal bereavement and long-standing and full-blown depression (dysthymic disorder, major depressive disorder). The symptoms may look the same, but we expect normal bereavement to resolve in a short time, typically within a year, and without the need for treatment. In fact, it's usually not a good idea to push the newly bereaved to see a counselor. However, if the symptoms of depression persist over time, a referral for counseling could prevent a chronic disorder.

Cognitive therapy helps put a loss into perspective. Hansen (2007, p. 23) sums up the advantages of cognitive therapy, "Older clients appreciate its practical common sense. They get it: The way you think about what's happening to you determines how you feel, and how you feel determines how you behave." Challenging irrational beliefs with Socratic questioning and teaching clients how to replace cognitive distortions with adaptive thoughts are techniques that have a proven track record. What are examples of cognitive distortions? Perhaps the client's grief is complicated by guilt: "I should have insisted that she go to the doctor with that." "If only I had been less critical of him." When there is unfinished business in a marriage (and there often is), realizing that you will never have a chance to make it up to your spouse is a recipe for depression.

Knight (2004) is emphatic that helping the bereaved express emotion is a necessary first step before attempting cognitive or behavioral interventions. While eliciting emotion requires little of the counselor other than active listening skills, Knight cautions that young or inexperienced counselors may try to rush it or avoid the expression of emotion altogether. No one wants to upset elderly people and make them cry! Perhaps counselors are uncomfortable hearing emotion-laden stories about the failures of the health care system and about the many awful ways there are to die.

Pastoral counseling has much to offer religious clients. Faith traditions prescribe rituals that help us accept our losses and move on. For example, in my own Jewish tradition, upon first hearing of the death of a loved one, you rend your clothing. Next you sit *shiva* for a week, staying at home, accepting condolences and sustenance from others. This is followed by a daily recitation of the *Kaddish,* the prayer for the dead. At the end of one year, family gathers at the grave for an unveiling of the stone. From then on, there is an expectation that you will get on with your life and resume your responsibilities, but every year, on the anniversary of the death, you light a *Yartzeit,* a candle of remembrance.

Many of the cases in this book illustrate counseling interventions with clients grieving for losses. In "Counseling Flora: Adjusting, Grieving, Dating, and Moving On," the client sought Fred Stickle's help on three distinct occasions over eighteen years: (1) when her adult children left home, (2) when her husband died, and (3) when she began a serious dating relationship with a person of dubious character and of a different religion.

Catherine B. Roland ("An Absence of Light: The Case of Marie") uses client-centered therapy with a 66-year-old client who is losing vision. Coincidentally, the lights of Marie's life have flickered out with the accumulation of losses of family members.

In Susan A. Adams's case study, "Life Losses and Changes from a Transactional Analysis Perspective," a married couple must cope with the primary breadwinner's forced early retirement. This couple was not at all prepared for 24/7 togetherness. Complicated grieving for their deceased parents was an underlying issue.

Alcohol and Substance Abuse. Alcohol and substance abuse in seniors is significant but underreported (Myers & Harper, 2004). Alcohol is commonly used as a self-medication for bereavement and depression. As one would expect, late-life drinkers respond better to therapy than lifelong drinkers.

Peggy P. Whiting's case study, "Dad Just Fell Again: Out of AA and into Grief," demonstrates the connection between bereavement and alcohol abuse. Peter, 84, takes a fall, and personnel at the assisted-living facility realize that he is drunk. Peter's drinking is connected to grieving for his wife of sixty years. Whiting uses narrative reconstruction to encourage Peter to author a healing story about the meaning of his life as it unfolds without his wife.

Diagnosed as an infant with cystic fibrosis, Thelma Duffey's client, Jillian, 55, makes matters much worse by abusing alcohol. Four marriages and four divorces testify to dysfunction in relationships. Duffey comments, "When I met her, much to her surprise and that of others, she was still alive." Take a look at Duffey's case study, "Cystic Fibrosis, Alcoholism, and Meaning," if you want to see how she manages this dangerous diagnostic mix.

Lloyd, 70, has been drinking heavily since the death of his wife of fifty-two years. Mary Ballard ("Living with Dying: Alcohol Is Not the Answer") sees clearly that Lloyd is grieving. Operating from a strengths-based perspective, Ballard uses a solution-focused approach to get Lloyd back on track.

Multicultural Issues in Counseling Older Adults

Race, ethnicity, gender, and socioeconomic class are determining factors in every segment of American life, including how we age. For example, the aging poor find themselves at a disadvantage with regard to health care and housing. The elderly, as a group, encounter barriers to receiving counseling services. Not surprisingly, there is a correlation between having insurance and the utilization of mental health services (Myers & Harper, 2004).

In Barbara Herlihy's case study, "Mama Del: A Case Study of Counseling in Post-Katrina New Orleans," race and aging and disaster combine as a tragedy of Biblical proportions! After Hurricane Katrina floods New Orleans, Mama Del, an 82-year-old African American woman, is referred following a suicide attempt. Mama Del's home in a public housing project has been destroyed, and her identity as a community leader has been blown away. Herlihy finds that Erikson's developmental stages just don't fit Mama Del. She consults with Dr. Zarus E. Watson, a colleague and an African American who has lived most of his life in New Orleans. Dr. Watson knows that Mama Del was a legendary public housing and community activist. Watson suggests that Herlihy replace Erikson with a model for black racial identity development, and then Mama Del's experience begins to make sense.

Ana Blancarte's case offers a perspective on aging in the Hispanic culture. Blancarte's 72-year-old client, Dora, grew up in a U.S.–Mexico border town. Even though Dora is fluent in English, Blancarte's valuing of the Mexican culture and her ability to speak Spanish helps her client feel accepted and understood.

"Multicultural Counseling" is a required course in our program at the University of Texas at San Antonio, as it is in many programs. Should the elderly be one of the populations that are the focus of such courses? I think so, but then what should be included in the curriculum?

Being old is a culture of its own. Within that culture, people who are old and healthy live in a different world than those who are old and disabled. It's helpful to distinguish between two broad categories: the "young old" and the "old old," who are different from each other not so much by chronology as by health and self-sufficiency (Pipher, 1999). One of the competencies for counselors of the elderly should be a working knowledge of the chronic illnesses and disabilities to which the "old old" are especially subject.

A persistent question that arises when preparing gerontological counselors is: Can young counselors be effective with elderly clients? I don't think there is any reason that a self-aware and sensitive young counselor cannot work effectively with older people. On the other hand, age matters, and to act as if it didn't would be like saying that race doesn't matter. (How often have I cringed when a naïve student says, "I don't see any difference if a client is black, white, or polka dot.") I think that cross-cultural skills are best learned person to person. Daniel Eckstein, founder of a geriatric counseling specialization at Sam Houston State University, takes his students on field trips to nursing homes, where they interview residents. Residents provide the students with feedback on their interviewing skills (personal communication, Daniel Eckstein, November 12, 2008).

In order to highlight the impact, if any, of the "age gap," I asked all of the contributing authors to this book to disclose their ages. Here are some of their observations.

There is nearly a thirty-year age gap between Mary Ballard and her 70-year-old client, Lloyd. Although the age gap does not seem to matter to Lloyd, the potential for countertransference is of keen interest to Ballard: "Having a father Lloyd's age made me examine my motives more than once."

Marijane Fall includes ages in her case's title: "Help! She's Old and I'm Young but She's 57, and I'm 65." Fall admits feeling critical of Mary's uptight mannerisms, which seem to symbolize her passivity in the face of aging. This is certainly not the active path that Fall has forged for herself, and she yearns for Mary to revolt! But Fall, a seasoned therapist, recognizes a judgmental stance when she sees one, even in herself. She concludes, "I've got some thinking to do about this age thing."

Peggy P. Whiting is 53, and Peter, 84, is her client. In consultation with a colleague, Whiting sorts out how her feelings toward her own father readily transfer to Peter. "I discovered that I have a strong sense of protection toward others older than I am."

With the benefit of hindsight, Heather Trepal discloses that her relative youth made it difficult to relate to a 64-year-old grandmother raising her grandchildren: "When I was working with this client I was a relatively new counselor and I was young (about 26) and had yet to have my own children."

Advocacy is another key competency for counselors who work with the elderly. I can't imagine how I could presume to assist people in any vulnerable group if I were not committed to being their advocate. To be a gerontological counselor means standing up for clients who cannot speak forcefully for themselves. Huber, Nelson, Netting, and Borders's *Elder Advocacy: Essential Knowledge and Skills Across Settings* (2008) is a highly relevant book written by and for social workers. The authors present advocacy skills, such as how to approach complex delivery systems, clarify advocacy roles, investigate complaints, and mobilize resources. Regrettably, these skills are usually *not* taught in counseling and psychology programs. Perhaps there is an opportunity here for some cross-disciplinary course work. I'm not optimistic about this happening, because the academic "cultures" of counseling, psychology, and social work may prove as resistant to cooperation as anything encountered in society, at large. I want the reader to understand that although I typically refer to "counselor" and "counseling," this is done in the generic sense. I recognize that counseling with older adults is the appropriate territory of many disciplines, regardless of their professional identity as counselors, psychologists, social workers, or psychiatrists.

Bret Hendricks is a good role model for advocacy. In his case study, he was under contract to counsel residents of a nursing home, *and* he was a strong advocate for his 87-year-old client when staff complained about her "agitated depression" and wreaking havoc. He would sometimes overhear a staff member say that a resident was "having the usual problems adjusting to nursing home life." Hendricks maintains that he has not found any usual or predictable pattern to a resident's "adjustment." In the Reflections portion of his case study, Hendricks shares his personal experience in getting counseling for his own mother in a nursing home. "My own mother, who had been diagnosed with Parkinson's disease, was admitted to a skilled nursing facility as a result of a fractured hip. I became vociferous in my quest to make counseling available to the residents of this home. Each time I asked about counseling, I was told by administrators, 'We really should look into that sometime.' I am proud to say that I persisted in my quest, and six months after mother was admitted, a counselor (not me) began contract work for residents and their families."

In Conclusion

Should *you*, the reader, develop an area of expertise in counseling older adults? At Jewish Family and Children's Service, I saw older clients who for most of their lives played games with addictions, dodged the demands of a career path, and left a trail of wrecked relationships. Now in their 50s and 60s, these clients were looking to therapy to figure out how to salvage what was left. I found them rewarding to work with, because they meant serious business.

I enjoyed James Hollis's book, *Finding Meaning in the Second Half of Life: How to Finally, Really Grow Up*. Hollis, a Jungian analyst, says that *anxiety* is our companion if we risk embarking on a new stage of our journey, *depression*, if we opt for security. You decide: Anxiety is an elixir, while depression is a sedative. Hollis says that not to consciously choose a path guarantees that our psyche will choose for us, and then there will be hell to pay. Clients, old or young, do not seek us out to help them remain the same. We are agents of their change. Nor do they wish to remain destructively unaware of their true motives. We, as counselors, shine a light in the dark corners of their minds.

Finally, consider what Beverly Snyder says about counseling older adults as she reflects on her case study: "I have a sacred responsibility as a therapist to hold near and dear to my heart the growth of the vulnerable clients who cross my path. It is such a privilege to be part of the journey of older adults who look back across the lifespan and try to garner meaning from their lives as they look forward to the remaining years."

References

Bee, H., & Boyd, D. (2003). *Lifespan development* (3rd ed.). Boston: Allyn & Bacon.

Broderick, P., & Blewitt, P. (2004). *The life span: Human development for helping professionals* (2nd ed.). Upper Saddle River, NJ: Pearson Merrill Prentice Hall.

Butler, K. (2007). Refeathering the nest: From dutiful daughter to self-aware caregiver. *Psychotherapy Networker, 31,* 26–33, 54–55.

Erikson, E. (1982). *The life cycle completed: A review.* New York: W. W. Norton.

Gatz, M., Fiske, A., Fox, L., Kaskie, B., Kasl-Godley, J., McCullum, T. J., et al. (1998). Empirically validated psychological treatments for older adults. *Journal of Mental Health and Aging, 4,* 9–46.

Glover, R. (1998). Perspectives on aging: Issues affecting the latter part of the life cycle. *Educational Gerontology, 24,* 325–332.

Hansen, M. A. (January/February 2007). Retired couples: Therapy with older people. *Family Therapy Magazine,* 20-23.

Hollis, J. (2005). *Finding meaning in the second half of life: How to finally, really grow up.* New York: Gotham.

Huber, R., Nelson, W. H., Netting, F. E., & Borders, K. W. (2008). *Elder advocacy: Essential knowledge and skills across settings.* Belmont, CA: Thomson Brooks/Cole.

Kelch-Oliver, K. (2008). African American grandparent caregivers: Stresses and implications for counselors. *The Family Journal: Counseling and Therapy for Couples and Families, 16,* 43–50.

Knight, B. G. (2004). *Psychotherapy with older adults* (3rd ed.). Thousand Oaks, CA: Sage.

Lowe, W. (2005). In praise of the older therapist. *Psychotherapy Networker, 29,* 38–43, 54, 70.

Myers, J. E., & Harper, M. C. (2004). Evidence-based effective practices with older adults. *Journal of Counseling & Development, 82,* 207–218.

Paterson, J. (January 2008). Better late than never. *Counseling Today,* 12–13.

Pipher, M. (1999). *Another country: Navigating the emotional terrain of our elders.* New York: Riverhead/Penguin Putnam.

Tornstam, L. (1997). Gerotranscendence: The contemplative dimension in aging. *The Journal of Aging Studies, 11,* 143–154.

Zalaquett, C. P., & Stens, A. N. (2006). Psychosocial treatments for major depression and dysthymia in older adults: A review of the research literature. *Journal of Counseling & Development, 84,* 192–201.

Suggested Readings

Coberly, L. M., McCormick, J., & Updike, K. (2005). *Writers have no age* (2nd ed.). New York: Haworth.

Daire, A. P., & Mitcham-Smith, M. (2006). Culturally sensitive dementia caregiving models and clinical practice. *Adultspan Journal, 5,* 25–35.

Degges-White, S. (2005). Understanding gerotranscendence in older adults: A new perspective for counselors. *Adultspan Journal, 4,* 36–48.

Dorfman, L. T. (2002). Stayers and leavers: Professors in an era of no mandatory retirement. *Educational Gerontology, 28,* 15–33.

Golden, L. (2005). Max's Newsletter of Advice on turning 60. *The Family Journal: Counseling and Therapy for Couples and Families, 13,* 81–82.

Golden, L., & Davis, C. (2005). A dialogue between a young lesbian counseling student and an older straight male counselor educator. *Journal of Creativity in Mental Health, 1,* 99–105.

Harper, M. C., & Shoffner, M. F. (2004). Counseling for continued career development after retirement: An application of the theory of work adjustment. *The Career Development Quarterly, 52,* 272–284.

Hill, R. D. (2005). *Positive aging: A guide for mental health professionals and consumers.* New York: W. W. Norton.

Ingersoll-Dayton, B., & Campbell, R. (2001). *The delicate balance: Case studies in counseling and care management for older adults.* Baltimore: Health Professions Press.

Laidlaw, K., Thompson, L. W., Gallagher-Thompson, D., & Dick-Siskin, L. (2003). *Cognitive behaviour therapy with older people.* Chicester, West Sussex, England: John Wiley.

Lichtenberg, P. A. (1999). *Handbook of assessment in clinical gerontology.* New York: John Wiley & Sons.

Montgomery, R. J. V., Rowe, J. M., & Kosloski, K. (2007). Family caregiving. In J. A. Blackburn & C. N. Dulmus (Eds.), *Handbook of gerontology: Evidence-based approaches to theory, practice, and policy* (pp. 426–454). Hoboken, NJ: John Wiley & Sons.

Pennick, J. M., & Fallshore, M. (2005). Purpose and meaning in highly active seniors. *Adultspan Journal, 4,* 19–35.

Schwiebert, V. L., Myers, J. E., & Dice, C. (2000). Ethical guidelines for counselors working with older adults. *Journal of Counseling & Development, 78,* 123–129.

Snyder, B. A. (2005). Aging and spirituality: Reclaiming connection through storytelling. *Adultspan Journal, 4,* 49–55.

Stickle, F., & Onedera, J. (2006). Depression in older adults. *Adultspan Journal, 5,* 36–46.

Whiting, P., & Bradley, L. J. (2007). Artful witnessing of the story: Loss in aging adults, *Adultspan Journal, 6,* 119–128.

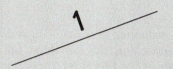

1

Like a Stab in the Back

John M. Littrell

Kay is in her early 50s. After her company laid her off, she embarked on a new career as a counselor. This involved years of retraining. Among her clients at her first counseling job are two individuals who present nightmarish problems. When Kay develops sleep disturbances, she seeks help from John Littrell, nationally known as an advocate of brief solution-focused therapy. John skillfully adds metaphoric storytelling into his therapeutic mix.

Kay Edwards, a woman in her early 50s, exhibited an exhausted seriousness. Although she was slightly overweight, she described her health as good but complained about stress. As I listened, I was not surprised. Two years ago, Kay's company downsized and laid her off. This prompted her to enter a two-year master's degree program in marriage and family therapy; currently, she was just two weeks from graduating. Kay has primary responsibility for assisting her demanding mother, who is in failing health. A year ago, she began a new job as a mental health counselor. Within the last month, two clients she counseled in her work setting had severely challenged Kay.

Kay lives in a middle-to-upper-middle-class neighborhood with her husband and two teenaged children. Her husband is a software executive, and that job keeps him on the road during the week. One daughter is in middle school and the other in high school.

My primary employment is as a professor and program coordinator of Counseling and Career Development at Colorado State University. I obtained my doctorate in counseling at Indiana University in 1975. Three years ago, Kay took my course on brief counseling. Now, she had sought me out as a counselor based on our acquaintance and because she specifically thought a brief counseling approach was appropriate for her concerns. I met Kay in my university office. We contracted for a maximum of five sessions, with my work being *pro bono*.

Kay and I met for two fifty-minute sessions. I conducted a five-minute follow-up session four weeks after the second session. Based on my belief in brief counseling, I did not make a formal diagnosis; instead, I engaged in an ongoing situational assessment. If I had resorted to the DSM-IV-TR (American Psychiatric Association, 2000), Kay would probably be classified as having an adjustment disorder with anxiety.

Conceptualization

Initially, Kay's presenting problem was stress about two clients she had seen in her work as a therapist. Kay was not sleeping well. She would awaken at 2:00 AM and ruminate about a horrendous situation that Fran, one of her new clients, had described. In addition, she was coping with Tim, her first suicidal client. When combined with her approaching graduation and a new job, the stress had knocked her off balance. Kay felt as though these new clients' stories were stuck inside her. Her attempted solutions, such as counting sheep and a visualization technique, had not worked.

My theoretical orientation is as a brief counselor (Littrell, 1998). I draw on the brief therapy theories and techniques of the Mental Research Institute (MRI) approach (Fisch, Weakland, & Segal, 1982), and the solution-focused approach (Berg & Szabó, 2005; De Jong & Berg, 2002). Also informing my work is Rogers' person-centered counseling and neuro-linguistic programming (NLP). I especially like Milton Erickson's metaphoric stories. I'll try anything that might help my client.

Given Kay's age, I thought a lot about the role of developmental tasks, transitions, and challenges. Kay was sandwiched between her own aging mother and her growing children, all the while doing graduate work and learning a new job, tasks that are usually those of a younger person. Arnold (2005) found that as women moved into their fifties, these developmental themes found expression: stepping out of the mold, letting go, walking in balance, moving in new directions, redefining relationships, and experiencing a freedom "to be." What role did these themes play in Kay's life? However interesting these developmental tasks, transitions, challenges, and themes were to me, my client had selected a brief approach with the goal of solving an immediate problem. At one point during counseling, Kay said that she had issues with her mother, but that was not what she was in counseling to work on at this time. Throughout counseling, I drew on Kay's life experiences and knowledge, and her desire for goal-oriented practicality. Brief counseling fit Kay's frame of reference.

Process

Session 1. Kay had been my student, and that got us off to a good start. I began our first session by describing how I work in a brief, solution-focused way, the possible number of sessions, and the limits of confidentiality. I asked, "When we're successful, how would your life be different?"

Kay:	I'd be not so tired and exhausted at the end of the day from working with clients. I'd be sleeping better. I wouldn't be so emotional. I'd be more in control of my feelings, physically and mentally. I think it's being more aware of who I am.
Counselor:	When things are different, you won't be so tired, you won't be so exhausted at the end of the day from working with clients. What will it be like for you?
Kay:	I'd be getting through a night without waking up or worrying about a client. I'm having weird dreams. Usually, I go to sleep around 9:00 and get up at 5:30. Lately, I'm waking up at about 2:00 in the morning.
Counselor:	So at 2:00 you wake up, and then what?
Kay:	I watch TV or just lie there and then it's almost as if my brain starts going more. I'm really trying to figure out how not to think so much. I'm caught up in clients and with what's going on at work.
Counselor:	How long do you stay awake?
Kay:	I never seem to totally go back to sleep. Then the alarm rings and I can tell that I must have been asleep, but I don't know for how long. I'm really tired when I get up. I'm not very motivated to go to work. (Nervous laugh)
Counselor:	So you wake up exhausted and then it's like, "Oh no, another day!"
Kay:	Yeah. But then I'll have a nice night's sleep. That's what I'm trying to figure out. I know right now, with going to school, working, and trying to graduate, I know that has something to do with all this.

Kay told me that her husband is only home on weekends and she sleeps much better when he is present. Using a behavioral approach, I asked when the sleep problems began. Kay told me about the emotional trauma that had triggered her disturbed sleep.

Kay:	I've had some tough weeks with clients. I had a suicidal client, Tim, and I had another one, Fran, who told me. . . . Every time I tell this story, I don't do well. (Her eyes tear)
Counselor:	Why don't you give me the two- or three-sentence summary?

I do not believe that clients must relive their experiences in order to deal with them. In responding, Kay provided many details that are omitted here to preserve confidentiality.

Also, take note of my normalizing statement.

Kay:	Fran's young child was horribly abused and murdered.
Counselor:	And you wonder why when you wake up and think about that, you can't get back to sleep!
Kay:	I have weird dreams. Emotional ups and downs. The week after Fran told me was horrendous. Physically, when she told me the story—I've never had this happen before—I felt like I was being stabbed between my back shoulder blades. I actually felt pain. That whole week I couldn't function. It wasn't so much my concern for Fran but for the young child. I didn't know what to do with it. It was so horrendous I didn't want to share it with anybody. I didn't want anyone else carrying it. It was even hard to tell my family.
Counselor:	So if you start to think about that, goodbye restful sleep.
Kay:	Exactly. Because of where I'm working, every time someone comes around the corner there's a new story. I'm blown away by what people go through.
Counselor:	Whatever that emotion is, you take it out of the session with you.
Kay:	Yes, it's right there. (Points to her heart)
Counselor:	So it's not just Tim and Fran's child, but other clients also affect you.
Kay:	I'm afraid to say, "Tell me more about that." I don't know if that's good or bad. I'm really struggling with that. Several days later, I had a woman telling me about her son in prison and I said to myself, "I don't want to hear this story. Let's just move you forward." I know Fran needs to work through it. She's carrying a lot of guilt. She's never been in therapy. I'm real confused now.

I acknowledged that Kay was exhausted.

Kay:	I think what's exhausting me is, "How do I help these people?" We're running three to four clients a day, two hours each. They're all in crisis. I'm not sure it's mentally possible for someone to work with this many people and be effective. I don't feel like I'm effective, maybe because I'm just starting.

Kay was so shaken by Fran's story that she thought it might not be true. She checked on the Internet and found that it was even worse than Fran had reported.

This made Kay even more anxious about working with Fran. Also adversely affecting her sleep was her worry about suicidal Tim, "who wound up being arrested when I called 911, because he had a bench warrant out that I didn't know about." She added, "I remember not sleeping that night because I was thinking, 'Oh, my god. I've betrayed my client and now he's in jail.'" Following my summarization, Kay told me about positive aspects of the experience and how she was now focusing on her clients' strengths.

Counselor: You've gone into a job that gives you the worst look at humanity. You lose sleep over it. It affects you emotionally. You're drained. You're exhausted. You're not sure if you're giving your best. You don't even want to hear it anymore.

Kay: Then there is the other side. Tim, my suicidal client, now has a job and is doing really well. He's a different person. It's so exciting. I know that that was a lot of my hard work. Staying with him, calling him, and encouraging him to keep going. I'm working with Fran on getting her GED degree. I'm thinking, "Let's just move you forward. You've got other kids to take care of." I like that part and that's what I mean when I say it motivates me. That's why I like the solution-focused approach. I see more of people's strengths.

Kay provided an alternative to her worrying about clients. I believe my accurate empathy allowed her to acknowledge what she does well.

Kay: I want to help clients get the pain out. But their pain gets stuck in my heart.

Counselor: What do you do when it's stuck in your heart?

Kay: I don't know what to do.

Counselor: Does it just stay there?

Kay: Their story gets stuck in me.

Counselor: And it stays there.

Kay: Well, I'm better now.

Counselor: You feel better. So where did the pain go? I'm talking metaphorically.

Kay: Where did it go? I was reading Shakti Gawain's book, *Creative Visualization,* and tried to picture stuff going down me, but it didn't work. I know it's still there because I get emotional when I think about it . . . so I try not to think about it.

In the next section of dialogue, I applied NLP visualizing techniques to elaborate on her metaphor.

Counselor: If you were to close your eyes and visualize where the pain is stuck, does it have a size and a shape, a color?

Kay: I picture a heart and it's red. My heart.

Counselor: And how is that different from before you took their stories into you. What did your heart look like then?

Kay:	Excited about life. On the move. But I was blind-sided by her story. I was on a path moving forward, and it just came out of the blue. I need to figure out how to prepare myself.
Counselor:	I heard you say at one point, "I'm not even going to ask because if I don't ask . . ."
Kay:	. . . then I can stay detached.
Counselor:	Don't ask, don't tell.
Kay:	And I have been doing a lot of that lately. (She laughs)
Counselor:	I'm thinking that the two awful stories that affected you can't get any worse.
Kay:	I hope so, John. (Hearty laughter) Because I don't want to hear any more. It's like falling off your bike and not wanting to get back on. I got up that day and pretended as if I were shaking stuff off. I think I tried everything. I cried for three or four days.
Counselor:	And those things hurt.
Kay:	Yeah. And maybe it's just normal. Maybe I'm having a normal human reaction to all of this.

Kay normalizes her experience, which indicates a perspective shift. Then Kay told me a story about a stranger who had really listened to her. She said, "It was probably the nicest act of kindness I've ever experienced."

I followed this up by exploring how she could connect with supportive people.

Counselor:	So who are the people at work who can function like this?
Kay:	Claire is a mental health counselor at our agency. I did talk to her. She helped with a tip about leaving everything at your office when you leave. Our whole team is good. But it's hard to put all of that on them because they're dealing with enough of their own. It's difficult to go to Claire and burden her.
Counselor:	(Kay's answer above is a "Yes, but . . .") Is Claire a seasoned person?
Kay:	Very. She's been there a long time.
Counselor:	One possibility is that as a seasoned professional she's heard her worst.
Kay:	Right. I did go to Claire about my suicidal client. I talked with her several times.

I shifted gears and revisited Kay's heart metaphor.

Counselor:	I was struck with your image that it all seems to be stuck in your heart. It's almost as if your heart becomes congested by filling up with the horror of some people's existence. There's no shunt that pulls the pain away. It pools, rather than circulating.

In spite of her clients' horrifying experiences, they functioned to get Kay more fully involved. Earlier in the interview, Kay had stated, "I'm a resource seeker. I went right to books and started reading."

Counselor:	Despite all those horrible things happening to your clients, you became motivated. You somehow reached out and were useful to your clients.

Kay:	Yeah, the day after Tim was arrested, he came back and thanked me. He said that nobody had ever cared about him as much as I had. That was an experience!
Counselor:	Given the double whammy of those two clients, how is it that you didn't give up?
Kay:	I couldn't give up. Tim needed to see that I was going to be there, no matter what he thought or felt.
Counselor:	So despite your pain, you stayed in there.
Kay:	Yeah, and for Fran, too. I could see a future for her, and I think she can see it now. However, in the meantime, every time I see her, I remember her story. I don't want to think about her murdered child and what Fran's been through. I grew up in a very chaotic and dramatic family and I keep thinking, "Is this something I need to do? Do I need to dwell on this? Am I really that psychotic?"
Counselor:	We'll at least put you in the neurosis category as opposed to the psychosis one. (Kay got a good laugh out of my formulation.) Given the worst, it brought out the best in you.
Kay:	I don't know if it's the best in me, John. But it exhausts me. I can't do this job long-term if I can't figure this out. Because there is this side of me that wants to jump in and take care of people. I've got to make sure people are okay. However, it's still their lives. They still need to figure it out.

Kay took responsibility for her clients' change, but began to recognize that she had paid a price.

Counselor:	So with these two clients, how much are they doing the work and how much are you doing the work?
Kay:	I've done a lot with Tim. I did a lot with résumés. Up until now, I haven't really stepped back and said, "Come on, you're the one who needs to go apply for this job." And with Fran, I'm getting better at saying, "You need to do this, this, and this, and call me when you're ready."
Counselor:	You're learning what's yours and what's theirs.
Kay:	But I feel like I need to put on a front and provide hope to them. It's exhausting. They're pretty down in the dumps. I'm constantly saying, "Let's go."
Counselor:	Are you spending your time being a cheerleader? (Deliberate closed question)
Kay:	I'm trying to remind them of their strengths. Part of my style is to say, "Look at your résumé. Look at what you've done. Look at where you can go." I can't imagine not doing that.
Counselor:	So maybe the question is, how do you make sure that you're staying healthy and do what you do well?
Kay:	Exactly. Can you do both?

Later in the interview . . .

Counselor: What did you learn from Fran and Tim that is valuable for you?

Kay: It's a learning process. I just need to experience some of this so I know how to deal with it. Maybe if I hear a story like that again, it's not going to affect me the same way because I've heard the worst. And now I've worked with a suicidal client. Nah, I think it's still going to be hard, no matter what.

Counselor: I think those are going to be hard, regardless. How is it that you didn't just let their terrible problems overwhelm you and close you down?

Kay: I did shut down for a couple of days, but then I remembered a week or so later that Claire asked how I was doing and I said, "I'm actually doing better." I could feel that I was doing better. Maybe I just need to be patient with myself. I need to acknowledge that it's going to knock me off balance for a while.

Counselor: If I were thinking of a mental exercise for you to do at 2:00 AM, it would be this. Keep the story going to include what you did, how they've been helped, and how they're starting to make changes in their lives. In other words, don't keep the story stuck at only the first part. Instead of a snapshot, make it a motion picture.

Kay: Wow! I like that. It takes it from the child back into helping Fran. And that feels much better.

Counselor: The story may start with the child, but it doesn't end there.

Kay: It doesn't. Other children in that family also need their mother's help.

To reinforce Kay's new learning, I ended our first session by telling her a metaphor about other people's stories and how they had transformed their horrible experiences by adding new endings.

Counselor: You read stories about Mothers Against Drunk Driving, parents of children killed by drunk drivers. These mothers used their tragedies to educate youth about the consequences of drunk driving and, in the process, have saved lives. You can rewrite your story to include parts where you and your clients work together to make for a better ending.

I told Kay I'd begin the next session with, "What's better?" She said, "I'm already feeling better." I provided her a copy of my session notes to take home and review.

Session 2.

Counselor: So how did your session go?

Kay: I was digging for the right things to say, but I finally let it go and it went more naturally. I focused more on where we were going to go with Fran—forward. I didn't get lost.

Counselor: So it's where *we're* going to go.

Kay: Yeah! It wasn't about me. I like that. Wow! She does most of the work. I can be there to help guide her. If she's not willing to do that, it's her choice.

Kay then opened up another topic—patience with herself. Again, I asked her about exceptions. When is she patient with herself?

Kay:	When am I patient with myself? (Long pause) It makes my head hurt to think about that. I can't think of a time.
Counselor:	When are you just a little bit more patient with yourself?
Kay:	Probably with my kids. With them, if something is not right, I can let it go.
Counselor:	What about colleagues at work?
Kay:	Oh, yes, I am patient with other people. That's true.
Counselor:	With your kids and colleagues, you can be more patient. What's a small example of being more patient with yourself?
Kay:	Saying I can't do everything is a big patience for me.

In my work with clients, I relentlessly seek ways for clients' new learning to be cued to remind them about their increased choices. Because Kay was more visually oriented, I asked her, "Are you into flowing-water metaphors?" She answered enthusiastically, "Sure. I like flowing water." I reached across my desk and took down a postcard I had taped to the wall. The postcard showed a stream flowing rapidly across boulders. "Kay, place this card on your desk at work." She said, "It's beautiful." I planted a metaphorical seed:

Counselor:	Kay, when you look at the flowing water, it will remind you that in your work with clients that their experiences can flow from them and flow through you.

Four-Week Follow-up Interview. Kay and I met for five minutes to review her progress. I asked, "How are you sleeping?" She looked at me with an amazed expression on her face and said, "You know, I haven't even been thinking about that. I guess it's not a problem anymore." Kay talked about how, at work, she no longer dreaded the prospect of asking difficult questions, but asked without hesitation. She described our brief two sessions of counseling as "Just what I needed."

Outcome

When Kay and I first met, she struggled with an exhaustion that came from assuming too much responsibility for other people's experiences and forgetting to take care of herself. I was impressed by the contrast between Kay's resources and strengths, and how she stayed attached to the parts of her life that were overwhelming. I believe I succeeded in hearing Kay accurately and in getting her to redirect her focus.

The metaphor she originally presented of a client's horrible story being stuck in her heart was developed in the first session. In that session, my use of an NLP technique to change the visually represented photo of the child into a motion picture allowed Kay to move beyond the "stuck" image that congested her heart. The technique allowed Kay to process the experience in a new way by having an ending she could control. Her relief was immediate. This relief carried into the second session and allowed her to touch on another topic that was of concern to her, which she decided she would work on outside of counseling. Kay judged our counseling a success.

In brief counseling, the counselor sticks close to the client's agenda—what the client wants to work on. I believe Kay learned to deal more effectively with painful experiences. Prior to counseling, she had been stuck because she did not have a successful means of dealing with the pain she experienced when working with clients' most challenging stories. Through counseling, Kay discovered a new way to help herself in the future.

Adjusting to a new job involves learning how not to take one's work home. Because Kay was an inexperienced counselor and because of her prior coping patterns, Kay assumed too much responsibility for her clients. In two sessions, Kay gained insight into these patterns. She developed more effective ways of coping with aspects of her clients' experiences that troubled her. I suspect that Kay will continue to face this issue, but that she will find it much less problematic in the future. Kay has taken steps to seek collegial support. I hope that my encouragement to continue and increase this will be heeded.

Kay's complaint of disrupted sleep predominated because of the terrifying images she saw in the early-morning hours. I anticipate that Kay will sleep better now, as she has a method of making snapshots into motion pictures that provide her more control over troubling images.

Kay used guilt and worry as ways to deal with life situations. She referred to this pattern with her mother in particular. Kay indicated that although this was problematic, she did not want to use counseling as the way to work on it. She seemed content to feel relief at having dealt successfully with a challenging work-related situation. In my occasional and informal contacts with Kay, she continues to report that the issues that brought her to counseling are no longer problematic for her.

Reflections

As I listened to Kay, I definitely related to some of the issues she raised. Like Kay, I recently began a new job. Because of a new academic possibility, I left Iowa State University, where I had been a faculty member for twenty-four years, to work at Colorado State University. Although many of my job responsibilities remained similar, I was initially unsettled at having to learn a new work culture. Like Kay, I found that being the new employee involved a steep learning curve. Also like Kay, I was occasionally perplexed as to how much I should share with new colleagues. If I relied on them too frequently, was I burdening them? On the other hand, if I didn't reach out, was I going to stumble and make a fool of myself?

What did I learn about conducting therapy with older adults? Kay reaffirmed lessons I had learned in my mid-40s, when I had dealt with my own mid-life crisis. Then, I had found wisdom in Levinson's book (1978), *The Seasons of a Man's Life.* Levinson presented three major patterns that might emerge as responses to a crisis— use the crisis to get better, stay the same, or deteriorate. Getting better seemed the most sensible, so I took three actions: (1) I focused on my strengths and resources, (2) I drew on the help of people close to me, and (3) I employed techniques to escape becoming stuck. My increased awareness of how to help myself was reflected in my work with Kay. I helped her take a similar set of three actions as she struggled to make sense of this phase of her life.

As Kay's counselor, I drew on my own family-of-origin experiences to provide models of how to handle issues related to aging and its developmental challenges and opportunities. My own family of origin offered mixed models. My mother fought grow-ing old and viewed it as something terrible—something to be denied. In contrast, as my father aged, he forged new opportunities with which to display his talents. After re-tiring at 68, he surprised his four sons by immersing himself in the family's genealogy. When he died twenty years later, he left a legacy of twelve books he had written about various branches of the family tree. In working with clients, I make use of my father as a role model for aging gracefully. I help clients use their talents and strengths.

References

American Psychiatric Association. (2000). *Diagnostic and statistical manual of men-tal disorders: DSM-IV-TR* (4th ed., text rev.). Washington, DC: Author.

Arnold, E. (2005). A voice of their own: Women moving into their fifties. *Health Care for Women International, 26*(8), 630–651.

Berg, I. K., & Szabó, P. (2005). *Brief coaching for lasting solutions.* New York: W. W. Norton.

De Jong, P., & Berg, I. K. (2002). *Interviewing for solutions* (2nd ed.). Pacific Grove, CA: Brooks/Cole.

Fisch, R., Weakland, J. H., & Segal, L. (1982). *The tactics of change.* San Francisco: Jossey-Bass.

Levinson, D. J. (1978). *The seasons of a man's life.* New York: Alfred A. Knopf.

Littrell, J. M. (1998). *Brief counseling in action.* New York: W. W. Norton.

Suggested Readings

Berg, I. K., & Szabó, P. (2005). *Brief coaching for lasting solutions.* New York: W. W. Norton.

De Jong, P., & Berg, I. K. (2002). *Interviewing for solutions* (2nd ed.). Pacific Grove, CA: Brooks/Cole.

Fisch, R., Weakland, J. H., & Segal, L. (1982). *The tactics of change.* San Francisco: Jossey-Bass.

Littrell, J. M. (1998). *Brief counseling in action.* New York: W. W. Norton.

NLP Comprehensive Training Team. (1994). *NLP: The new technology of achievement.* New York: William Morrow.

Watzlawick, P., Weakland, J., & Fisch, R. (1974). *Change.* New York: W. W. Norton.

Biographical Statement

John M. Littrell, Ed.D., is a professor and program coordinator of counseling and career development at Colorado State University in Fort Collins. His two books are *Brief Counseling in Action* (1998) and *Portrait and Model of a School Counselor* (with Peterson, 2005). John's e-mail address is John.Littrell@colostate.edu.

2

Cystic Fibrosis, Alcoholism, and Meaning

Thelma Duffey

Diagnosed as an infant with cystic fibrosis, Jillian, 55, made matters much worse by abusing alcohol. Four marriages and four divorces testify to relationship dysfunction. Thelma Duffey comments, "When I met her, much to her surprise and that of others, she was still alive." Duffey uses the central relational paradox and relational-cultural theory to make sense of this complex case. The central relational paradox is a dynamic wherein, in spite of a yearning for connection, we engage in behaviors that, paradoxically, keep us from the very connection we desire. Duffey uses the lyrics of popular songs to encourage creativity. It should be noted that Thelma Duffey is the founding president of the Association for Creativity in Mental Health.

Jillian, 55, came to me for therapy following an accident in which she was driving while intoxicated, severely injuring a passenger in another car. Jillian had been referred to my office by her attorney, who knew of my work with addiction and with grief and loss.

Diagnosed as an infant with cystic fibrosis, Jillian has also suffered from related illnesses including diabetes, chronic bacterial chest infections, pneumonia, an enlarged spleen, and infertility. Jillian has abused alcohol since she was a teenager. When I met her, much to her surprise and that of others, she was still alive.

Jillian has married and divorced four times. Bearing children had not been an option, and she commented on how much worse her life would have been had she been able to bear them. In Jillian's words, "If I had had kids, I would have had to work all my life or I would have had to stay married to someone who would."

One of the great tragedies of her life came when her father died, when Jillian was 25. Her mother died several years later. Jillian has one sister, Shanna, and four nieces and nephews. She describes a very close relationship with her sister and her family, who live close by.

Jillian graduated from college and received a master's degree in college counseling. She is retired from a community college counseling center, where she provided mostly academic counseling. Jillian inherited a sizable trust fund and is economically advantaged. She lives in a modest home and also owns a lake house.

At the time that I met Jillian, I had been practicing as a licensed professional counselor for several years. I was owner and operator of a multidisciplinary group practice.

Conceptualization

For Jillian, reaching 55 with cystic fibrosis (CF) represents something of a miracle. She feels lucky to have lived such a long life and enter the age of retirement, when most, if not all of the CF kids in her age cohort died early, as predicted. She credits her positive attitude and her ability to live life rather than having her illness live it for her. Ironically, another person lay in the hospital, unconscious and near death, as a consequence of the accident in which Jillian was the drunk driver.

Jillian's parents learned that she had the dreaded CF shortly after her birth. Their daughter had a life expectancy of twenty to thirty years, at best. Her parents encouraged her to live as unencumbered as possible. The family had a lake house, a boat, and jet skis. Jillian's father taught her to water-ski and fish. Her mother gave her free rein, and Jillian grew into a playful, quick-witted, and charmingly comedic child.

Jillian's sister, Shanna, was two years her senior. While Jillian was gregarious and spirited, Shanna was reserved and reflective. It appeared that Jillian developed a "live for today" attitude while Shanna was her rescuer. Jillian was hospitalized on several occasions when she was in college for intoxication as well as for complications from illnesses. While she was in college she was also involved in a near-fatal car accident. In contrast, Shanna was the responsible sibling and transferred colleges to be close to Jilli and look after her.

Jillian had intended to become an attorney, like Shanna, but acknowledged that the effort appeared too great. She entered a profession she thought she could do easily, one that would "pay the bills." When asked about her choice of careers, she simply responded, "Everyone has to have a job." She made it clear that she worked to have fun. Having fun was a driving force in Jillian's decisions. By her sister's account, Jillian cultivated a cohort of aggressively social drinkers and a lifestyle that threatened her health and her personal growth.

Jillian and Shanna described their father as a man who succeeded at everything he attempted. They marveled at how driven he was, his strong work ethic, and his no-nonsense strength and vigor. Father fought for their rights at school and took their point of view when they had conflicts with others. Mother, too, protected them, but particularly Jillian. The sisters described their mother as one who worried about her children at the same time that she enjoyed letting her hair down and being playful with them.

Jillian received these messages: "Your days are numbered, so make the most of life while you have it. *You* are the priority." Jillian came to hold a belief that she was entitled to live life unfettered and that anyone who needed any form of reciprocity was really asking too much. She negotiated relationships that required little from her.

What for some might be considered a reckless lifestyle—excessive alcohol abuse, late-night partying, sporadic care of her fragile body—she explained as living into her comfort zone. "This is who I am." In Frank Sinatra's words, she "did it my way" and was proud of it. She was frustrated with the bad luck that had placed someone in the intensive care unit of the hospital and forced her to do what she enjoyed least—talk to a counselor about uncomfortable subjects.

When I took a close look at Jillian's history, I suspected that although she prized autonomy, she was a prisoner held hostage by alcoholism, relational dead-ends, and a voracious need for options, freedom, and unencumbered choice. Given the developmentally disabling psychological, emotional, and relational consequences that early alcohol abuse and addiction brings, it was not surprising that her level of maturity was stunted. While Jillian appeared worldly, confident, and competent, she was self-centered and limited in her understanding of her impact on others. She behaved much as a person in preadolescence would in the face of conflict. Her sensitivity to others was referenced by her own pain. This did little to help her understand the real pain of others, unless it resonated with feelings of her own. And yet, thanks to her training as a counselor, she was clever at *responding* empathically, which was seductive. Ultimately, her surface-level social skills backfired, particularly when they required true reciprocity.

Jillian admitted to me that her husbands complained that she did more to please others than she did to please them. After a while, they left her, confirming her beliefs that relationships are not to be trusted and that unconditional love is an experience that died with her parents. Alcohol, on the other hand, gives unconditionally. But, of course, there is a price.

I wonder whether much of Jillian's challenge and defensiveness come from a core of shame. My surmise is that the differences and conditions imposed by her illness contributed to these feelings. When I asked about whether spirituality played a role in her life, Jillian told me that she gave up on God when her parents died. She mocked the need for spirituality. However, it is not uncommon for people to search for meaning during difficult times or as they approach later life. I had the good fortune to meet Jillian as she neared what authorities on cystic fibrosis call the "miracle" of an expanded life span. She was weary and frightened and ready to drop the defenses that had kept her seemingly protected. Jillian's spirituality was wounded and at the core appeared to be grief and shame.

My theoretical frame is integrative with relational-cultural therapy (RCT) as a philosophical base. I am also influenced by systemic, existential, cognitive, and narrative therapies. Primary to my work with Jillian was establishing a growth-fostering therapeutic relationship.

Therapeutic goals included fostering mutual empathy, working through disconnections, creating a safe place for authenticity, honoring vulnerability, working through shame, and challenging strategies of disconnection that get in the way of intimacy.

I wanted to help Jillian work through the *central relational paradox,* a concept described by relational-cultural theory. The central relational paradox is a dynamic whereby, in spite of a yearning for connection, we engage in behaviors that, paradoxically, keep us from the very connection we desire. My hope was to help Jillian work through and release feelings of shame, become accountable to herself, and facilitate an accountable relationship with people who have invested in her. That, in my opinion, is the way to create a life of meaning and value. Readers who wish to learn more about RCT may wish to consult the publications listed in the References and Suggested Readings at the end of the chapter.

Process

Jillian and I met twice a month over the course of two years. She came to her initial counseling appointment on time. She was well groomed, casually dressed, talkative, eager to tell her story, and concerned about whether a visit with me would help her with the drunk-driving court case she faced. She expressed appreciation that I was able to work her into my schedule on short notice.

In one breath, Jillian described her childhood in glowing terms and minimized her experience with lifelong chronic illness. Her eyes lit up as she talked about her parents and sister. She told stories about friends with a jovial chuckle and seemed oddly upbeat, given the gravity of her situation and the critical condition of the person her automobile had struck. I also saw flashes of anger as she described living with her illnesses.

Although Jillian denied problems with drinking, she talked at length about her enjoyment of alcohol. She jokingly described her drinking patterns: "I'd rather have a bottle in front of me than a frontal lobotomy!" Her expression clouded when I asked about the accident, and she insisted that it was simply a terrible mistake, an aberration. She acknowledged that drinking and driving was an error that she seriously regretted. She acknowledged that her last boyfriend and some former spouses accused her of being an alcoholic. But, in her defense, she said that all one would have to do is look at her professional success and her clean record up until the accident to see that she was not an alcoholic. The accident resulted from a bad choice, bad timing, and bad luck.

Jillian's casual attitude would shift when she received word that the person she injured while intoxicated had taken a turn for the worse. Jillian's fears raged and her need for support heightened. She committed to attend individual therapy sessions. Jillian also wanted Shanna to attend sessions with her from time to time. Shanna, however, was ambivalent about this. She did not want to place another useless "Band-Aid" on Jillian's emotional wounds and thereby enable her drinking. Nonetheless, Shanna participated in the work.

There were several relapses during our work together. For example, Jillian went drinking with old friends who came into town. Shanna described how Jillian was less sensitive, thoughtful, or responsive following her visits with these friends. This prompted Jillian's defensiveness, and she said that she felt controlled and mischaracterized by Shanna. Shanna, again, felt helpless, as she experienced Jillian retreating into old patterns.

Shanna attended only occasionally, but her participation was helpful. Shanna described her lifelong worry for Jilli and the choice she made several years ago to pull back from being so involved. She told me how their parents supported Jilli and provided what, to this day, Jillian describes as "unconditional love."

The following is an excerpt from one of the conjoint sessions that occurred about a year into therapy. I have included this excerpt because it illustrates how Jillian acquired a valuable insight.

In the following, Jillian responds after Shanna tries to explain how Jillian's accident affected her (Shanna).

Jillian:	I don't know why this has to be such a big deal. *I made a mistake!* (Shouting) Do you think I like this?
Shanna:	Every time something happens, it's a mistake. You never take any responsibility in it. Even when someone else gets hurt, you end up feeling like a victim.

Jillian flinched. I wondered what this felt like to her. It was important that she hear it, and I did not want to interrupt this exchange.

Jillian:	I am *no* victim! I'd like to see you deal with what I've had to deal with.
Shanna:	You're right. I don't know what it feels like to wonder if my next breath is going to kill me. But I do know what it feels like to wonder when your next breath is going to kill *you.* And it makes me so angry to know how much you contribute to your own demise. You're alive in spite of yourself. Why do you think that is? Why do you think you are still here?
Therapist:	You have both suffered. Jillian, we can't know what this has been like for you. Shanna, it is painful to watch someone you love do hurtful things to herself or others.
Jillian:	(in a whisper) I am no victim.
Therapist:	What would being a victim look like to you, Jilli?
Jillian:	You would not be able to do things for yourself. You would need others to take care of you.

Suspecting that Jillian's primary fear was to be physically disabled, I wondered if she had any context for how *emotionally* dependent she was.

Shanna:	Everyone needs to be taken care of sometimes. If you'd only see how *much* help you really need to understand your anger and your fears, maybe you could let some of those feelings go. Then you wouldn't be a victim. Who wants that?
Jillian:	I am not a victim.
Therapist:	Sometimes, when we have been told that we will have no choice but to depend on others, our independence can seem amazingly important, and the last thing we need is to feel like we *need* to depend on someone; that, in itself, can feel victimizing.
Jillian:	Yeah.
Therapist:	And so, when you *do* need something or someone, and it feels victimizing to have that need, it would make sense that you could protect yourself from seeing that. Who would want to feel like they are living out their worst fears?
Jillian:	Yeah.
Therapist:	So, since we are simply human, and we all need someone or something at times, and if we are hardwired to be repelled by that need, what do you think we do then?
Jillian:	I don't know. That's a shitty place to be.
Therapist:	And if it doesn't feel good, but you still need it, what do you do to feel better?
Jillian:	I don't know. I've got to figure it out.
Therapist:	And you figure it out by....
Jillian:	Hell, you just don't let yourself think about it. You dull your mind. You stop yourself from feeling badly. You check out. You watch television. You have a drink. You call a friend. Hell, you go to sleep. There's no end to things you can do.
Therapist:	Yes. There are all sorts of things you can do to divert attention. And sometimes, it feels good to take a break.
Jillian:	Yeah.
Therapist:	But what happens if you take a break *every* time something difficult comes up...if you change channels, so to speak, *every* time an uncomfortable thought or situation comes up for you?
Jillian:	Then I don't have to think about it at all!
Therapist:	And if you *never* have to think about uncomfortable things and something comes up that is *so* intrusive that you truly can't switch the channel, how good do you think you're going to be at dealing with it?
Jillian:	I don't know. I guess if you never do it, you can't be very good at it.
Therapist:	And, what I really hear you say when you tell us you don't want to be a victim, that you are not a victim, is that you don't want to be helpless. You don't want to be in a situation where you have no control. Is that right?

Jillian:	Yes. That's right.
Therapist:	There are things we have control over and things we don't. One of the things we have control over—that you have control over—is how you respond to things that hurt. However, if the only practice you have in responding to hurt is to pretend it doesn't exist, or find diversions, or blame someone because you *do* hurt, how much control do you think you really have?
Jillian:	I'm not sure. I've never given much thought to that.

In subsequent sessions, I continued to work toward the goals of helping Jillian increase her capacity for empathy, accountability, and grace while, at the same time, reducing shame.

I used novels, music, and the media and drew from Jillian's favorites, such as Victor Hugo's *Les Miserables,* the music of Townes Van Zandt, and even the superhero movie, *Hellboy*. For example, one of Jillian's favorite songs is Van Zandt's "To Live Is to Fly." He sings, "Living's mostly wasting time / And I waste my share of mine / But it never feels too good / So let's don't take too long" (Van Zandt, 1972).

Given the odds Jillian beat to be alive at this age, even *she* found her favorite lyrics to be ironic. One of the lines in the song seemed to capture Jillian's long-held coping patterns: "But it don't pay to think too much—on things you leave behind. Well, I may be gone, but it won't be long, I'll be bringing back the melody and the rhythm that I find" (Van Zandt, 1972). Still, the grief she carries permeates her being and is palpably close to the surface:

> We all got holes to fill
> Those holes are all that's real.
> Some fall on you like a storm,
> Sometimes you dig your own. (Van Zandt, 1972)

Jillian used the music to reflect on her life. The lyrics gave words to feelings and fears she had long repressed:

> The choice is yours to make,
> Time is yours to take;
> Some dive into the sea,
> Some toil upon the stone. (Van Zandt, 1972)

Clearly, Jillian was more comfortable diving into the sea and appeared to have contempt for people who "toiled upon the stone." She would say how that would take too much effort—and effort wasn't something she especially liked expending.

▪ Outcome

Jillian fought to hold onto her denial of reality. Our work involved creating enough safety in our relationship that she could be honest with herself and with me. She couldn't ignore her fear of helplessness as her medical prognosis became even graver. During our two years together, we worked to reframe these experiences and put them in some form of productive context.

Weaning Jillian from alcohol wasn't as difficult as I had thought it would be. When she made up her mind that she would no longer drink—at least for the time being—she was able to do so. She began this effort by avoiding people and places where drinking was a shared activity. Although she did not want to participate in a Twelve Step program because of conflicts with her spiritual beliefs or lack thereof, she did agree to attend Rational Recovery (RR) sessions, based on Albert Ellis's rational-emotive therapy. Even though she liked RR's emphasis on cognitive control, the benefits were fleeting.

At one point, Jillian became interested in a man and appeared to find safety in the fact that he was married. We discussed how the relationship worked for her, because it was clear that he would not expect her to commit more time, attention, or care than she was willing to give or receive. Jillian made half-hearted jokes about their arrangement. I thought it was important for her to see how the affair was affecting this man's marriage and children. Although she eventually understood and stopped the affair, it was not before damage had been done to the marriage and to her own self-esteem.

In time, Jillian gained insight and discovered ways of participating in relationships to a greater degree. However, she continued to struggle with understanding how her actions affected others, and she could still become put off when someone challenged her decisions. She brought alcohol under control. Although she would drink with friends from time to time, she did not drink and drive again. In addition, Jillian grew patient with Shanna and learned to reciprocate in ways that were helpful.

Jillian continues to see me in counseling when the need arises.

■ Reflections

I was 40 when I first began my work with Jillian, and yet age did not seem to be an issue. We used shared experiences with an early coastal life and water activities and enjoyment of music and the media to connect with each other and, in time, collaborated on designing creative interventions to facilitate our work.

I have had experiences that help me understand both aging and illness. As a little girl, I grew up living next door to my maternal grandparents. I was used to sharing space with elderly relatives. I also experienced my grandmother's long-term fight with cancer and accompanied her on occasion to M.D. Anderson Cancer Center in Houston. I spent considerable time with her in the nursing home until she died. When my own children were small, I volunteered at a nursing home, playing Bingo and singing with a group that sang Cole Porter songs. I've found it humbling and meaningful to spend time with people in the last stage of life.

Andy Lipman, in his book, *Alive at 25: How I'm Beating Cystic Fibrosis,* describes his remarkable victories, but we are also left to wonder what life might have been like for Andy if his family had been able to talk openly about his disease (Lipman, 2002). Without placing blame, the book addresses the need for families to genuinely deal with their feelings of loss surrounding the news that one of the children carries a debilitating illness and describes the consequences that can come when parents normalize the situation without giving it context.

Certainly, as much as parents try to protect their children who face chronic illnesses, there are times when children can be protected out of a capacity to emotionally and relationally manage their life and their relationships. These issues become particularly salient as people age and as their fears of isolation and loss are more likely to become realized. Jillian showed great courage in her willingness to confront this task. It has been a privilege to walk this walk with her.

References and Suggested Readings

Comstock, D., & Qin, D. (2005). Relational cultural theory: A framework for relational development across the lifespan. In D. Comstock (Ed.), *Diversity and development: Critical contexts that shape our lives and relationships* (pp. 25–45). Pacific Grove, CA: Thomson Brooks/Cole.

Duffey, T. (2005). The relational impact of addiction across the lifespan. In D. Comstock (Ed.), *Diversity and development: Critical contexts that shape our lives and relationships* (pp. 25–45). Pacific Grove, CA: Thomson Brooks/Cole.

Duffey, T., Comstock., D., & Reynolds, J. (2004). From disconnections to connections: The effects of relational cultural therapy and the Enneagram personality typology in couples counseling. *VISTAS: American Counseling Association, 1*, 237–242.

Jordan, J. (2000). The role of mutual empathy in relational/cultural therapy. *Journal of Clinical Psychology, 56,* 1005–1016.

Lipman, A. (2002). *Alive at 25: How I'm beating cystic fibrosis.* New York: Longstreet Press.

Miller, J., & Stiver, I. (1997). *The healing connection: How women form relationships in therapy and in life.* Boston: Beacon Press.

Van Zandt, T. (1972). To live is to fly. On *High low and in between* [record]. New York: EMI Records.

Walker, M., & Rosen, W. (2004). *How connections heal: Stories from relational-cultural therapy.* New York: Guilford Press.

Biographical Statement

Thelma Duffey, Ph.D., is a professor of counseling and counseling program director at The University of Texas at San Antonio. She is a licensed professional counselor and a licensed marriage and family therapist in the state of Texas. She maintains a private practice working with individuals, couples, and families, and has done so for seventeen years. Dr. Duffey is editor of the *Journal of Creativity in Mental Health* and serves as founding president for the Association of Creativity in Counseling, a division within The American Counseling Association. Her book, *When the Music Stops: A Dream Dies,* was published by The Haworth Press, Taylor & Francis Group, in 2005. You may reach Thelma at tduffey@satx.rr.com.

3

Help! She's Old and I Am Young but She's 57 and I'm 65

Marijane Fall

Mary, 57, never left home without her husband Frank, lest she suffer heart palpitations (for which there was no medical basis). Behind the psychosomatic symptoms, Marijane Fall saw depression as Mary struggled unsuccessfully to adjust to inevitable change. Fall used cognitive behavioral therapy and prescribed regular exercise, both proven remedies for depression.

Fall admits feeling critical of Mary's uptight personal mannerisms, which seemed to symbolize her passivity in the face of aging. This was certainly not the path that Fall has forged for herself, and she yearned for Mary to revolt. But Fall, a seasoned therapist, recognizes a judgmental stance when she sees one, even in herself. She concludes, "I've got some thinking to do about this age thing." Don't we all!

Mary entered the counseling office with a tentative gait, as if uncertain of her footing. She was tall, perhaps 5′8″, and stood very straight, as if at attention in a military uniform. She was dressed in perfectly pressed white slacks, a long-sleeved yellow-and-white blouse, nylon stockings, and white sneakers. She had a white sweater over her shoulders despite the temperature outside being 82 degrees. Her blouse was clasped tightly at the neck with a cameo broach. Her hair was short, close to her head, turned under at the ends. She looked around, smiled tightly at me, and clasped the broach at her neck in a reflexive type of action. "Hi. You must be Mary. I'm Marijane," I remarked. She smiled and nodded yes while fingering the broach. I put out my hand to shake hands and she replied in kind, her hand having no life or energy. I gestured toward the chairs. She stepped very carefully over to the closest one, sat down, smoothed her clothing, and looked up at me. She fingered the broach at her neck. She still had not spoken. I sensed how hard this was for her and that it was going to be tough for me too. And that was the beginning of Mary's and my relationship, one in which I was to learn as much about myself as she was to learn about herself.

I am a licensed clinical professional counselor and a counselor educator. My clinical practice is small, only one day a week. Mary was referred by her family physician in a neighboring town. She had heart palpitations and flutters, panic, sweating, dizziness, and insomnia. As a result, she rarely left home, and then only with her husband. She feared she was having a heart attack or had a cancerous tumor around her heart. The family physician referred Mary to therapy after determining that there was no physical reason for her symptoms of distress. Mary had never seen a therapist before and was frightened at the prospect but willing to do anything to get to the bottom of the problem. I noted with curiosity that she didn't have a goal of alleviating the symptoms. And while Mary was very apprehensive about coming to see a counselor, I was fueled with tension and excitement. This is usual for me. Who is this new person? What brought her here today? Will I be able to help her? I quickly added more questions. She is so silent and scared. Will she speak? Will our work calm her or make it worse? Is she okay?

Mary had filled out the intake document at home with precise penmanship. She stated that she never left home without her husband Frank, lest she lose consciousness as result of dizziness or palpitations. She was a homemaker, married for thirty-nine years, and had never worked outside of the home. Mary and Frank had married when they were both 18, just three days after graduation from high school. They lived comfortably in a home inherited from Frank's parents.

Mary stated that there were no problems with alcohol or drugs, that she had never contemplated harming herself, and that her health had been relatively good until this episode. She had no friends outside of family. She confessed that she had dreamed of working in a small dressmaking shop down the road from her home when her children were grown, but she had never inquired to see if they were hiring. Besides, she had a routine that took all her time every day, and she worried that she could not work even one day a week and complete the work at home. She listed no recent losses, moves, changes, or deaths.

Mary's parents were deceased. She had never known her father, and her mother had died of cancer when Mary was 5. She remembered her mother as a tiny woman who was always lying down, smelled funny, and loved flowers. Once Mary brought a bouquet of field daisies to her, which delighted her. Mary had tried to find some daisies for her when she died. There was snow on the ground and she couldn't find any. Mary remembers feeling "funny" when her Mom died.

Mary and Frank have three married sons; each family has one or two children, with five grandchildren all together. They all gather at Mary and Frank's home on Sundays between 10:00 and 11:30 for breakfast as a Sunday ritual—a lot of work now, as that means thirteen people for breakfast. Everyone wants different things to eat, and Mary never has time to visit. "Frank tells me just cook one meal and make them eat it or go without, but I always give in and cook what they want." In the summer the families go camping together. Mary waits for camp all year.

Despite a forty-minute drive for Mary, Dr. Jones still thought that I might be the best therapist because of our similar ages. Our ages? Mary was 57 going on 100. I was 65 going on 50, or so I thought at the time. How could she be younger than I was chronologically and seem to me to be so much older? What did that mean for me?

Conceptualization

I saw Mary once a week for twelve sessions of therapy. Considering that week 1 was an intake and week 12 concerned next steps, it was a very short time. It was as if Mary needed to find the opening, but she traveled out of her tunnel-of-the-unknown fears very fast once she could see the light. I was a bystander, watching her journey in the present with tiny steps and new thinking. I provided the map and the gas for the car. Mary drove.

Our original goals were to get to the root of why Mary was having physical symptoms. There were several parts of her present behaviors that needed attention. Mary had symptoms of mild to moderate depression as well as several features of panic disorder. Because she did not have insurance that would cover her visits to me, we did not need an immediate diagnosis. However, we talked of these features and discussed medication. Her physician had already agreed to prescribe medications for the depression and the panic features if Mary wished. My goal was to understand how this behavior met her needs and assist her with new behaviors that were more consistent with her present needs. She had decided to wait before taking any medication and ultimately ended up not using the prescription.

One question that I entertained was whether to see Mary alone or with Frank. He drove her to therapy and waited outside in the car, so it would be an easy decision to include him. I decided against including him initially, as I was struck by how often Mary answered questions in the intake session from other people's perspectives. In one example, when I asked her about friends, she replied, "Frank doesn't think we need any friends outside the family. We have three sons and grandchildren." When I asked what *she* thought, she replied, while fussing with her broach, "Frank says I think too much. He's probably right." As a second example, when I asked what a typical Saturday would look like, she replied, "Frank says we shouldn't go to the stores unless it's quiet, so we go at 7:00 in the morning Saturdays, well, we leave the house by 6:40 and get there when it opens at 7:00. People are not shopping then." Where was Mary's voice? It seemed as if establishing her voice might be more easily done if she was in individual therapy. Later she could decide if she wanted to include Frank.

A second question concerned how much she would do outside of the session. When clients have depression symptoms, I usually give them homework the first session. I suggest some form of exercise, typically walking, for at least twenty minutes every other day. What would happen if I suggested that to Mary? I decided that I would try it and include Frank in the outing if she chose to go outside. We discussed walking to the corner of her street with Frank each night if she felt able. I suggested that the exercise would aid her strength and assist with the depression at the same time. I also said that the goal was to try. If it didn't work one night, simply try the next. It would be a process to get her body and mind ready to do this. She asked if I could explain this to Frank (he would be coming inside to pay the bill), as otherwise he probably wouldn't do it. I suggested that she tell him while I was there. I was even more intrigued.

I chose to work with Mary from a relational theory base. She seemed personally unconnected with her family and even herself. Her social life consisted of Sunday morning breakfasts for all three sons and their families, for which she did all the cooking and cleaning. On the surface it appeared that she was busy and connected, yet in reality she was far more connected to television characters than to her own family. Certainly no one asked about her or knew of her, including Mary herself.

Because cognitive behavioral therapy is well documented as being helpful to clients with clinical depression, I wanted to include cognitive behavioral small guided steps to change Mary's depressive life stance. This theory also allows for demonstration of behaviors that are a part of self-efficacy, which was extremely low for Mary. Her beliefs in her ability to perform in ways that meet her needs would get a foundation in successful performance of small tasks and my verbal reinforcement of her enactment of behaviors.

It might appear that our work in the relational and cognitive behavioral theories would be disjointed, but it wasn't. Being empathic, nonjudgmental, and open to a very different way of life was the base from which I wished to work. Having said that, the reader will notice right away that I was far from nonjudgmental. Although I didn't express it overtly, I felt critical of Mary's dress—the broach, the tightly buttoned-up collars, the nylons and polished white sneakers, the pressed sharp creases in the pants. I was conscious of Mary's subservience to her husband and her lack of voice. I wanted her to revolt!

I am plagued by a persistent question with all of my clients: How does a particular behavior or symptom meet the client's needs? Mary's symptoms kept her at home. She never left home without her husband. How did that help her? She described her daily schedule, down to fifteen-minutes intervals. Such a schedule would not work for most people. For Mary it appeared to be a source of comfort. She always knew what was coming next.

What about me? I wanted to be nonjudgmental, yet I found myself judging Mary's way of life. Her only control was over her schedule of housework. She seethed at Frank's "selfish behaviors" but would respond to this situation only by days of silence. Frank had no idea what got her to the point of silence, nor did she ever disclose this. Mary resented that her sons and their families never hugged her, yet she didn't ask for hugs. All of this judgment got in my way of understanding totally what it was like to be Mary. Why couldn't I let Mary be Mary?

Of course, the answer is always within myself. I thought about the journey I was on. Where was I headed? I was at the age when most of my friends had retired. What was holding me back besides the too-easy answer of finances? Was it easier to remain in the established pattern than to develop a new one? What would it be like to let go of the teaching and research and head off without encumbrance to being fully present in the world of 66-year-olds? And, by the way, what was it like for people to be with me? What habits did I have, such as fingering a broach or wearing nylons with sneakers, that were indicative of my rootedness in years gone by? Would I ever appear as old as Mary? What did age mean? Perhaps I could not see what others saw. Working with a supervisor helped me to address these nagging thoughts, all the while becoming more engaged in the relationship with Mary.

Process

Session 1. The intake session was scheduled for two hours. Mary had filled out the intake form at home and brought it with her. I asked questions to get further depth on biographical data, present family and family of origin, history, health, social connections, mental status, and present-day issues. It was here that I began to respect this woman who sat before me, nervously fingering her broach, constantly looking away, giving very short answers to my queries, and always trying to please me. This was so hard for her, she was so fearful, yet here she was. She had courage.

Session 2. I was surprised to hear that Frank had had a heart attack and subsequent surgery four months previously. Mary had never told me about this. She brought it up because she was particularly worried about Frank's condition and their summer plans. The whole family had always gone away camping most summer weekends. They had already reserved campsites. Would Frank be able to do this? Could he do the driving? Could he set up camp? What if he had another heart attack and only she was around? Further, she didn't drive, couldn't go shopping, and didn't know about their checkbook or bank accounts. How would she handle it? As we worked on a timeline, it was clear that many present physical symptoms began shortly after Frank came home from the hospital.

A second surprise was that Mary had starting going for walks at night. She did not share this information until I asked, but then seemed ever so slightly proud when she mentioned that today she had walked by herself, without Frank, before coming to our session. These walks continued throughout our twelve sessions and quickly built up to a mile a day. Neighbors were speaking to her on her walks, and she was responding! She had only to get started on something and she would surge forward with giant steps instead of the tentative baby steps that I had expected.

<u>Session 3.</u> This was the most important session of all. Although Mary had not marked any losses on her intake form, I suggested we take a look. She told me about the death of her mother when Mary was 5 years old. Her grandmother took care of her then. Grandmother required Mary to sleep with her in case she (Grandmother) died or needed help in the night. Indeed, Grandmother did die in the night when Mary was 10. Then Mary went to live with an aunt and uncle who had five children of their own. She tried to be especially good so that they would keep her, and she lived there until her marriage eight years later. We discussed her loss of an unborn child. Now that her sons had left home, that was still another loss. The list continued.

- She would not always be able to depend on Frank.
- She no longer knew how to cook for Frank, as he now required a special diet.
- No more anticipation of the summer camping.
- Financial insecurity.
- Loss of trust in a predictable future.
- Fears about her own heart health. After Frank's illness, it was as if her own body was giving up.

Near the very end of that third session, sitting demurely in the chair, fingering the clasped broach at her neck, in a hushed voice, she said, "I remember when my grandmother and my mother died." I asked her about sensations of smell, sight, and touch, and she grew more tender and less physically rigid. Her eyes glassed over with tears as long-forgotten feelings surfaced. It was tentative, it was quiet, and it was so important. I wished the session could have continued, but our fifty minutes were up. Would this continue in the next session?

<u>Sessions 4–11.</u> Frank's illness had shaken Mary. Frank did the driving, paid the bills, and made all the decisions. When Frank was in the hospital, her boys had taken her to visit and had helped with shopping. But what would happen when Frank was gone for good? Mary was vulnerable at the very core of her existence, and the life force of her body, her heart, became the focus of anxiety and fear.

Mary had been vulnerable during the third session. Would she back away from me in the fourth? Mary came in the door for the fourth session and remarked, "You have such pretty clothes." She was connecting with me around fashion, a typical thing to do with a woman friend. "I suspect we both like yellow," I answered. I can still remember the high energy with which she replied, "Yes!" And we were off and running once again. Last week's connection was rekindled. We were a team, two women in yellow working to discover Mary.

Subsequent sessions began with Mary sharing what she had done differently each week. This gave me a chance to acknowledge her successful performance (in self-efficacy terms) and to create an "Accomplished" list, which we added to throughout the sessions. Mary began to chuckle over the list and how long it was getting to be. Sometimes she would mention that an item wasn't new, but instead built on another item. Thus she demonstrated to me that she was keeping track of the list, much as she did with her household schedule.

While all this progress was exciting, I wouldn't want the reader to get the wrong impression. Mary still slipped silently into a room, still had a hesitancy even to her steps, still depended on Frank. But she took steps every week. She asked Frank to show her how to write a check and show her what he did with the bank statement. She told her children that she wanted hugs. She went out to lunch with a neighbor. Some of the hardest things were identifying feelings, figuring out what *she* wanted when Frank had another opinion, and standing up for herself. The day she told Frank that she would like to write a check, she left a triumphant message on my answering machine.

<u>Session 12.</u> Our last session was a celebration. Mary and Frank were going to be camping for the rest of the summer, so it seemed logical to stop now. Mary could come back later if she wished. Was it a bit earlier than I would have wished? Yes, but it fit their lives. We celebrated with going over the list of losses and Mary even added a new one—the loss of our meeting every week. We then went over her "Accomplished" list. It was long. When I asked for her reaction, Mary said she was "kinda proud" of it. We made copies of both lists, one for her, one for me, and talked of next steps. She said she would continue moving forward with her lists, and I believe that she will.

Outcome

The outcome is interesting to ponder. Certainly there were changes in Mary's behaviors and her sense of self. She came to recognize an identity for herself that was both a part of and separate from her family. She began to ask quietly for what she needed, on occasions, and she stopped relying on her husband. She left the house by herself and took short walks. She developed a friendship and went for lunch, "just us girls." She no longer felt that she was utterly dependent on Frank. However, she still washed clothes every Monday at 7:30, ironed every Tuesday at 9:00, and had hot muffins for all the family on Sunday. Some things never change. She liked it that way.

Mary noticed a difference as she acknowledged emotions. She laughed now with a slight chuckle and could express words of sadness. Tears did not flow easily, but had made an appearance. She was surprised to find that she wanted Frank to hug her on occasion, and she asked him to do so. She could tell the grandchildren to behave better. Once she even unbuttoned the top button of her blouse, though she said it made her uncomfortable because of the draft of air. And when she left the last time, she gave me a hug.

Reflections

I love hindsight. It is so much more fun than muddling my way through this maze of therapy. If I had known that I only had twelve sessions, I might have suggested a few more role-plays to assist Mary with social skills. I like to use immediacy and to share observations with clients about "us," about what is happening between the client and me. But timing is of the essence, and I waited for the right time and it never came. Maybe I held off because I was learning so much about myself?

I would have liked more time for Mary to build her social skills and to continue her knowledge of herself. She had a lifetime of unacknowledged feelings and thoughts. Twelve weeks was only a brief beginning. I am not sure if I would have tried to go any faster—at times I wished I had slowed down more—but having knowledge of the end would give me more freedom to plan what was most important.

I was disappointed that Mary didn't get out of those constricting nylon stockings and kept fidgeting with that strangulating broach around her poor neck! But these articles of apparel were comforting for her, and they were obviously my problem, not Mary's. When I was young, I had an ancient grandmother who often wore a broach. "So what?" is the question. The only answer I can come up with is that my personal awareness of age, of changes required by age, and of losses concerning body changes are increasing. Am I the one whose style is out of sync for my age? Should I button up my collar so that my older skin would not show? I've got some thinking to do about this age thing.

Suggested Readings

Kottler, J. (2003). Client and therapist: How each changes the other. In *The Gift of Therapy* (pp. 1–24). San Francisco: Jossey-Bass.

Myers, J., & Harper, M. (2004). Evidence-based effective practices with older adults. *Journal of Counseling & Development, 82,* 207–218.

Schwiebert, V., Myers, J., & Dice, C. (2000). Ethical guidelines for counselors working with older adults. *Journal of Counseling & Development, 78,* 123–129.

Scogin, F., & McElreath, L. (1994). Efficacy of psychosocial treatments for geriatric depression: A quantitative review. *Journal of Consulting and Clinical Psychology, 57,* 403–407.

Townsend, K., & McWhirter, B. (2005). Connectedness: A review of the literature with implications for counseling, assessment, and research. *Journal of Counseling & Development, 83,* 191–201.

Yalom, I. (2002). *The gift of therapy.* New York: HarperCollins.

Zalaquett, C., & Stens, A. (2006). Psychosocial treatments for major depression and dysthymia in older adults: A review of the research literature. *Journal of Counseling & Development, 84,* 192–201.

Biographical Statement

Marijane Fall, Ed.D., is a professor at the University of Southern Maine. She is a licensed clinical professional counselor and a registered play therapist supervisor. In addition to her university duties, she has a small private practice. Marijane has authored many journal articles and book chapters. She co-authored a book with John Sutton, *Clinical Supervison: A Practitioners Handbook.* Marijane subscribes to the adage, "Perhaps it does not matter what I am, so long as I do the job for the client that is needed, and am mindful of getting my personal work done elsewhere." Marijane welcomes your correspondence at mjfall@usm.maine.edu.

4

The "Transition" Experience: Group Counseling for Baby Boomers

Mary Finn Maples

Logistically, small groups are more efficient than individual sessions, and they have the advantage of offering mutual support for people who find themselves in the same boat. In this case, the "boat" is pending retirement. Maples brings together six professionals ranging in age from 56 to 78, who valued work as their meaning in life and so regarded retirement as a fearful prospect.

As a former president of both the American Counseling Association (ACA) and the Association for Spiritual, Ethical and Religious Values in Counseling (ASERVIC), Maples is in a strong position to comment on the state of the profession; you may be interested in her comments about gerontological counseling in her Reflections section.

In a recent conversation with a colleague at the university where I have been a professor for thirty years, he mentioned that he was considering the possibility of retiring from his post as a chemistry professor. During our discussion, I noted that his facial expression could only be described as "pained." He said he was not looking forward to retirement, because the university had been "his life." The next day and, coincidentally, several times over a period of a couple of weeks, I encountered six or seven other friends and colleagues who were close in age, and the topic of retirement emerged again and again.

Not being a right-brained "creative" individual, yet a counseling professional, I credit one of my colleagues with the idea of starting a counseling group of professionals who are being seriously challenged by thoughts of retirement. Although I have researched, published, and presented for years on the topic of gerontological counseling, I had never counseled a "retirement" group. Gathering all the data that were available was daunting because of the dearth of information.

I e-mailed an invitation to several leaders of nearby organizations, agencies, and businesses requesting that they pass my invitation to professionals in their employ who might have concerns or questions or simply the need to meet with other "like-minded" professionals.

Conceptualization

The invitation explained that because this was an "initial experiment," the size of the group was limited, but that other opportunities might arise for participation in future groups. The time frame was to be eight one-hour sessions. I decided that a group of five to seven would be appropriate. I described the purpose as "an opportunity to share and discuss with 5–7 professionals who have given more than a 'fleeting' thought to what retirement might be like." I received 109 responses from the invitations.

I asked respondents to answer questions about what kind of life one would have without work or enjoyable hobbies. In all, there were ten open-ended questions to help me discern how a small cohort might interact in a group. I narrowed the finalists to ten potential members who lived within thirty or forty miles of my counseling home office. In a sense, it was taking a risk, because I knew there would be dropouts before the group even started. In fact, I wound up with six. I have led a lot of groups, and I don't especially like even numbers because of such issues as partnering, cliques, and taking sides. I took the chance.

Of the six, there were four men and two women. They ranged in age from 56 to 78, with a median age of 60. The 56-year-old began the first session with, "This is the first time in twenty years that I've been the youngest in a group." With regard to education, two members held terminal degrees (M.D., Ph.D.), three had master's degrees (education, business), and one held a bachelor's in finance and was chief financial officer of a national conglomerate. With regard to family, two were divorced; one single, one windowed, and two were married (for over thirty years). All but the single member had adult children, and three had grandchildren.

Because this group was experimental, I decided to offer it on a *pro bono* basis. However, the group subsequently reached a consensus to donate to a charity that served the needs of older persons.

Before going ahead with a description of group process, I want to review some of the research that makes gerontological group counseling a wave of the present and future. Consider some of these facts about "Baby Boomers" (Maples & Abney, 2006):

- They are living longer than any prior generation, thanks to the many advances in medical science, and, in attention to health issues, fewer smokers.
- They have lower rates of disability. Again, medical science, as well as advances in science itself—new physical prostheses, as one example, perhaps because of the necessity for caring for wounded in the various military actions that their generation has experienced.
- They are achieving higher levels of education. Much more financial aid was and is available to them. They are continuing their formal education far beyond that of their parents.
- They are living less in poverty, therefore they are financially more secure; even though the cost of living, housing, and fuel costs are rising, their education helps them to advance educationally and economically
- They are experiencing many different family structures than prior generations. Consider, for example, the increase in divorce rates, the acceptance and flourishing of gay marriages, or partnerships of both genders, and adoption of children by single persons, none of which were common in earlier generations
- They are taking better care of themselves than any generation before them. The upswing of health and physical fitness organizations has created huge investment opportunities for Boomers, both physically and financially (Maples & Abney, 2006).

Further, consider that, prior to 1800, there were no known persons in the United States who could be verified to have lived to the age of 100. Currently, the fastest-growing population in the United States is 85+. By 2030, one in five Americans will be over 65 years of age, and at least 50 percent of Baby Boomers, born between 1946 and 1964, will see their 100th birthday (Stickle & Onedera, 2006). Knowledge of these facts, along with the changing nature of life in later years, helped to make this adventure in "transitional" group counseling a very exciting one.

Process

Session 1. Words are important. I described the group as an "experience," and John said, "Then let's call it that!" Steve, who turned out to be a valuable group facilitator, requested (rather than suggested) that we not allow the word "retirement" ever to be used by any group member, or the counselor, throughout the experience. To make that agreement more interesting, Teresa suggested that we fine anyone one dollar for using the forbidden word. John further suggested that we donate the proceeds (the fines) to the charity that we had discussed earlier in the session. From a group-process perspective, I was delighted, because I figured we would be more avid listeners if we were trying to catch someone using the prohibited word. All agreed, also, that the rules could be flexible and could be changed throughout the experience, with mutual concurrence. We agreed that homework between sessions would be helpful.

We also talked about rules of confidentiality, as they would apply in our group. I explained that there were ethical issues if members were also in counseling with other mental health professionals. I required those who were taking psychotropic medicines to have written permission from the prescribing physician to participate. Only one member fit this last category, who wound up withdrawing from the group after the third session.

As might be expected, the first session was devoted to becoming acquainted. I decided against formal icebreakers because the group members were pretty sophisticated about counseling and probably had already experienced these types of activities. I did, however, conduct a contest to name the group. Each participant wrote a suggestion anonymously, and it was noteworthy that four members used a form of the word *transition*. We agreed to call ourselves the "The Transitioners," hence the title of this case study.

During this first session, I explained some of the stages we might encounter during a group experience, and I assured them that each stage was integral to normal group development. I told them that I hoped that in time we would come to feel more like a team than a group of separate individuals.

Finally, in this first session we discussed commonalities and differences, family configurations, professional backgrounds, activities outside of work, travel experiences, time constraints, and the like. What I had planned for a one-hour session became three hours, and no one left early!

Session 2. It had become clear in the first session that these folks respected those members who provided input and feedback. Steve, who functioned like a facilitator in the first session, was the most vocal and also appeared to be the most respected. All members had contributed in the first session, but I was cautious about Sally. Much of what she had said was merely reinforcing Steve.

With a preliminary review of why we had come together, I distributed a blank slip of paper and played a five-minute audiotape of relaxing soft music and woodland sounds. I stopped the tape and asked, "When you hear the word 'retirement,' what one word describes how you feel?" Immediately, Joan reminded me that I owed a fine! I put one dollar in a cup on the table. However, I continued to play the tape and asked them to close their eyes before writing the word that came to mind.

Almost unbelievably, after collecting and shuffling the papers, three of the six had written the word *fear.* Two of the others wrote *apprehension,* and the last, *confusion.* I read aloud each of the responses and realized from their nonverbal reactions (facial expressions, deep breathing, open sitting postures) that this was an "OK" activity. The remainder of Session 2 was an open discussion of the words. I learned more from that meeting, I am certain, than any of the participants.

Time now for homework. I sent the group home after the second session with an assignment: Please describe three issues, concerns, or problems that caused you to identify with that one word you put on your paper.

Session 3. It was reinforcing to me that all had devoted extensive thought to the assignment. They expanded on *fear, apprehension,* and *confusion* to include these comments:

- Loss of my identity.
- Loss of friends, colleagues, meaning in life.
- Time—too much—what will I do with 24/7, instead of weekends?
- To whom will I be significant now?
- I have nothing else that means anything to me, and I don't want to spend *all* of my life with family.
- What will happen if I lose my spouse and am *really* alone?
- I write, give speeches, and travel extensively because there is great reward in them, not always monetary, but they increase my collection of friends, new colleagues, and I extend my own learning.
- Many people admire and respect me for who I am (professionally). Who will I be if I "transition" (laughter).

Not so coincidentally, every one of the members of the cohort identified with the majority of these issues. Unfortunately, so much so, that we lost Sally, the participant who had been on medication for depression. About three weeks after the last group session, she called to ask if she could be counseled individually regarding her feelings about "*potential transitioning.*" She made good use of individual counseling and has kept in touch with me.

At this point in time, at the end of the third session, the group asked me to share a bit of the research about Baby Boomers and about those who would be described as being from the "Silent Generation"—born between 1925 and 1946. Of course, I was happy to do so. Readers can refer back to the Conceptualization section for a review of these data.

As a homework assignment, I asked the five remaining members to e-mail me three topics before the next session that they felt were issues they had faced or were facing that might help them in their deliberations about their futures. Throughout the group experience, I was grateful for their Internet ability. Of course, we agreed to discuss and deal with the issues from the original homework assignment, as well—i.e., loss of identity, loss of meaning, friends, too much time on their hands, loss of spouse.

Sessions 4 and 5. One of the challenges of working with this group could only be called "staying on task." They were such highly intelligent people with so many life experiences that they digressed. We agreed to work on only one issue at a time, beginning with general issues and then moving to specifics.

Taking the results of the first homework assignment, we agreed that the main issue was *loss.* We devoted the entire session to past and current losses. I asked how each might react differently if they were to experience past losses now. Meaninglessness, life worth, friendships, living on a regular schedule, knowing what each day would bring, spouses or partner losses were also seen as major "loss" issues. I encouraged members to share feelings rather than thoughts. John's comment, "Thoughts are so superficial but it's tough for me to share feelings with people I've only met a few weeks ago, but I know that I learn more about me and where I am when I can share my own feelings." He also noted that he wrote "fear" in the original assignment because he feared sharing his feelings about the impending idea of "retirement." Oops! Another fine for the "R" word. We had collected fifteen dollars in fines, so far.

Sessions four and five actually blended, and writing about them at this point is difficult, because they simply seemed to be a continuation from one week to the next. There was a considerable outflow of feelings about the words they had written in their assignment. Although these sessions cannot be described as cathartic, by the end of the fifth session all five described themselves as feeling relieved that they were not alone in their fear, apprehension, and confusion about the future, and that the sense of loss was not as ghastly or frightening as it had been before the group began.

Sessions 6 and 7. The task was setting goals for the future. The group had reached the point at which I felt they were really listening to each other and paying respectful attention. I was contributing less verbal input with each session. As a homework assignment for the sixth session (and it appeared to be so important to them that it consumed the seventh, as well), the group was asked to discuss the future with their significant others. During ordinary group counseling experiences in the past, I have found this to be somewhat risky. What if someone doesn't have a significant other? However, I knew that with this group, all had important people in their lives, and that even the single member had a loving partner. The focus of the final session, I hoped, would be positive. But one never knows.

Session 8. At the beginning of the final session we devoted considerable discussion to the word *transition*. Questions emerged such as, "What transitions have I already made in my life?" "What ones were difficult?" "Why?" I had no idea how intense this topic would be. In a true sense, each was reliving his or her life. As each person shared, I developed the hope that they would see the future as their most important transition, that of *retirement* (yes, I paid again), as one for which they had had considerable opportunity to reflect already.

The reader may be noting at this time that we had not appeared to devote much time to the topic of finances and/or financial security for the future. In fact, in one of the earlier sessions we had indeed discussed money. Only the 56-year-old had some minor concerns. All had pensions, 401(k)s, Social Security, and had saved through investments sufficient to consider themselves financially secure, if not wealthy, barring unforeseen future circumstances. One of the major problems in that particular discussion was getting them off the topic of stocks, bonds, and mutual funds, and their successes and failures in these ventures.

During the last part of this session, having earlier discussed some serious issues in their lives, we devoted time to fantasizing about such questions as "What might make you the happiest person in the world ten years from now?" "To what extent did you meet your childhood goals as an adult?" "If you could 'transition' right now, what would you do?" While considerable humor was shared in this discussion, it did bring the group into a futuristic mode.

Now that we were concluding the transition experience, I asked each of the five participants how they felt about the last eight weeks. One of their comments stayed with me: "Since I now look forward to the end of my paid working life as another transition, of which I have had many and all successful, why should I fear this one?" Others reinforced this statement vigorously. It almost appeared to me that they had seen the idea of retirement as some sort of death or disabling experience. I could see that it had been a mystery, no matter how many friends, colleagues, and relatives they had watched go into retirement.

Outcome

This experiment in "Transitional Group Counseling for Baby Boomers" was, at best, risky for me, despite the prior research I had done and prior groups I had counseled. My goal was to relieve the mystery, apprehension, and fear about retirement among professionals who valued their work as their meaning in life, and who felt that their lives would be meaningless once they retired. Each member of the group evaluated the experiences as highly meaningful, and each planned to maintain contact with each other after the experience was over.

One of the most interesting outcomes of the experience was their discussion and decision about what to do with the "fines." We had collected $37.00 from the group for their use of the forbidden word *retirement* (yet not one dollar after the fifth session). They had decided, in the seventh session, that because there had been no charge for the group experience, they would each return with an unmarked envelope for the last session, which would contain a donation to the charity of our choice. The group agreed that there would be a $25 maximum.

About twenty minutes during the eighth session was devoted to deciding the charity to which we would donate the money, and that turned out to be a real challenge, because everyone had his or her own ideas (never again, in the last session!). We finally agreed, and as I opened each envelope, I discovered that all five had contributed the maximum amount. The fact that the group was unanimous in wanting to continue beyond the eight weeks tells me that it was a success!

Reflections

I see this form of group counseling as meeting a great need for the Baby Boomer generation, but if that need is to be met, there is a far greater need for *trained* counselors to work with these intelligent, gifted, and important (to the future) people. I am disappointed that the Council for the Accreditation for Counseling and Related Educational Programs (CACREP), which is the national accrediting agency for counselor education programs, will no longer accredit gerontological master's degree programs (Council for the Accreditation for Counseling and Related

Educational Programs, 2006). This is understandable, because, until recently, there were only two of these CACREP-accredited graduate programs in the country. Creative solutions to this problem, such as post-master's-degree certification, should be considered.

I am reminded of a session I participated in at the American Counseling Association's national conference in 2006. Helen Chapman was a panelist on the subject, "A New Age of Aging," and her research focused on the joys and fears of aging (Chapman, 2006). Helen highlighted the joys as family, grandchildren, travel, hobbies, volunteering, pets, and social activities, and the fears as insufficient funds to last a lifetime, loss of independence related to physical illness, inability to maintain control of their life, and the expense and pain of a terminal illness. While Chapman's joys and fears were certainly integral to our group, as to any older person, "my" group" just didn't seem that fearful, perhaps because most were younger and/or more optimistic than the persons in Chapman's study.

Engaging in a transitional group experience appeared to provide both reinforcement for the concerns expressed by participants and reassurance that they were not unique. The experience clarified the need to feel "comfortable in their discomfort." Did this experience prepare them for their ultimate transition into retirement or any alternatives? Only time will tell.

References

Chapman, H. (2006, April 2). Aging: Fears and joys. Presentation at the Annual Convention of the American Counseling Association, Montreal, Canada.

Council for the Accreditation of Counseling and Related Educational Programs. (2006, March 30). Report to the American Counseling Association Annual Conference, Montreal, Canada.

Maples, M. F., & Abney, P. (2006). Baby-boomers mature and gerontological counseling comes of age. *Journal of Counseling and Development, 84*(1), 3–10.

Stickle, F., & Onedera, J. (2006). Teaching gerontology in counselor education. *Educational Gerontology, 32,* 247–259.

Suggested Readings

Brewington, J. O., & Nassar-McMillan, S. (2000). Older adults: Work-related issues and implications for counseling. *The Career Development Quarterly, 49,* 2–15.

Glover, R. (1998). Perspectives on aging: Issues affecting the latter part of the life cycle. *Educational Gerontology, 24,* 325–332.

Harper, M. C., & Shoffner, M. F. (2004). Counseling for continued career development after retirement: An application of the theory of work adjustment. *The Career Development Quarterly, 52,* 272–284.

Hollis, J. (2005). *Finding meaning in the second half of life: How to finally, really grow up.* New York: Gotham.

Maples, M. F., & Abney, P. (2006). Baby-boomers mature and gerontological counseling comes of age. *Journal of Counseling and Development, 84*(1), 3–10.

Pennick, J. M., & Fallshore, M. (2005). Purpose and meaning in highly active seniors. *Adultspan Journal, 4,* 19–35.

Snyder, B. A. (2005). Aging and spirituality: Reclaiming connection through story-telling. *Adultspan Journal, 4,* 49–55.

Biographical Statement

Mary Finn Maples, Ph.D., NCC, is professor of counseling and educational psychology at the University of Nevada, Reno. She is a former president of both the American Counseling Association (ACA) and the Association for Spiritual, Ethical and Religious Values in Counseling (ASERVIC). Dr. Maples has researched, presented nationally, and published extensively on issues related to the Baby Boomer generation. She can be reached through her website at http://wolfweb.unr.edu/homepage/maples/maplesindex.html or through e-mail at maples@unr.edu.

5

The Existential Issues of Freedom and Responsibility: Every Year It Is Getting Harder to Deny Them!

Collie W. Conoley and Jane Close Conoley

As we enter the realm of old age ourselves, we live as well in the kingdom of extreme old age inhabited by our parents. Helen, 60, wanted help from Collie and Jane Conoley with her parents, Phyllis, 84, and Fred, 87. The Conoley team brought the key players into solution-focused therapy, even including the housekeeper. Helen was especially worried about her mother's insistence on driving. She hoped that her parents would move to an assisted-living facility. Lamentably, the very elderly lose their freedom through loss of physical and cognitive abilities, and they can't earn it back.

I received a call from Helen, a 60-year-old woman, who began crying as she described why she needed my help with her 84-year-old mother, Phyllis. Although Helen was clearly communicating her sadness and pain, the problems that prompted her call were not initially clear. She was worried that Phyllis, who had always been intellectually sharp, was forgetting things and not understanding issues as clearly. Also, Helen was worried that her mother was unable to care for Fred, Phyllis's husband and Helen's father. Fred, 87 years old, was not as mentally alert or as physically mobile as Phyllis. Finally, Helen was upset about her mother's insistence on continuing to drive a car.

I am a family psychologist, in practice for thirty years. My career has consisted of being a professor and a practitioner. My partner, Jane, for thirty years, is a psychologist also. She and I have a radio show once a week addressing family mental health questions from callers and presenting usable and/or entertaining mental health research. Helen was calling me at my university office because she liked our radio show.

"So you are uncertain about how to be helpful to your mom and your dad . . . but you are seeing indications that you need to do something more or different. Is that right?"

Helen responded, "Yes! You are so insightful, doctor!" Wow! With such an intelligent client, I knew that success was just around the corner. Compliments can lure me into cases that I should run from! Jane and I were enthusiastic about working with this family, however, to investigate how family dynamics in aging families might differ from our more common client families of middle-aged parents and adolescent children.

Our new clients were the McCormick family. They were an upper-middle-class, college-educated family of English, Irish, Scotch ancestry. Their family had been in the United States for at least ten generations. The elderly parents were Phyllis, age 84, and Fred, age 87. They were retired high school English teacher and insurance company manager, respectively. Both took medicine for depression, high blood pressure, high cholesterol, and blood thinners for stroke prevention.

Phyllis was steady in her gait, able to hear well, not able to read for extended periods, sharp in her reasoning, and slightly forgetful. Phyllis still drove, but Fred did not. There was disagreement about whether Phyllis's driving and memory were worsening noticeably. Phyllis was reported to have been depressed at times in her life, but never sought therapy or medicine prior to five years ago. The physician assured her that all old people took antidepressants.

Fred could not hear without great effort, and he walked unsteadily with a walker. His memory was noticeably impaired, and poor eyesight hampered reading. He had no history of mental health difficulties. Fred may have had an alcohol problem in his 30s, but he cut back and "it hasn't been a problem since."

Helen and Anne were their only children. Helen, age 60, was a business manager with an MBA. She was married to George, age 62, who was also a business manager in the same company. They had no children. They reported no physical or mental health problems.

Anne, age 57, was a high school mathematics teacher who was married to Chuck, age 57. Chuck taught Spanish in the local college. They had a daughter in the Peace Corps, living overseas. Anne reported having had some problems with depression, for which she had sought help several times. For the last fifteen years, the depression had seemed manageable with medication. Chuck and their daughter reported no physical or mental health problems.

■ Conceptualization

My initial impression was that the problems were developmental. Most of the time, I view problems as developmental. By *developmental* I mean that we have issues to deal with at every step of our path through life. When the path is blocked, we are not certain which fork in the path to take, or we stumble along the path and experience psychological problems. Feeling the responsibility to make decisions for her parents' safety was Helen's particular developmental issue, which caused her to feel frustrated (angry) and impotent (depressed), leading her to initiate family therapy. Both adult children feel increasing responsibility for addressing the difficulties of their elderly parents. I anticipate that the adult children disagree about the extent of their parents' problems as well as about what should be done to help. I always predict disagreements when two or more people feel that they are in charge of the welfare of another person, who is experiencing problems. I expect that Helen and Anne disagree about their need to intervene with their parents.

Depression in the family system with elderly parents is not unusual. Developmentally, a predictable issue for the family is the present real and anticipated future loss. The diminishing physical and mental functioning of the elderly is a real present loss. The anticipation of death that diminishing functioning reminds us about is the anticipated loss.

In the initial phone conversation, we decided to meet with Helen, Phyllis, and Fred at Phyllis and Fred's house. Helen's husband did not want to attend, stating that it was Helen's "project." Helen's younger sister, Anne, and her husband, Chuck, decided to attend. Also, one of the housekeepers, Linda, would attend. I was excited to get as large a cast of solution contributors as possible! Early in my career I was trained in structural family therapy, wandered to brief therapy, and now enjoy solution-focused therapy. I believe that families and adopted families (caring housekeepers) make powerful contributions by helping to build on strengths.

Solution-focused therapy also seemed ideal because I anticipated that the family members disagree about what is a problem. Defining a contentious problem expends precious time and can feel like a demeaning confrontation to those labeled as problematic. Members of a system have varying perspectives of what is problematic. Power struggles often occur in systems when deciding whose perspective of the problem has privilege over another. The therapist can spend a great deal of time negotiating acceptance of multiple perspectives without making progress toward the goal of therapy.

In this situation, Phyllis would fight the label of *unable to live autonomously*. That label would leave her vulnerable to solutions that she greatly feared. Helen would fight the label of *over involved* or *meddlesome*. She was certain that tragedy was close. Avoiding this conflict through moving to the solutions seemed viable and wise.

Process

I was excited to be meeting in the McCormicks' home. Home sessions reveal even more than the proverbial million words of a picture. The values and functioning level of a family can be communicated much more clearly than during an office visit. Everything from accessibility of bathrooms to strategies for regulating medication becomes precisely clear. The processes of the family become alive as well. At times the distractions of the uncontrolled environment of the home try my therapist's need-for-control. Most often, however, any inefficiency is outweighed by the rich information. The McCormicks' house was clean but cluttered and in need of upkeep. It was the home of an upper-middle-class family that valued reading material but could not part with old magazines, newspapers, and books. (Hmm. . . . Too bad I'm not psychodynamic. I could say something about the issue of loss. Well, no theory covers everything. Theories have to simplify the process so we know what to pay attention to! I feel better now.)

Session 1. I started the initial interaction to establish a relationship by focusing on what they enjoyed doing as well as what they liked about themselves individually and about each other. The communication established rapport quite successfully. I theorize that their connection with me was based on their viewing me as a facilitator of their strengths and what they like best about themselves. I did not ask about any problematic issues, and I complimented them as often as possible.

The family was easy to engage, except for Fred, the father. Fred vacillated between being good-natured and irritated. His inability to hear even with a hearing aid left him isolated and bored. When he was unable to hear, sleep became his immediate escape.

Phyllis enjoyed eating, and going out to eat was her favorite activity. She would often visit with friends, the wait staff, and the managers during meals. Restaurants typically gave them extra food to take home. She clearly experienced the food gifts as treasures. Phyllis's other, less enjoyable, regular activity was visiting physicians. Fred's and her health had become her full-time job. She reported that at least once a week they went for a physical health checkup. Eye, ears, skin, heart, headache, physical therapy. . . . All kinds of ailments were checked out.

Once I felt comfortable about the relationship with the family, I moved toward goal setting. What were each family member's goals for counseling? Typically, people seeking counseling are focused on what they do not want—the symptoms—rather than what they do want. The McCormicks were no exception!

"So, in a year, when you look back on our meeting, what will you say was the best part about us having met together? What will you be doing or having or thinking in a year that is not happening now? What is the something that will make a helpful difference in your life?" I asked. Each person is expected to contribute to the goals that evolve. I usually take brief notes to remember each perspective. The trick is to maintain eye contact most of the time, so that people feel important and engaged.

Helen began. She hoped that her mother and father would move into an assisted-living facility. She stated that her mother never listened to her. She then began to cry. I paraphrased the goal part of the statement: "I think I understand what you would like, Helen. You want to feel that what you say is important to your mother. (I now drop my voice to address the sadness in the tears.) Also, you want your parents to be safe. (My voice goes back to normal now.) The best solution you have in mind is an assisted-living situation. I'll write that down now. Let's not talk about whether anyone thinks this goal is good or bad right now. I just want to know everyone's goal. I do not expect that you will agree on your goals."

My statement was an attempt to avoid jumping right into an argument. Understanding each person's perspective is an important first step toward establishing shared commitments for action or more positive assessments of each person's intent and motivation toward the others.

After attempting to quell any disagreement over assisted living created by Helen's goal, Phyllis spoke. "I do not know why I have to spend my last few years dealing with this! As it is, I have nothing to look forward to. . . . Will you leave me nothing?" Phyllis began crying. Fred, her husband, became agitated, saying, "Why the hell are you upsetting Phyllis?"

Meltdown was just around the corner, it seemed. I had just gotten a peek at how the family did not accomplish their goals.

I quickly said, "Thank you, Fred." Then, to Phyllis, "Phyllis, I think your goal is to have something enjoyable to look forward to almost every day? I want you to get what you want. Do I understand you?"

"What do I have to look forward to? Nothing! And Helen wants us to leave our home!" Phyllis said.

"I see. So an important issue for you is that you would like to have something to look forward to each day? And you would like to stay in your home? Could we say those are your goals?" She agreed. Not a fully committed agreement, but enough to proceed.

Anne stated that she wanted her parents to be safe and happy, which received a "You betrayed me" look from her sister. Chuck, Anne's husband, stated that he wanted the same. Fred stated that he just wanted things to be happier and easier. Fred would not be clearer other than to say that Phyllis had been crying more lately, which disturbed him a great deal.

The goals were restated to the family as based on increased communication that would affirm several issues:

- The love and respect they have for each other;
- The safety issues regarding Phyllis and Fred's living situation; and
- The need for Phyllis to have something to look forward to each day.

These goals, although not overtly phrased as such, held promise as remedies to the safety concerns, Phyllis's depression, and the rejection, anger, and lack of respect experienced by Phyllis and Helen in their interactions.

After gaining agreement to the goals, we negotiated assignments for each person to accomplish before the next session. I wrote down each person's assignment, so each would remember. Anne and Chuck were to drive Phyllis and Fred to a psychiatrist who works with the elderly to check the prescriptions that had been given by the family practitioner for depression. Specialists for the elderly can be especially important because of the number of prescriptions typically involved as well as dosage issues.

Also, Anne and Helen would call Phyllis every day to tell her something enjoyable they did that day. Also, Anne and Helen would recommend something for Phyllis and Fred to watch on TV. Phyllis and Fred enjoy watching television, especially travel and nature shows. Phyllis and Fred stated another thing that they enjoyed doing was remembering when the children were young. So they were asked to bring up one fond memory a day to discuss with each other at breakfast time. Finally, Helen was to think about whom she would trust to report on her parents' safety.

They each committed to the goals and responded well to my parting words. These parting words are prescribed by solution-focused therapy: Compliment the clients and link their goals to the homework assignments. I told them that clearly theirs was a loving, committed family, dedicated to doing what helped each other. The problem was that they were stuck in not knowing how to move in a safe, helpful way, and their communication had not clearly expressed the love they felt for each other. However, we are on the road now.

Between-Session Phone Calls. Before the next session, I called all the people involved, to keep up their motivation and to adjust the assignments. A major issue that surfaced was that Phyllis and Fred were not feeling like getting out of bed. The only day that they did was when friends from their church brought them lunch. I suggested asking for more frequent visits from the church group. Phyllis rejected this notion because she objected, ostensibly on health issues, the habit the churchwomen had of kissing Fred as a way of greeting and leave-taking. When speaking with Helen, I added the suggestion that she contact the local Office of Aging and scour the Internet for ideas that she might find acceptable.

Session 2. We met again two weeks later. "What did you like that happened in the last two weeks?" is my typical session starter. The emotional tone of the group was much warmer. They attributed their increased caring feelings to the phone calls. When Helen and Anne purposefully shared the positive aspects of their lives, Phyllis felt more involved with their lives. Phyllis's enjoyment influenced her daughters' experience of the conversations, so the daily phone call felt better to them as well.

The medicine that Phyllis was taking for her depression was altered by the geropsychiatrist. Phyllis and Fred did not, however, talk about their past happy memories as agreed. I took the blame for it being a bad idea. They did, however, ask the church visitors to come three times a week, which did facilitate them getting dressed in the morning. I complimented them profusely on their follow-through. Phyllis decided she was feeling better.

Remaining issues, besides Phyllis's depression, were Helen's concerns about the safety of her parents living at home and her mother continuing to drive. Helen's research did lead her to some ideas. She thought that having a home health aide come in every day to visit, check on medicine, and check on her parents' functioning, was a great idea. Phyllis and Fred had housekeepers come in every day. They had become attached to the housekeepers and enjoyed their company. However, Helen did not trust the housekeepers' judgment in reporting her parents' safety.

Phyllis quickly drew a line in the sand, stating that she would not allow strangers into her house who would be talking about her. We discussed her current solution of being able to live at home with the personable housekeepers supporting them. Phyllis trusted the housekeepers and enjoyed visiting with them about their families. The home health aides, on the other hand, were outsiders, whom Phyllis sensed would be cold, distant, and intrusive.

The initial positive feelings with which the session had begun were approaching nuclear once again! Firmly, I redirected the conversation back to the success Phyllis and Fred had with the housekeepers—complimenting them on the clever way they dealt with keeping the house and meals going smoothly. Perhaps the success with the housekeepers was a solution we could build on.

Many people do not become friends with their housekeepers. How had the McCormicks accomplished this unusually positive situation? Phyllis had taken charge of selecting the housekeepers. The evolution of multiple persons happened over years. As Phyllis and Fred needed more help, they hired a new person if the existing worker was unable to provide more hours. As it evolved, the adding of new people was fortuitous, because if one housekeeper was ill or needed time off, another could stand in. Also, having more people around created more conversations and friendships. Perhaps the home health aides could be selected in the same manner.

The existing strengths of the McCormicks were found by exploring their existing solutions. Using their existing solutions led to achieving the new goal of ensuring safety. The family agreed that having the home health aides could be an addition to the family that would provide safety in a personal way. Helen believed that the home health aides could be trusted to tell her when Phyllis and Fred needed extra attention. Phyllis believed that she could use her proven skills in hiring personable home health aides.

I followed the solution-focused therapy suggestion of ending the session with:

- A compliment;
- A statement that ties their goals to the activities that are assigned; and
- New homework that is tied to their goals.

The compliment was that they continued to show a great deal of caring and concern for each other. (This general statement needs to be followed up with specific examples of their behavior. It makes the compliment believable and underscores their strengths, which are also solutions to continue using.) For example, when Helen and Anne communicated their daily life joys through their frequent phone calls, Fred and Phyllis felt happier by living vicariously through their daughters and feeling like successful parents. The phone calls also serve to reassure Helen and Anne as a check-in with their parents. Second, I complimented their great idea of hiring personable home health aides who would help maintain Fred's and Phyllis's health while reporting to Anne and Helen about their parents' functioning level.

Finally, the issues of getting dressed in the morning and Phyllis continuing to drive were left for the next session. The homework assignment related to driving was for everyone to think about what might reassure everyone that Phyllis was driving safely. I stated presuppositionally, "No one, including Phyllis, wants to endanger anyone by taking risks with unsafe driving." This was a maneuver to get the whole family on the same side of the issue. Just for future reference, I also suggested that everyone think about how Phyllis and Fred would get around town when Phyllis was no longer driving. The statement seemed to jar Phyllis. It was as if she thought she would die before becoming unable to drive. Issues of losing control over their environment, bodies, and minds seemed to lurk in the background of family discussions. Phyllis reacted strongly to all intimations that dealt with loss. The presence of old newspapers and magazines took on new meaning as my understanding of Phyllis's struggles with loss grew clearer.

Between-Session Phone Calls. I again phoned each of the family members between sessions. Each reported progress. The home health aide idea was not, however, progressing as planned. The aides worked within an agency in this small city. The agency would not agree to the selection of certain workers. The agency wanted to retain scheduling flexibility. Fortunately, Phyllis knew that one of her neighbors was a registered nurse. Phyllis liked and trusted this person. Both Phyllis and Helen spoke with her about visiting Fred and Phyllis regularly for checkups. The idea of having a registered nurse versus a home health aide seemed to appeal to the family because of the increased expertise that would be available. Also, serendipitously, the nurse worked for a family physician who was particularly responsive to emergencies. Although the initial plan failed, the goal was accomplished.

The safe-driving issue, however, hadn't progressed. Everyone saw this issue as potentially explosive. I asked Anne to call the Department of Public Safety and Office of Aging as well as search the Internet for ideas. In the last ten years, dents on Phyllis's car had mysteriously appeared with a frequency of two to four a year. According to Anne, her mother was not forthcoming about the causes of the damage.

The church visitors had continued their luncheon meetings three to four times a week. The fortuitous occurrence was that the visitors and Phyllis enjoyed playing the game Scrabble. Much to Phyllis's delight, after lunch they would play a game. Phyllis did not complain about the women kissing Fred anymore. The attention seemed to be spread about more fairly.

Session 3. Three weeks had passed since the last session, and there was plenty to talk about. Progress is the first topic that I entertain in a session. The phone calls between Phyllis and her daughters continued to be an enjoyable new tradition. The positive topics made the contact pleasant for the daughters and the parents. The registered nurse had visited each Monday, Wednesday, and Friday to take vital signs, listen to symptoms, and recommend physical therapy. There was considerable foot dragging on physical therapy, but having a professional listen and provide information was very well received. The family had a new but less explosive power struggle over what Fred and Phyllis should be doing to remain healthy—physical therapy.

Phyllis and Fred enjoyed the church women's visits. These contacts provided another reason to get up every day. They were also going to a luncheon for the elderly that was sponsored by the community. They visited long into the afternoons. Symptoms of depression were fading.

I introduced the issue of safe driving. What insights had occurred? That old dreaded wall of silence appeared. Finally, Anne said that she had called the Department of Public Safety for advice. They recommended frequent driving tests as a solution. Anne added that the Internet chat groups suggested that when a dent appears in the car more often than once a year, it's time to hang up the keys. More silence. . . .

I said, in the most innocent voice I could produce, "What interesting ideas! Fred, Phyllis, what do you think of them?" Fred said that Phyllis had been responsible for innumerable dents in dozens of cars since she'd started driving sixty years ago. She would never have a driver's license if the rule was that more than one dent per year revoked a license. Everyone laughed. . . . Whew! Even as Phyllis denied the assertion, she laughed.

"So, Fred, you have your doubts about the dent rule. What about the driving test as reassurance of good driving ability?" I asked.

"Well," Phyllis firmly asserted, "there are many bad drivers on the road who pass a test. What would taking the test prove?"

Expanding Phyllis's literal message, I said, "So, Phyllis, you would like to be certain that you are better than average drivers, because you are not impressed by the number of dangerous drivers on the road." No commitment to testing was made, but a conversation about proof of competence replaced the conversation of loss of independence.

Between-Session Phone Calls. Before we met again, Fred had a medical problem leading to a three-week hospital stay. Therapy was terminated by this event. Telephone contact continued for two additional months.

Outcome

A few goals were accomplished in the brief family counseling process, but some remained. I thought the processes of solution-focused therapy worked well. Enjoyable communication increased. Conversations facilitated more positive moods and more frequent telephone calls. The safety net of frequent contact with Fred and Phyllis made independent living more acceptable to Helen and Anne. The danger of Phyllis continuing to drive and the advisability of Phyllis and Fred living independently continue to be difficult issues.

Reflections

The absurdity of solving a problem engages my imagination with this case. The problem of losing our abilities was not solved. The balance of overreacting and under reacting to the dangers of aging were represented by the family members.

This case highlighted the existential issue of personal freedom. The contrast of the personal freedom issues of adolescents with those of the elderly intrigues me. I have had a great deal more experience with adolescents. With the adolescents I think of the process of earning greater personal freedom as one of demonstrating readiness via responsible behavior. The elderly lose their freedom through demonstrating their loss of physical and cognitive abilities, and they can't earn it back.

As our future grows shorter, a question becomes more clearly framed: What are we willing to risk to live fully versus what are we willing to give up in order to live longer? The freedom that Fred and Phyllis enjoyed as adults is slowly being curtailed by their family. When the values or the safety judgments of Helen and Anne are different from those of Phyllis and Fred, a power struggle that erodes Phyllis's and Fred's autonomy develops. Even if Helen and Anne believe their position was not adopted, the nonaffirming message was communicated to Phyllis and Fred.

Phyllis and Fred hold a mirror for me to examine my own behavior when considering the existential issue of freedom. Also, they remind me to enjoy my ability to walk, hear, see. . . . What wonderful gifts! I believe that if a theory of counseling and the process of counseling helps me become a better person while it is helping the clients, then it is a worthy theory. My interaction with the McCormicks did help me become a more grateful person (for health) and one with a clearer grasp on the preciousness of autonomy and of a caring family. Solution-focused therapy allowed an uncovering of the family's strengths. These strengths serve as models for me to emulate as I care for aging parents and as Jane and I age.

Suggested Readings

Adler, G., Rottunda, S., Christensen, K., Kuskowski, M., & Thuras, P. (2006). Driving SAFE: Development of a knowledge test for drivers with dementia. *Dementia, 5*(2), 213–222.

Cohen, S., & Pressman, S. D. (2006). Positive affect and health. *Current Directions in Psychological Science, 15*(3), 122–125.

Conoley, C. W., Graham, J. M., Neu T., Craig, M. C., O'Pry, A., Cardin, S. A., Brossart, D. F., & Parker, R. I. (2003). Solution focused family therapy with three aggressive and oppositional acting children: An *N* = 1 empirical study. *Family Process, 42*(3), 361–374.

Dahl, R. (2000). The use of solution-focused therapy with an elderly population. *Journal of Systemic Therapies, 19*(4), 45–55.

DeJong, P., & Berg, I. K. (1998). *Interviewing for solutions*. Pacific Grove, CA: Brooks/Cole.

de Shazer, S., Dolan, Y., Korman, H., McCollum, E., Trepper, T., & Berg, I. K. (2007). *More than miracles: The state of the art of solution-focused brief therapy*. New York: Haworth.

Golub, S. A., & Langer, E. J. (2007). Challenging assumptions about adult development: Implications for the health of older adults. In C. M. Aldwin & C. L. Park (Eds.), *Handbook of Health Psychology and Aging* (pp. 9–29). New York: Guilford Press.

Juengst, E. T. (2005). Can aging be interpreted as a healthy, positive process? In M. L. Wykle, P. J. Whitehouse, & D. L. Morris (Eds.), *Successful aging through the life span: Intergenerational issues in health* (pp. 3–18). New York: Springer.

Levy, B. R. (2002). Longitudinal benefit of positive self-perceptions of aging on functional health. *The Journals of Gerontology. Series B, Psychological Sciences and Social Sciences, 57*(5), 409–417.

Reed, J. E. (2007). Social support and health of older adults. In C. L. Sieloff & M. Frey (Eds.), *Middle range theory development using King's conceptual system* (pp. 92–104). New York: Springer.

Steeman, E., Godderis, J., Grypdonck, M., De Bal, N., & De Casterlé, B. D. (2007). Living with dementia from the perspective of older people: Is it a positive story? *Aging & Mental Health, 11*(2), 119–130.

Biographical Statement

Collie W. Conoley, Ph.D., is a professor of counseling, clinical and school psychology, at the University of California, Santa Barbara. He is a Fellow of the American Psychological Association and a member of the National Health Service Providers of Psychology. He has over 150 written and presented works. His practice and research areas are family psychology, multicultural counseling, and positive psychology. You can reach Collie at CConoley@education.ucsb.edu.

Jane Close Conoley, Ph.D., is dean and professor at the Gevirtz Graduate School of Education at the University of California, Santa Barbara. She is a Fellow of the American Psychological Association and a member of the National Health Service Providers of Psychology. Her research interests are in creating positive school environments for student success, teacher development, and family involvement. Jane is the author or editor of twenty books and seventy articles and book chapters. She serves on ten editorial boards and has received numerous research, teaching, and service honors. You can reach Jane at Jane-conoley@education.ucsb.edu.

6

Sandtray and Artwork: The Woman Who Created Herself

Beverly Snyder

Caroline, 60, is mentally ill (bipolar disorder, anxiety disorder, compulsive self-mutilation, family history of schizophrenia). All of her life, she has had difficulty holding jobs and maintaining relationships. At the Blue House, the agency where Beverly Snyder works, "Caroline became my client simply because it was my turn to receive the next client who called for an appointment." In this random way, an incredible journey began. Snyder was practicing play therapy with children and believed that the techniques could work with adults as well. In a tray of sand, Caroline creates a world.

A challenging case walked through the door to the Blue House, where I was working shortly after gaining licensure as a mental health counselor. It came in the guise of a woman who was fairly functional in a quiet sort of way. However, it seemed she almost diminished in size as I met her, as if she were shrinking inside. Caroline Sims was 60 years old, just over 5 feet tall, and had a look suggesting she very much wanted approval. She was nearly pleading with her eyes, asking me nonverbally to help her become more functional in her life. Her presentation was clean and not remarkable in any way except for a certain lack of "pizzazz" or *joie de vivre*. I did notice that her energy level seemed very low as she walked with rounded shoulders toward my office.

I became curious about this little woman who was almost birdlike in her walk and manner, and I wondered what our work together would be like. I slowly began the lengthy process of building a relationship with her to discover who she was, and I promised myself to be gentle. I have a tendency to be very direct, but I didn't think that would work well with her. As we began to talk, Caroline had difficulty maintaining eye contact. She glanced my way and then hastily beat a retreat to focus on the hands clenched in her lap. I read over the presenting problem: bipolar II disorder, generalized anxiety disorder, and a compulsion to self-mutilate. I wondered where to begin.

I began by gathering information and essentially did an informal social history. Getting details from Caroline was difficult, as she answered in very short sentences, abbreviating her responses as much as possible. However, I did learn that she had taken a few college courses over the years, though none recently. Because of her lack of professional direction and other issues, she held low-paying jobs that did little to improve her financial status. She had no additional training, so her job skills were minimal. Money was frequently an issue in later sessions, as she struggled to keep her head above water. She had no physical limitations, just the emotional ones that kept her trapped in her own world.

At various times in her adult life, Caroline had been hospitalized to keep her safe from the suicidal thoughts that sometimes swamped her. She believed her future to be void of opportunity for success, and I could feel her discouragement and growing helplessness. Other than short-term hospitalizations Caroline had no other institutional affiliation. She worked with a psychiatrist who accepted her government insurance, but she only saw him once every three months for a meds check unless there was an emergency. Caroline lived in a tiny one-bedroom apartment in subsidized housing and had an old car she could drive to work. Gaining a picture of her lifestyle, I continued to probe for significant life details that had led to her serious diagnoses.

Caroline became my client at a United Way–supported mental health agency, the Blue House, where I worked part-time in the evenings and on Saturdays. Caroline became my client simply because it was my turn to receive the next client who called for an appointment. I was also licensed as a mental health counselor, which seemed necessary in order to file for Medicaid insurance. At the Blue House we served the low end of the socioeconomic population, and the sliding fee scale went down to $5.00

per session. We received additional funding from United Way and an occasional grant that supported special programs such as multifamily groups for status offenders. All in all, it was a difficult setting, with clients who had multiple areas of dysfunction requiring willing and empathetic therapists.

Caroline paid the $5.00 each session, and there was no limit to the number of sessions she could receive. I actually worked with Caroline for just over a year before I moved to another state and couldn't see her anymore. She came every other week and usually kept her appointments. It seemed as though coming for therapy was a highlight in her life, and she didn't like to miss one.

In digging for family details, I discovered that Caroline's family had a long history of schizophrenia. In fact, both parents and one grandparent were schizophrenic, as well as two older siblings. Sifting through what Caroline was willing to share, I learned that mixed messages from everyone she lived with created a "crazy-making" atmosphere that contributed to her tenuous grasp on reality. Repeatedly, she had been placed in double-bind situations that left her confused and uncertain about how to manage relatively simple life tasks. Her self-esteem and confidence eroded during her youth, but she was able to graduate from high school and move out to live on her own. That she was able to move out was quite remarkable itself, given the level of family dysfunction. Much of the credit is owed a high school teacher who had Caroline in a typing class and who felt especially compelled to help her. This woman guided Caroline in a job search when she graduated from high school and helped her gain an entry-level position in a large insurance company. That mentoring experience became a highlight of her life and may have contributed to any success she encountered.

The years passed while some obstacles were overcome and some were not. In her early 20s, Caroline was diagnosed as bipolar after a bizarre weekend experience of frantic activity with very little sleep. What followed was a lengthy period when her manic and depressive episodes interfered with her holding a full-time position, ultimately resulting in the loss of jobs. The years became a blur as she lived from one episode to another; her medications did not seem to be effective in keeping her stable. To exacerbate her feelings of low self-esteem or of worth to the world, she did not receive adequate medical care. There was no continuity of service through the social welfare system, with many changes of doctors. Caroline reported that her family was virtually no help; indeed, they seemed to contribute to a toxicity that grew when she was around them.

Caroline's presenting problem was a combination of her bipolar disorder, generalized anxiety disorder, and her compulsion to self-mutilate by scratching her arms and legs raw in spots that eventually bled. She was greatly shamed by the open sores on her arms and legs and tried to hide them under long sleeves and pants. She tried to redirect my attention elsewhere by recounting some unimportant life event. I didn't dwell on her self-scarring but tried to develop some coping strategies to use instead. When she became lonely (or hungry, angry, or tired . . . the acronym HALT), it seemed she lacked sufficient emotional support or enough external encouragement to try something else. When her anxiety became intolerable, she would give in to binge eating and then scratching.

◼ Conceptualization

As I conceptualized Caroline's case, it became obvious that she was socially isolated and without meaningful relationships. The woman across the hall in her apartment complex was her only friend. They went to breakfast every Sunday morning, and this was the sum totality of Caroline's involvement with a normal existence. Although she was able to express herself in therapy, she had minimal social skills. Reaching out to someone else seemed like an insurmountable task, and she gave up before trying. I began to see the truth of Adler's (1964) work and his measure of mental health when he said that a person's involvement with others is the best measure of how well adjusted they are.

I reflected on her family of origin and marveled at how well she was doing despite the total chaos among her parents and siblings. How in the world could I possibly help her to find meaning and purpose when she was barely surviving? Existing on the lowest level of Maslow's hierarchy, she experienced minimal belonging and love and, consequently, no validation. I decided the place to begin was to work on self-esteem. I believe that self-esteem grows when you learn something new. My goal with Caroline was to find something to excite her so she would become engaged in life beyond her work and apartment.

Glasser (1999) says that we must have freedom, fun, power, and belonging in our lives to feel good about ourselves. I didn't find many of any of those characteristics in Caroline, so I added an umbrella goal of increasing socialization. We brainstormed about possibilities. Church was not an option, because that would take away her only activity with a friend on Sunday mornings. We eventually settled on her taking an accounting class at a community college. She thought it might help her find a better-paying job, and I concurred, thinking she would at least be with people. Emotional development of older adults continues, and most adults experience more satisfaction with their interpersonal relationships than they have throughout their lives (Craig & Dunn, 2007). In other words, it is never too late for emotional growth.

Although my philosophical orientation tends to be psychodynamic, my actual treatment plan was cognitive-behavioral with a large dose of play therapy. Our sessions consisted of a few minutes of discussing goals and behaviors and then the bulk of the time was spent on experiential therapy and developing a sense of playfulness that was at the same time serious. I was practicing play therapy with children and believed the techniques would work with Caroline as well.

My theory was that Caroline needed a way to reach inward for unconscious material. Her conscious verbal skills for expressing herself were undeveloped. By working with the right side of her brain, the left (which criticized and belittled) could be bypassed. The natural medium of communication with most adults is verbalization, but Caroline was far more comfortable with experiential expression and the imaginative exploration of her emotional world.

I want to explain the use of sandtray play therapy. In the tray of sand, in the serious spirit of play, clients make a world. The open space is large enough to hold a segment of the client's world, but it has firm boundaries around the edges to contain it. Clients feel free yet protected. Clients select any number of miniatures to use in the construction of their world in either the dry or the wet sand. Dora Kalff (1971), who introduced sandplay to the C. G. Jung Institute of San Francisco, is known to have said that if the inner world can be created in the sand, it can be left in the sand. And thus, the process of making the unconscious conscious begins. Kalff notes that a preliminary condition for the unfolding of inner forces is what she called the creation of a free and protected space. This protected space is often considered sacred and leads the client to a deeply moving experience wherein the unconscious can be explored safely. Sand worlds are left intact and not dismantled until a photo is taken and dated, after clients have left the playroom, so they can more easily take the image of what they produced with them.

My experience in using sandplay with adults coincides with Kalff's three stages of ego development: animal-vegetative, fighting, and adaptation to the collective; this held true for Caroline as well. Up through session 7, Caroline experimented with art materials, but after she began developing sand worlds, it became apparent that she had regressed to a much earlier stage. My intuitive sense was she had not had much opportunity to play as a child. I believe that play is an apprenticeship for adult life, and it is through this experience that individuals become integrated into society. Play opens thoughts and feelings. Because Caroline had not played much in childhood, she had had little apprenticeship for adult life and lacked the skills for dealing with rejection, cooperation, and competition. It is no wonder, then, that she was not integrated into society.

Older adults have a heightened sense that time is fleeting. I hoped this might create a sense of urgency that would motivate Carolyn to make the most of therapy. I subscribe to the view that older adulthood is different from earlier stages and is not just an extension of what has come before. There is continuity *and* there is change. Readers who want to pursue my line of thinking should read the work of Levinson (1996) and Atchley (1989). Their research supported my faith in Caroline's ability to grow, and my goal became to connect with the inner core that we all use to define ourselves.

Process

I worked with Caroline for about a year, averaging two sessions a month and sometimes more if she started crashing. We used cognitive-behavioral techniques to look at her progress toward goals as well as monitoring her thoughts. She kept a journal and usually wrote about mundane things. Most of our time was spent in a modified playroom with two sandtrays, one dry and one wet. I had a wide bookcase with dozens of miniature figures, animals, and abstract items to be used in the construction of the sandtrays. There was also a painting easel with tempera paints, and various decks of cards with archetypal symbols to use as a vehicle for discussing her life in a metaphoric way. There were puppets. A library table provided a comfortable place to work while we talked. I did not include the wide variety of toys typically found in a children's play therapy room but made available many craft items that could ignite the imagination, such as markers, crayons, colored pencils, scissors, magazines, and easel paper.

Caroline was free to use whatever materials she chose, and she focused on the craft items and paints during the first few months, not venturing toward the sand-trays. Eventually, Caroline used the sandtray to "make her world in the sand" (Lowenfeld, 1939). The technique is referred to by the terms sandtray, sandplay, and sand world; each term serves a function in describing the process. *Sandtray* refers to the vehicle, *sandplay* to the activity, and *sand world* to the product.

<u>Sessions 1–4.</u> I took many notes as Caroline told me about her current situation in life. I noted the lack of emotional resources, the ragged work history, her penchant to use an eraser to make holes in her skin when she became very lonely. She was on medications and was generally stable until she spent weekends alone. This often resulted in binge eating and self-scarification with a corresponding self-hatred for her weakness. She described her childhood in a schizophrenic home.

I treated the binge eating and self-scarring as addictions and used art as an instrument to help Caroline visualize her illness. This provided objectivity and distance from the chaos of her inner experiences. Some directives I used were:

- Draw your addiction.
- Draw what happens to you when you are under the influence of mood altering foods.
- Draw the unmanageability of your addiction to erasing pieces of yourself when you are lonely.
- Draw what it is like when you feel powerless.
- Draw the effects of powerlessness in your family.

Art therapy can break down defenses quickly and less traumatically than talk therapy (Wilson, 2003). Once Caroline understood what she was doing to herself, I hoped she would recognize the reality of her experience and become a candidate for cognitive-behavior therapy.

<u>Sessions 5–7.</u> Artwork continued, with Caroline focusing on current issues of self-care and her work. Many pictures were created, mostly chaotic scenes of dark clouds and darker landscapes, devoid of people. She drew huge, menacing birds. Caroline took her pictures with her at the end of the sessions. The day Caroline told me about her friend and the ritual of Sunday morning breakfasts, her picture was of a bright sun and flowers.

During the fifth session, I suggested that she draw a picture of "all you have lost as a result of your illnesses." Putting a face to her reality did connect her to the consequences of her staying stuck, and we talked about the possibility of her taking baby steps toward establishing a few social connections. By session 7, I had her create her paper bag self in which she placed pictures of aspects of herself that she was willing to share with others on the outside; in the inside, she placed pictures of aspects she was afraid to let others see. We discussed what it would take to share these with her Sunday friend and approached the topic of trust.

I helped Caroline become aware of situations that triggered binge eating. I asked her to draw the triggers to acting out. Then I had her draw the tools of recovery that could help her deal with loneliness: taking a walk, sketching in the park, visiting the library, window shopping at the mall. These ideas were Caroline's own, and I was eager to see if she could implement them.

Sessions 8–9. Talk continued about self-defeating thoughts. We set a goal of finding a college class, and eventually she registered for an accounting course. Caroline was afraid to drive across town and getting lost on campus, but she agreed to do a trial run.

During session 8, Caroline approached the sandtray for the first time and asked how to use it. I showed her the miniatures and instructed her to "create her world in the sand." She created a very early childhood world using prehistoric animals and vegetation. At the very center, Caroline buried a creepy-crawler animal that she said represented herself. This suggested to me that she did not have much ego at all. She then created a dark area to the right of center by scraping away the sand to reveal the dark blue floor of the tray. This became a water hole for the animals to gather around. I perceived this as an experience of giving to herself, a step toward actively obtaining self-nourishment and higher ego autonomy. She created mounds of sand and later told me they were the feelings she could never express. We had begun the adventure of self-exploration!

During session 9, Caroline arranged the prehistoric dinosaurs and birdlike creatures in a semicircle around herself, facing outward in protective stances. She was in a corner of the box surrounded by these animals; her family was at the other end of the box and enclosed by fences, closing them off from herself. I believe the fences represented her recognition of the need for restrictions associated with her own ego development; it was a clear boundary between her and hurtful people. It could also be seen as the way in which she continued to function in the world and that she had not grown past this level of development. There was no discussion of her attending class at the college.

Sessions 10–11. In session 10, Caroline told me she made it to the first two classes, but then declared, "I quit. It's too hard on me to find parking and then the classroom." She withdrew from school and spent weekends bingeing and scarring. Caroline was depressed. I felt we had taken a few steps backward. It was difficult to engage her in using the craft materials. I worked with her and made a collage of her conflicting feelings. In session 11, we used beads to make a bracelet. This pleased her, and she took it with her as an anchor to remember our time together. She ended the session saying, "Next time I will try the sandbox again."

Sessions 12–18. In the next six months, Caroline made twelve different sand worlds and our routine shifted. She made a sand world the first half of the session and we talked the last half. The first seven worlds furnished a background to her illness and contained a figure of a young girl in a corner, surrounded by dozens of army figures aiming guns outward toward a family scene in the opposite corner. She seemed fixated on the need for protection. Occasionally she would bury an ugly insect or animal in the center of the box and place various objects around it, effectively shutting that part of her life off.

These repetitive sand worlds depicted conflict with family. Over time, the figure representing herself did not need so many defensive items around her. It was slow going, as she recalled "crazy-making" childhood experiences. Sources of energy appeared (a crystal, for example), suggesting to me that her ego needed more energy for the struggle between inner and outer forces.

In session 15, I decided to give Caroline homework and asked her to draw a picture of all the benefits she would experience if she could find a social outlet. She brought the picture to the next session and we discussed how hard it was for her to imagine taking steps to develop additional relationships.

At the end of session 16, I asked for more homework. This time she was to draw herself surrounded by people who nurtured her. She, of course, loved the feelings but still remained behind a wall of reluctance. The homework at the end of session 17 was to draw a picture of the qualities she would like to have in a friend. Our talk included the qualities she, herself, needed to become someone's friend.

I saw a parallel between the artwork she did at home and the sandtrays she created in my office. Both represented the struggle between the grown-up self and the baby self; the good and the bad, the courageous and the timid, the compliant and the rebellious, the sick self and the healthy self. During session 18, Caroline introduced a bridge into the sandtray, which I thought indicated an attempt to make connections between where she was in life then and where she wanted to go. Binge eating was greatly reduced by then, and Caroline's affect was more open. She was considering engaging someone in conversation, perhaps a stranger in a grocery line or at the library. However, still no action.

Sessions 19–21. In sandtray play during session 19, Caroline identified herself with the figure she placed in a tunnel made of a toilet paper cardboard cylinder covered with sand. She placed the figure well inside the mound and added defensive rocks around the entrance to the tunnel. She told me, "She has to go way inside so no one can find her." Oh no, I thought to myself, more regressing away from our goal of social interaction. So I assigned her the task of drawing a picture of seeing herself walking toward a person to whom she would speak.

The next session, she brought a straw from home and again made the tunnel with the figure inside; this time, she used the straw to allow air into the tunnel, opening herself to the world in a small way. When we talked about the drawing she had done at home, she admitted it was nebulous and she couldn't see a face on the stranger. I intuitively felt that this was the time to introduce the idea of a Higher Power. She told me that she had experienced a connection earlier in life but not much since. I encouraged her to think about faith and how that could help her see herself receiving help from her Higher Power so that she wouldn't have to take the difficult steps we talked about all alone.

The following session, Caroline made a flag she placed next to the straw in the tunnel, suggesting a victory. We talked about the growing strength the girl figure seemed to have, and Caroline remarked, "She is not so worried about the people on the outside. She can take care of herself." She had begun a practice of daily prayer. We began using the term God, and she could see herself being successful with His help.

At last, I thought to myself, we are making progress! The work we had been doing together began to coalesce.

Sessions 22–24. Caroline's next three sessions were dominated by a conscious struggle to extricate herself from bondage to her schizophrenic parents. She wanted to grow. She read avidly in her eagerness to understand psychology and how she had been affected by her early life. She made a clay figure of herself at home to use in the sandtray and tried to apply what she was learning to break through a net of confusion around ideals and reality, of lies and truth, masculine and feminine aspects of self, sex, religion and spirituality.

She used the figure of a queen in her last sandtray. She cleared that tray and placed her clay figure of herself in the center of the tray—all alone. She created a flowing river in the sand with a small boat and said, "I can go by myself. See, the rock is behind me," and she placed a stone in the river, behind her, where it prevented any of the events of her earlier life to reach where she was now. It was truly a dramatic turning point. No longer did she have to defend herself from her family, and she knew she could make it on her own. She had grown strong cognitively, emotionally, and spiritually.

Session 25. We had one more session together before I left for my move to the West. She brought glue from home to mend a tear in the boat she had used the previous session. She created the stream again and added a pool in which she placed the mended boat. Next, she created a mound of sand in the center of the pool of water and on top she placed herself. She placed trees behind and to the side of her figure and added treasures: a piece of turquoise, a clump of quartz crystals, and a tiny book. And farther away from herself, beyond the stream of water that led to her past, she placed all the human figures she had used in the previous twenty-four sandtrays. It was a triumphant ending.

Outcome

Session 25 was the last time I saw Caroline. Before I left, I gave her referrals to therapists I knew would be willing to work with her using experiential materials and to incorporate her growing spirituality. I think it is important for the reader to know that much of the discussion we had during the last several sessions was about coping strategies in her real world. What amazes me the most about this experience of seeing Caroline's growth through her artwork and the sand worlds she created was that she possessed inside herself all she needed for her own healing. She was able to contact her inner core and begin to bring the beauty of who she was out into the real world. She truly became a woman of her own creation. I did not give her my forwarding address, and I have not heard how Caroline is doing since I left.

Reflections

In reviewing my work with Caroline, there is not much that I would do differently. As I continue to believe today, the most important goal of therapy is to develop a trustworthy relationship with the client that is based on unconditional positive regard.

This was my constant focus with Caroline whether or not she met a weekly goal or cut herself or binged. Bit by bit, we developed a strong relationship that modeled what loving relationships should look and feel like.

My own biological age is about the same as Caroline's, yet there is a world of difference in our developmental stages. My family was supportive and encouraging, hers was not; indeed, hers pulled her into its chaos and toxicity. Mine demanded gaining an education, hers never discussed what an education could mean to her future. Mine offered socialization, opportunities, travel, sports, music, intelligent discussions; hers offered none of these, so it is not hard to see how her life and mine differed so greatly. My biological and extended family created a safe place in which I was able to negotiate Erikson's (1964) developmental stages up through adolescence before leaving home. Caroline had unfinished business at every early developmental stage to work on before she could move into the stage of intimacy, so necessary for deep relationships. I like to imagine Caroline traveling successfully through these stages if she found the right therapist.

There was so much pleasure and insight for me in working with Caroline. She taught me the lesson of patience and accepting that clients will "move" when they are ready to do so and not before! I have a sacred responsibility as a therapist to hold near and dear to my heart the growth of the vulnerable clients who cross my path. It is such a privilege to be part of the journey of older adults who look back across the lifespan and try to garner meaning from their lives as they look forward to the remaining years.

On a recent sabbatical, I conducted a study of retired persons, asking them about how they found purpose and meaning in their lives since they were no longer working and had raised their families. Most of them told me that they just got up every morning and moved from day to day without much thought. Depressing, I thought to myself, concluding they were either stuck in self-absorption or in despair (according to Erikson). But I also met individuals who were excited about life span and had found new things to occupy themselves. Many found new work, either paid or unpaid. So what I took to heart is this: All of us have the chance to prepare for the future; some of us have had more support than others, but all can take charge and make choices so that we can find purpose and meaning. Caroline did this.

Conducting therapy with older adults is such a joy, it eclipses the work I have done with children, adolescents, young adults, and families. Older adults have so much life experience they offer a richness and depth that I have found nowhere else. The very fabric of their lives is woven with success and failures, triumphs and disasters, that all contribute to who they are when they come into our offices. Some simply need a boost, whereas others need significant work that leans toward personality reconstruction. All offer us the opportunity to enrich our own lives through their life experiences.

References and Suggested Readings

Adler, A. (1964). *What life should mean to you*. New York: Capricorn. (Original work published 1931.)

Atchley, R. (1989). A continuity theory of normal aging. *The Gerontologist, 29*, 183–190.

Craig, G. J., & Dunn, W. L. (2007). *Understanding human development*. Upper Saddle River, NJ: Pearson–Prentice Hall.

Erikson, E. H. (1964). *Childhood and society* (2nd ed.). New York: W. W. Norton.

Glasser, W. (1999). *Choice theory: A new psychology of personal freedom*. New York: Harper Perennial.

Kalff, D. M. (1971). *Sandplay: Mirror of a child's psyche*. San Francisco: Browser Press. (Republished as *Sandplay: A psychotherapeutic approach to the psyche*. Boston: Sigo Press, 1981.)

Levinson, D. (1996). *The seasons of a woman's life*. New York: Ballantine.

Lowenfeld, M. (1939). The world pictures of children. In C. Schaefer & D. Cangelosi (Eds.), *Play therapy techniques* (pp. 117–123). Northvale, NJ: Jason Aronson Inc.

Wilson, M. (2003). Art therapy in addictions treatment: Creativity and shame reduction. In C. A. Malchiodi (Ed.), *Handbook of art therapy*. New York: Guilford Press.

Biographical Statement

Beverly Snyder, Ed.D., is professor and chair of the Counseling and Human Services Department in the College of Education at the University of Colorado at Colorado Springs. She is both a licensed professional counselor and a school counselor and has been teaching in higher education for fourteen years. An educator for more than thirty years, she is a national presenter on various playful topics with various groups and has many publications on school and mental health topics. She can be reached at bsnyder@uccs.edu.

7

Life Losses and Changes from a Transactional Analysis Perspective

Susan A. Adams

Joe was forced to take early retirement, but the news got worse. Joe's investments were lost when his company went bankrupt. Furthermore, Joe and his wife Lisa were not at all prepared for 24/7 togetherness. Grieving for dead parents was an underlying issue for both Joe and Lisa. Within a conjoint format, Susan Adams applied narrative therapy and Transactional Analysis (TA). TA worked wonderfully to unravel multigenerational issues for this couple. Wildly popular in the 1960s and 1970s, TA is somewhat ignored in today's counseling theories courses, and so I am grateful that Adams offers us a short course in this powerful form of intervention.

*C*hange is uncomfortable for everyone, but for some it presents more challenges than for others. For the Bakers (not their real names), Joe's early retirement was more than their coping skills could handle, and that brought them to counseling.

Joe was a senior sales executive who was used to his opinions not only being valued, but accepted without question. With his last promotion twenty-five years ago, he began a commuter marriage with his wife, Lisa. Joe flew from Dallas to Houston on Monday and made the reverse trip on Friday to spend weekends at home. Throughout the forty-one years of their married life, Joe had been largely absent, but he viewed this as the price for providing for his family. Lisa was lonely, but she adapted.

As for family of origin, both Joe and Lisa were reared in two-parent families with clearly defined traditional roles. They reported similar religious training, and participation in an organized church was not optional. They continued these same patterns in their own family relationships.

Joe had unresolved issues with his father's strong, dictatorial personality. He felt like a failure for not meeting his father's expectations. Examples included not making enough money and not driving the right car or living in the best neighborhood. Lisa felt like a failure as well, because she did not keep the house clean enough or raise the children according to her father-in-law's standards.

Joe and Lisa were both college graduates and in good health for their age. They did not report any physical limitations other than those caused by the normal aging process (e.g., "can't work as hard," "not as much energy"). The couple described their relationship with their adult children and grandchildren as warm, but noted that the children were closer to Lisa than to Joe.

Someone in my Bible study class at church referred Joe and Lisa to me. The couple had the same presenting problems: grief issues related to losing parents and difficulty adjusting to Joe's retirement. When I met them, both were in their early 60s.

I have a doctorate in counselor education and a current license as a Professional Counselor in Texas. I have taken nine hours of graduate academic bereavement courses and have attended numerous workshops and conferences about grief. I have led more than three dozen workshops about grief over the past ten years, and I teach a graduate-level course on bereavement.

I do not accept insurance in my private practice. However, I do complete paperwork for clients who want to seek reimbursement from their insurance providers. The Bakers paid my full fees, and there was no limitation on the number of sessions I provided.

Conceptualization

Lisa's parents had both died within the past two years, within five months of each other. There were legal complications related to the settlement of the estate because her mother's will had not been probated, and her father's will been changed before he died. Lisa said that she and her younger brother were working things out amicably.

Joe's 87-year-old father has Parkinson's disease and Alzheimer's. In addition, he has life-threatening elevated blood pressure, congestive heart failure, and type II diabetes. Joe's 85-year-old mother was attempting to take care of his father on a daily basis even though his father was in a nursing home within a special Alzheimer's intervention unit. Joe expressed resentment that his father's demanding personality was ruining her health.

When Joe retired, the Bakers owned a beautiful suburban home with a lakeside view, a boat, a recreational vehicle, and expensive cars. Joe invested heavily in company stock options so that he could continue to provide an affluent lifestyle during his retirement. When Joe's company downsized and he was *forced* to take early retirement, they were both excited about their new life as a couple. However, their vision of happy retirement was soon shattered.

Joe's retirement investments were lost when his company went bankrupt as a result of mismanagement and embezzlement. When the couple began working with me, there were legal battles going on to recover a part of the retirement funds. The Bakers had to sell their boat, camper, and high-status home, which they replaced with a far more modest house in another part of Houston. This move separated them geographically from friends and their church. Their familiar doctors, dentists, and grocery stores were gone. Joe felt a sense of shame because he thought he should have known better. Joe was now a failure in his eyes, his father's eyes, and those of his own family. At least that was his perception.

Although Lisa did not blame him, she did not have a clue how to reach out to him to build a new dream. She was struggling with what she described as an "invasion of my territory" now that Joe had retired. Lisa had female friends, and she volunteered in the community. However, none of this included a "we" identity.

I like a mix of narrative therapy and Transactional Analysis. Narrative therapy focuses on the story that clients make out of life events, as they attribute meaning and purpose to their existence based on their personal life history and culture. The story is just a story, however, and it can be reframed in a way that is more empowering to the client.

Now for a short course in TA. Transactional Analysis identifies three ego states that describe familiar roles in each of our lives. The *Parent* (P) ego state is comprised of two parts, the *Nurturing Parent* (NP) and the *Critical* or *Controlling Parent* (CP). Both of these clearly identify the behaviors and verbal self-talk associated with these labels. The Nurturing Parent provides a sense of validation for the individual and comfort in times of stress and/or distress. The Critical Parent is the negative internal voice that is often reflective of voices in the client's past. This voice is often harsh and full of criticism (e.g., you are so stupid, you didn't do that right); however, it can also be a positive influence (e.g., it tells us not to eat too much, to stop at a stop sign, to obey the speed limit or we will get a ticket).

The *Child* (C) ego state also has a dual identity. The *Free Child* (FC) is the spontaneous, often irresponsible, self-indulgent childish ego state that defies rules, often pushes the social norms, and generally enjoys living. The Free Child has both a positive and a negative side. For example, healthy individuals need to have "play times"; however, if this ego state is allowed to dominate, then the individual is described as irresponsible. The other half of the Child ego state is the *Adapted Child* (AC). This ego state has learned rules of engagement with others (friendships, business relationships, personal relationships, etc.) from childhood and from the person's primary caregivers. The Adapted Child was obedient as a child, and when the Critical Parent speaks (internally), this ego state often is triggered. This ego state also has both a positive side and a negative side. Examples of the positive side are when we say "Excuse me" when we burp in public, or when we say "Please" and "Thank you." An extreme of this negative side becomes evident when an individual has few boundaries and lives in a state of always needing to please others.

The *Adult* (A) is the cognitive, nonemotional ego state that can be compared to a computer doing processing. The Adult's role is to evaluate messages that come from both the Parent ego state and the Child ego state to determine if these messages are still valid and applicable. This unemotional ego state may best be described as a "Mr. Spock" from the television series *Star Trek*. The Adult referees among the other ego states; its job is not to eliminate any of the internal roles, but rather to maintain balance among them.

Each individual has all five ego states; problems occur when they get out of balance and the wrong ego state responds inappropriately in a given situation. The Child ego state is the emotional aspect, the Adult is the thinking ego state, and the Parent is the action or behavior ego state. All are necessary, and all are part of a healthy individual. They create a healthy cognitive and emotional blend that serves the individual well as he or she creates a meaningful life story. The key is to find balance and engage the appropriate ego state in different situations.

A major goal is to liberate clients from limiting childhood scripts. TA defines a *script* as a pattern of behavior that is beyond awareness but is directed to a personal payoff. Even a subtle rewriting of a script can change a relationship. I hope this is clear. If the reader wishes to learn more about TA, I recommend the classics: Berne's *What Do You Say After You Say Hello?* (1972) or Harris's *I'm Ok—You're Ok* (1969).

Both narrative therapy and TA examine the language clients use to express their internal conflicts. As their use of language and choice of phrasing provides insight for the counselor, the counselor enters the client's frame of reference to explore how these thoughts, feelings, or behaviors are influenced by the past and projected in the present. Only as clients become aware and gain insight can they target these faulty and negative thinking patterns and alter future interactions.

Process

There were thirty-eight sessions in all, twenty of them with the couple and the remaining eighteen divided equally between Joe and Lisa.

Two-Hour Intake Session (Conjoint). Following are some observations from the intake session. My office has three chairs and a couch. Joe and Lisa each staked out opposite ends of the couch. I describe it that way because they put assorted objects (her purse, his datebook) on the couch between them, as if to create a boundary. This pattern continued until the very end of our work together.

Lisa's nervous, rushed speech, rapid hand gestures, and crossing and uncrossing of her legs were greatly reduced by the end of the first session. Joe was clearly uncomfortable whenever the discussion turned to emotions. He would not or could not establish eye contact with me; he shifted frequently on the couch, and sometimes he tuned out.

Joe was cognitive and straightforward. He was interested in listing facts, checking them off, getting them done, and moving on. Lisa, on the other hand, talked about options and consulted with Joe. Lisa's incessant questioning irritated Joe. He said that he could have already made a decision and accomplished the task by the time Lisa got through talking about options. Lisa felt unheard when Joe rushed her to make a decision. She was fearful of upsetting Joe or questioning his decisions. I saw this fear on her face, and I explored the possibility that there might be abuse in their marriage. Fortunately, this possibility proved groundless.

I did not tell them about my hunch that Joe's values of husband as provider were behind a lot of his anger toward his father and himself. I also suspected that his sense of failure and loss of control might be contributing to his daily interference with Lisa's life.

Session 2 (Conjoint). I started the second session with "How was your week?" Joe responded quickly that it was okay, but Lisa gave an example of feeling excluded. She admitted the example was insignificant, but she identified the bigger issue for her as him "doing his own thing" rather than a couple concept. Joe said he felt like she was attempting to control him because she needed to know every little detail in his life. Although neither could identify any feelings associated with these positions, Joe's face was red, and he looked angry. Lisa had increased difficulty making eye contact as Joe spoke, and I identified the look on her face as fear. (Note: I would identify this pattern repeatedly over the next few sessions.) I used a white dry-erase board to teach them the basic concepts of Transactional Analysis in order to plot out their disagreement.

Sessions 3–7 (Conjoint). During each of sessions 3–7, Joe and Lisa returned to therapy with the "issue of the week" on their agendas. Neither made use of the insights from previous sessions. During session 7 I asked them to rate their communication on a scale of 0 to 100 (100 being "best ever"). Lisa gave it a 65 and Joe a 40. I asked them what the "pink elephant" in the room was and explained this term as "something one or both of them felt or thought was acting as an unacknowledged barrier between them." Neither came up with anything. I decided that I might be rushing things. I drew a 4 × 4 grid on paper, and across the top labeled the columns "Internal" and "External." The rows were labeled "No Control" and "Control." We worked together to divide their identified life problems (retirement, issues with their children, loss of financial security, chores, etc.) into one of the four squares to help them understand what was beyond their control (so let it go) and what was controllable (so do something or do something differently). Their homework assignment for the week was to make a list of at least ten issues they both agreed were problematic and put them in the grid for us to discuss at our next session.

Session 8 (Conjoint). Session 8 began with an admission that they had not done their homework. They argued when they attempted to do it, rehashing a volatile issue that happened several weeks ago and that had been discussed in a previous session. Joe thought it was settled, but Lisa had brought it up again. She said they were having fun working in the yard until she questioned where he wanted to plant a particular bush. Then Joe got angry, and she became afraid. Joe reported that "She asks a thousand questions, and I could have it done by the time she gets through with her questions." After exploring their argument from a Transactional Analysis perspective, Joe realized he has no Free Child so it is hard for him to "play." They were going to visit his parents the next week, so I asked them to let their Free Child do something fun together on their trip. They agreed to try.

Session 9 (Conjoint). Lisa reported that "the trip was boring and uncomfortable" but Joe said, "I got things done and we had some good activities." She realized she stays in the Nurturing Parent/Adapted Child ego states, and he realized he stays in the Critical Parent/Adult ego states, which create conflict. They were picking up on TA concepts. In this session I was very much aware of fear on Lisa's part, so I asked about the "safety" of both on a scale of 0 to 100. Lisa reported about 30 and Joe reported about 35 to 40. As a result of these responses, I asked if it might be helpful to have some individual therapy for a few sessions. Both quickly agreed.

Sessions 10–19 (Lisa). During Lisa's individual sessions I explored "safety" issues because I was worried about the possibility of actual abuse. Although Lisa reported that Joe had never been abusive, she was "afraid of him and his reactions." This seemed to be more a fear of his disapproval, which would be the Adapted Child fearful of the Critical Parent. (Note: This proved to be the better explanation throughout counseling.)

Lisa said that although she was glad that Joe was home now, she felt like it is an invasion of her space. She described her leaving home to attend college as an escape from someone else's expectation. "I'm afraid to give that up, now because I might lose myself."

We developed a plan of empowerment using three questions that could be answered *Yes* or *No:*

1. Do I *need* to do it?
2. Can *I* do it?
3. Do I *want* to do it?

When we explored what Lisa "needed" from Joe, she identified her primary love language (see Chapman, 1995) as acts of service and Joe's as words of affirmation. She was able to see how she set up a pattern (TA identifies this as a *script*) with Joe that had been blown out of proportion. We plotted out the scripting that was taking place using some construction-paper circles, representing the five individual ego states, and a small rectangular block to represent "blockers" (deliberate thought stoppers that allow a person to choose an alternative ego state to receive and respond to a message and thus change the script).

<u>Sessions 10–19 (Joe).</u> In his individual sessions Joe said that he no longer felt in control. He made a list of key people and the percentage of importance they had to him. His parents were 30 percent, his wife was 40 percent, his adult children were 10 percent, and he was 20 percent. Next, we drew a square divided into four equal parts. Across the top columns we wrote "Internal" and "External." Along the side rows, we wrote "Control" and "No Control." Joe wrote life events into each of the squares according to how he perceived them. As he linked each of these events, he saw how much he allowed other people and other things, which he had zero control over, to dominate. When he did not perceive that he was in control, he felt angry, but he admitted that he "stuffs his feelings."

Joe felt he was "less of a man" because he was aging. He identified his primary love language as acts of service (see Chapman, 1995). Although he was not too sure, he guessed that Lisa's was words of affirmation. He saw how they wrote a script to satisfy those love languages for each other. I did not point out the discrepancy between their perceptions of love languages in the other, but I introduced the topic when they returned for conjoint sessions.

<u>Session 20 (Conjoint).</u> Back together in a conjoint session, we discussed boundaries and having space and knowing what the rules are. However, the couple stuck with an old familiar script. In this script the person distorts things to match the preferred way of making meaning and discounts evidence to the contrary. I saw it as my job to raise awareness in these clients.

I had them plot out their transactions (TA script) from a recent argument. They saw how they were both reacting from their Adaptive Child and actually sounded like two 3-year-olds! We re-created the scenario—the argument—but this time they could use their blocker and make a different choice of how to respond.

<u>Session 21 (Conjoint).</u> Lisa allowed her Adult to challenge Joe when his Adapted Child complained about "the rules" at home. She said she felt pressured to make decisions about her parents' estate just because Joe thought she should. As I explored what completing the estate details meant to her, Lisa started crying, but Joe sat immobile at the other end of the couch. I asked Joe, "What is it like for you to sit there and see Lisa in pain?" Joe admitted that it hurt him and frightened him because he "could not fix it." Even when I asked where his Nurturing Parent was, he could not relate to this concept or make any move toward Lisa.

Finally, I asked Joe if he would be comfortable making some sort of contact with Lisa and he said, "I would be comfortable putting my arm around her." When he did, Lisa's response was, "It feels good, but I don't trust the consequences at home." However, after exploring these "consequences," she realized that her fears were more imaginary than real. Joe admitted that he wanted to be there for Lisa, but was afraid that he would fail at that, too.

We came up with a code word for when they needed an intimate connection. Both agreed not to discount such a request even if it wasn't complied with.

We then took a four-week break because of travel commitments. They thought the timing was good because it would give them time to try out this new code system.

Joe also admitted that he was struggling with depression, "not from a suicidal perspective, but from a just-coping-with-life perspective." I suggested he discuss this with his medical doctor.

Session 22 (Conjoint). When Lisa and Joe returned from the month-long break, Joe said he had gone to the doctor and started on a mix of drugs following a thorough physical and EEG. He reported the medication was helping his mood swings; however, the couple brought up a miscommunication that showed that they were back in their corners again (responding according to old scripts). Each blamed the other. I raised the specter of the pink elephant again. Their homework was to figure out what this beast was and give it a name.

Session 23 (Conjoint). Joe and Lisa identified the pink elephant as Lisa's fear of abandonment and Joe's fear of emotions. The elephant left them both feeling vulnerable. Lisa said, "I don't think we should continue with this right now because I don't want to push Joe over the edge, and I know he's dealing with a lot." She even suggested we stop therapy for a few weeks at least.

I challenged her desire to protect Joe and suggested that she ask him what <u>he</u> wanted. Joe's response shocked her, as evidenced by the look on her face, but her expression turned to joy, "I am so far outside my comfort zone now that it doesn't matter. I just want to keep working and get through this because I care about you!" Then he started crying and could not stop, but Lisa did not move from her end of the couch. When I asked Lisa what it was like for her to see him cry like that, she said, "His guard is down, and I can connect with him." Then she moved over and put her arm around him.

Joe said, "I feel like a complete failure because of all the retirement problems, Lisa's fear of me, and I can't seem to do anything right."

Lisa said, "I feel shut out when you isolate from me. I am afraid you'll leave me."

I shared Maslow's hierarchy pyramid with them, and we looked at the layers that had to be satisfied before they could reach a sense of love and belonging (Maslow, 1968).

Session 24 (Conjoint). In session 24 the couple sat next to each other, which was a first. We discussed how to shift from an "individual" to a "we" concept of TA scripting and explored how to use healthy "I messages" in conversation.

At the end of the session, Lisa and Joe looked at each and grinned. Joe asked Lisa, "Are we going to tell her?" Lisa responded, "We graduated! We're sitting next to each other and you didn't notice!" They both grinned at the thought that they had "caught" me. When we processed their move, they both said the previous session about the "pink elephant" had been pivotal for them.

Sessions 25–28 (Conjoint). Joe reported progress on the retirement front. Relationships with their adult children were also improving because of what they were learning in therapy about their own relationship.

Session 29 (Two-Hour Conjoint). In their final session, both Lisa and Joe reported that they were able to communicate without fear of escalation or isolation. They were using their "code words" to connect, but they didn't need them very much. They were settling into a new routine. They did not have a specific time to get up every day, but they were usually up by 8:00 AM. They preferred not to schedule any activities or appointments for first thing in the morning, so they had their combined devotional time over breakfast at the beginning of their day. Then they each had an hour for individual Bible study, to respond to e-mails, and to plan their day. They coordinated their schedules.

Both said that the TA circles (ego states) had been helpful. The pink elephant metaphor was another key piece. They were ready to terminate therapy, but wanted to be able to return "as needed" in the future.

Outcome

Joe and Lisa subscribed to traditional male and female roles, and they were having difficulty blending together as a couple after being so separated for most of their married life. I think seeing these two people as individuals for a few sessions allowed them the freedom to voice their individual concerns and thoughts without "losing face" with their partner. I was surprised at the result of my confrontation of identifying the pink elephant. I knew it was different from their perception, but it was more of a "gut reaction" on my part based on observation of their behavior and verbal reaction patterns during the sessions.

I would label the case a success based on their reported changed attitudes and behaviors plus the changes in their interactions over our sessions. They looked at each other and talked to each other—not through me. They both appeared more relaxed and even joked appropriately with each other. They recognized that they would always have struggles and that they would have to continue to work on their relationship or they would fall back into their old pattern.

Reflections

From a TA perspective, it is important to recognize that "playing" is always a healthy part of living. Life's routines numb people and rob them of spontaneity and a sense of adventure. Aging presents physical challenges, and it is important to remember that we need all five ego states in healthy balance to navigate through the aging process.

Although the Bakers are a few years older than I am, I was very much aware of my own life situation as I worked with them. My husband is partially retired, and I am learning to deal with the changes in our activity patterns as I am still working full-time. Changes in our physical abilities and energy levels have decreased our activity, and I had to be cautious not to project that onto the couple. I also took a step back and looked at how I have settled into a "routine" with my husband, which has created complacency in our own relationship. We have just gotten "comfortable" with each other, and I examined that pattern to see if this was really how I envisioned our relationship when we reached that particular phase of our life.

My husband and I do not hold with "traditional" gender-role systems, and I realized how that might affect my own impressions and attitudes when working with couples close to our age. This does not seem to be a problem for me when I think of "older couples" (couples that are more in my parents' generation), because my parents subscribed to traditional values, and I tend to think of couples in their generation as holding more to those traditional roles. I know this is a projection on my part; however, it does not pose much of a concern for me. It is important to note that traditional gender roles are not usually the key when working with the challenges of aging from a TA perspective. The significant factors are to hear the clients' story, help them identify their established patterns (i.e., TA's life scripts) that may need to altered or redefined, and find a way to create new meaning in their life story.

References

Berne, E. (1972). *What do you say after you say hello?* New York: Grove Press.

Chapman, G. (1995). *The five love languages: How to express heartfelt commitment to your mate.* Chicago: Northfield Publishing.

Harris, T. A. (1969). *I'm ok—You're ok.* New York: Avon Books.

Maslow, A. H. (1968). *Toward a psychology of being* (2nd ed.). New York: Van Nostrand Reinhold.

Suggested Readings

Berne, E. (1964). *Games people play: The basic handbook of Transactional Analysis.* New York: Ballantine Books.

Chapman, G. (1992). *The five love languages: How to express heartfelt commitment to your mate.* Chicago: Northfield Publishing.

Deits, B. (1992). *Life after loss: A personal guide dealing with death, divorce, job change and relocation.* Tucson, AZ: Fisher Books.

Gladding, S. T. (2005). *Counseling theories: Essential concepts and applications.* Upper Saddle River, NJ: Pearson Education.

Kaufman, G. (1992). *Shame: The power of caring* (3rd ed.). Rochester, VT: Schenkman Books.

Magnuson, S., & Norem, K. (1999). Challenges for higher education couples in commuter marriages: Insights for couples and counselors who work with them. *Family Journal: Counseling and Therapy for Couples and Families, 7,* 125–134.

McCullough, M. E., Pargament, K. I., & Thoresen, C. E. (2000). *Forgiveness: Theory, research, and practice.* New York: Guilford Press.

Myers, J. (1989). *Aging children and aging parents.* Alexandria, VA: American Association for Counseling and Development.

Plant, P. (1997). Careerist, wage-earner, or entrepreneur: Work values and counseling. *Journal of Employment Counseling, 34,* 165–170.

Potter-Efron, P. S., & Potter-Efron, R. T. (1999). *The secret message of shame: Pathways to hope and healing.* Oakland, CA: New Harbinger.

Potter-Efron, R., & Potter-Efron, P. (1989). *Letting go of shame: Understanding how shame affects your life.* Center City, MN: Hazelden Educational Materials.

Powell, J. (1998). *Why am I afraid to tell you who I am?* Allen, TX: Thomas More Publishing.

Wylie, B. J. (1996). *Life's losses: Living through grief, bereavement and sudden change*. Toronto, Ontario, Canada: Macmillan Canada.

Biographical Statement

Susan A. Adams, Ph.D., is an assistant professor in the Counseling and Development Program in the Family Sciences Department at the Texas Woman's University in Denton, Texas. She is a licensed professional counselor. Susan has a limited private practice in Denton and has published professional articles and presented extensively about grief in life situations. You can reach her at dradams@centurytel.net.

Counseling Flora: Adjusting, Grieving, Dating, and Moving On

Fred Stickle and Jill D. Duba

Fred Stickle saw Flora on three significant occasions over eighteen years: Round One, empty nest; Round Two, death of a spouse; Round Three, a dating relationship with a person of dubious character (as Fred sees it). One constant over the years was Fred's standard operating procedure: Start with client-centered counseling and then move to cognitive-behavioral therapy. Jill Duba, Fred's supervisor, takes her turn to comment on how counselors can respond when clients appear to be on a destructive path, as well as how religion plays out in counseling (see Reflections).

I saw Flora in counseling for the first time when she was 46 years old. She was having a hard time adjusting to an empty nest when the last of her three sons left home. I saw her again sixteen years later when she was 62 and grieving over her husband's recent death from cancer. She came back for counseling at age 64 to consult with me about getting remarried. Hopefully, our counseling relationship will see us both into old age. I (Fred) was the counselor, and I consulted with Jill Duba about this case.

Conceptualization

My approach to counseling typically consists of beginning with a client-centered approach. It is important to me to develop a level of rapport with the client. After building rapport, I move into a cognitive-behavioral approach to help clients choose constructive behaviors. Such was the case with Flora. Over the eighteen years that I worked with this particular client, I haven't changed this two-pronged approach: Starting with client-centered and then moving to cognitive-behavioral continues to be my standard operating procedure because it works for me.

Flora was 46 years old when I met her, and she was in generally good health despite having arthritis in her hip that affected her movement. This difficulty caused trouble in taking long walks, but she remained positive. Both Flora and her husband were educated and middle-class. Flora had a master's degree in education, and her husband Alex was a medical doctor. Basically, Flora wanted me to help her deal with loss. In one way or another, depression and loss were concerns during each of our three rounds of counseling.

I am in private practice, and I am a Licensed Marriage and Family Therapist (LMFT) and a Licensed Professional Clinical Counselor (LPCC). The client paid for her sessions with insurance and small co-pay. I diagnosed Flora with an adjustment disorder. There were no limitations to the number of sessions the client could be seen. This mode of compensation, established at the beginning, continued during all three rounds of counseling.

Process

The First Round of Counseling. Flora and her husband Alex had three sons, ages 24, 22, and 18. They were a tight-knit family and did as much together as possible. Although Flora was a certified school teacher, she remained at home full-time while the boys were growing up. Flora and her sons took care of their family farm and were active in 4-H. When the boys were in school, Flora was either involved in church activities or waiting for them to come home in the afternoon. Now they were grown, and she was left with an empty nest. Although she was happy to see her sons involved in their own activities in college, dating, and career goals, she felt "left behind." She realized that this was a normal part of life, but it still did not help the way she felt.

We met bi-monthly for six months. For the first two-and-a-half months, Flora used much of our time together to talk through her feelings about the physical loss of her sons, as well as guilt and self-blame related to not being able to handle their departure better. As Flora worked through these feelings, she then began to talk about what she might *do* to fill the void of her sons leaving home. It was then that I took a more active role with a cognitive-behavioral approach.

We discussed outside interests that Flora had enjoyed in the past. Through a gradual process of getting herself "out there," Flora's participation in outside organizations increased. We talked about ways to divert her attention from her sons to her husband. By the end of treatment Flora had decided to use her education and become a part-time teacher's aide. She volunteered to fill a leadership position on a church committee. Flora told me that she could actually have fun with her husband without her sons being around.

The Second Round of Counseling. Sixteen years later, at the age of 62, Flora returned to counseling. She told me that her husband, Alex, had died just four months after being diagnosed with cancer. The couple had just celebrated their forty-first wedding anniversary. During my initial assessment, Flora reported that she "cries all day long" and is awakened periodically throughout the night by her "own crying." Flora mentioned that she had no energy or interest in babysitting her grandchildren, something she normally loved doing. Finally, Flora expressed guilt regarding how many of the problems in the marriage had gone unresolved. She told me that she "should have just let things go" and that if she had known Alex was going to die, she "would have bent over backwards for him."

As before, I began with a client-centered approach. It was important that Flora be assured that she was not being judged, interpreted, or rejected by me. Flora vacillated between tears of sadness and regret, then moved to anger. She was angry because Alex had only limited involvement in her and her sons' lives, and she was angry because he "left me behind and lonely." I encouraged catharsis in order for her to truly experience all of the feelings and thoughts associated with her husband's passing.

As usual, I moved from a client-centered approach to that of a cognitive-behavioral one. We took a deeper look at: (1) specific times of the day that presented Flora with the most trouble and (2) what specific things could move her to thinking about something else. Together we devised a plan in which Flora could replace her sad feelings and demeanor with specific actions or behaviors that were likely to improve her mood.

I took a psychoeducational approach and taught Flora that she could choose when and how to grieve. I talked to her about the importance of limiting her grief, specifically to "how long" and "how often" in order to get relief from her presenting symptoms.

Flora told me that Sundays were the most "painful days of all days." She agreed to limit her depressive symptoms to Sunday evenings from 6:00 to 6:30 PM. Further, I instructed her to designate a grieving place in her house. Flora chose the chair in the living room in which Alex used to sit. Over the course of a few sessions, I encouraged Flora to begin "filling the grieving space" by focusing on other thoughts unrelated to her grief. For example, she took a great deal of interest in the upkeep of her garden and yard. Thinking about gardening left little room for thoughts about loss. Actually working outside helped even more.

By the end of that year Flora was in counseling, she was still grieving the loss of her husband but she was more in control of the more extreme feelings of guilt and depression.

The Third Round of Counseling. Flora returned to counseling one-and-a-half years after the death of her husband. She had met Jon, a used-car salesman, while shopping for a car. Flora said that Jon felt like her soul mate. She had concerns, though: his lack of education, his social status, and their differences in ethnicity. As I mentioned previously, Flora had a master's degree in education. Jon had not attended college and had significantly less earning power than Flora. Jon and Flora's ethnic backgrounds also differed; Jon was born and raised in Iran. He came to the United States during his early 30s but still consistently practiced his Islamic faith. Despite their differences, Flora's feelings toward Jon were very strong. The following week, Flora reported that she and Jon had slept together. Although she was still aware of the danger signs, she believed that he really cared for her.

Flora returned to see me weekly for another month and a half to talk about whether she should continue her relationship with Jon. Flora also reported experiencing periodic sadness related to the loss of her husband, as well as "having to start over again." At the one-month mark of therapy, she decided to go "with her feelings"; she began dating Jon steadily and then stopped coming to counseling.

Eight months later, Flora returned to counseling. We met for six weekly sessions. Flora was feeling anxious, depressed, and confused as to whether she should continue the relationship with Jon. Jon had refused to go out in public with Flora or to introduce her to his children from a previous marriage. He also told Flora that he would never marry her. Ultimately, he was ashamed of Flora's Christian background, and because of this he refused to introduce her to his family or close friends.

Although I was concerned about the relationship, I tried to be nonjudgmental. Flora was again sad and angry as she realized that Jon was not as loving and interested in the relationship as she was. She reported that her "life was full of losses," and she was worried about "being alone once again."

After four weeks of counseling Flora reported that she "was not ready to lose another relationship," no matter what. I reflected that Jon was hurting her; after all, she had said as much in various ways. After two more weeks of counseling, Flora never returned. I suspect that she did not want to examine the negative pieces associated with the potential marriage very closely.

──────────── ■ Outcome

I have been in private practice for twenty-five years. A good number of individuals have returned after several years for additional therapy. Looking back, it is obvious to me that my overall approach to counseling has remained the same over time. During the first session or sessions I function as a person-centered therapist. This is followed by a strong cognitive-behavioral approach.

I was discouraged (although I did not tell Flora so) with her decisions to continue with a relationship that seemed destined to be painful to her. Providing counseling in the area of mate selection, whether it be with a teenager or a woman in her 60s, is difficult if clients come for counseling *after* making a decision about pursuing a particular potential mate. Although the person may be older and more mature, love is still blind. I was careful to leave the counseling relationship open, and I would not be surprised should Flora call for additional appointments.

Reflections

Now it's my turn. I (Jill) functioned as Fred's supervisor on this case. In our supervisory relationship, we discussed the importance of remaining consistent in a counseling approach that is therapeutically aligning, as well as evidence-based. The case of Flora also points up for me the importance of understanding systemic and family issues.

One of my focus areas in supervision, as well as academically, is how religion plays out and how this surfaces in counseling. This case provides a great reference point and an interesting dimension as it relates to interfaith relationships. Fred and I had conversations about how to deal with couples in such situations. Because Flora was not married to Jon, Fred had opened the conversation with her regarding how these very different religious faith perspectives and traditions might cause problems within the relationship. Because Flora was so intimately tied with the relationship and resisting being alone, it was difficult for Fred and her to talk deeply about the challenges of an interfaith relationship. Furthermore, it was difficult for them to process potential ways for Flora and Jon to work with such differences by addressing new communication patterns, arrangements that incorporate facets of both religions, and how the two could create mutual rituals and traditions reflective of both Christianity and Islam (Lara & Onedera, 2008).

Before opening up a discussion and assessment of the influence of religious differences on the relationship, it would have been important for Fred first to address Flora's apparent resistance to "being alone again." After processing this issue, Fred might have moved Flora into a dialogue about the religious differences and the possible effects on the relationship. Given the opportunity, Fred and Flora might have identified differences by exploring Jon and Flora's level and adherence to their particular religious beliefs, each partner's identification with his or her faith base, and how each partner views the other partner's religious faith, and perhaps other issues as well. Discussing such matters might have brought Flora increased awareness and understanding of her own faith and practices, as well as those of Jon. With such awareness, she would have a foundation from which to make a conscious decision to pursue the relationship with Jon or terminate it based on irreconcilable religious differences.

My supervision with Fred looked at the question of how to work with clients when the counselor disagrees with the choices they are making. Obviously, Fred was unhappy with Flora's determination to go forward with an apparently destructive relationship. It appears as if the timing of Flora's willingness to engage in deep exploration of her resistance to being alone, as well as the presenting differences in religious faith, was not particularly conducive to continuing therapy. From what Flora was sharing with Fred about Jon, there were reasons to suspect a potentially hazardous relationship. Based on the rapport that Fred had developed with Flora over the course of therapy, it seemed appropriate to me that he discussed his concerns with Flora. He had her best interests and emotional safety in mind.

Perhaps one way of preventing Flora from terminating therapy on her own might have been to begin exploring differences in the relationship that did not pose an unbearable threat to Flora. In order to do so, Fred might have introduced this process by saying something like, "Since you have identified some foundational differences in your relationship with Jon, why don't we talk about some of those? Perhaps, if nothing else, you might gain additional awareness and feel better about interacting with Jon when it comes to working through such differences. . . ." During this process, Fred might have normalized any intense feelings that Flora experienced as she discussed the differences and explored her own religious beliefs and related behaviors.

Reference

Lara, T., & Onedera, J. D. (2008). Inter-religion marriages. In J. D. Onedera (Ed.), *The role of religion and marriage and family counseling*. New York: Taylor & Francis.

Suggested Readings

Goodman, J. (1990). *Empowering older adults: Practical strategies for counselors.* San Francisco: Jossey-Bass.

Knight, B. G. (2004). *Psychotherapy with older adults* (3rd ed.). Thousand Oaks, CA: Sage.

Kuther, T. L. (1999). Competency to provide informed consent in older adulthood. *Gerontology & Geriatrics, 1*(20), 15–30.

Myers, J. E. (1990). *Empowerment for later life.* Ann Arbor, MI: ERIC Counseling and Personnel Services Clearinghouse.

Myers, J. E., & Schwiebert, V. L. (1996). *Competencies for gerontological counseling.* Alexandria, VA: American Association for Counseling and Development.

Nussbaum, J. F., Pitts, M. J., & Huber, F. N. (2005). Ageism and ageist language across the life span: Intimate relationships and non-intimate interactions. *Journal of Social Issues, 61*(2), 287–305.

Onedera, J. D., & Stickle, F. (2008). Successful aging. *The Family Journal, 16*(1), 73–77.

Schwiebert, V. L., Myers, J. E., & Dice, C. (2000). Ethical guidelines for counselors working with older adults. *Journal of Counseling & Development, 78,* 123–129.

Smyer, M. A., & Qualls, S. H. (1999). *Aging and mental health.* Malden, MA: Blackwell Publishing.

Sternberg, R. J. (Ed.). (1990). *Wisdom: Its nature, origins, and development.* New York: Cambridge University Press.

Stickle, F., & Onedera, J. D. (2006). Teaching gerontology in counselor education. *Educational Gerontology, 32*(4), 247–259.

Stickle, F., & Onedera, J. D. (2006). Depression among older persons. *Adultspan, 5*(1), 36–46.

Zucchero, R. A. (1998). A unique model for training mental health professionals to work with older adults. *Educational Gerontology, 24*(3), 265–278.

Biographical Statement

Fred Stickle is a professor in the Department of Counseling and Student Affairs at Western Kentucky University. He is a Licensed Marriage and Family Therapist and a Licensed Professional Clinical Counselor. Fred sees clients in his private practice.

Jill D. Duba is an assistant professor in the Department of Counseling and Student Affairs at Western Kentucky University. She is a Licensed Professional Clinical Counselor and a Marriage and Family Therapist Associate. Jill receives regular clinical supervision from Fred Stickle. The two authors have published articles together about successful aging and teaching gerontology in counseling.

The Second Time Around

Heather Trepal

Grandparents raising grandchildren is a growing phenomenon. Ginny, 64, took over the full-time care of three grandchildren when her daughter went to prison for prostitution and drug dealing. Now Ginny's blood pressure was up, as was her stress level. Heather Trepal tried to help Ginny improve her parenting skills and find help through support groups, church activities, and respite care. A complication was that Ginny feared any involvement whatsoever with "the system," fearing that Child Protective Services would take the children away.

was working in an inner-city nonprofit family agency in the Midwest. An older woman trudged wearily into my office. How slowly she moved! She was carrying a baby in an infant car seat on one arm while trying to keep a toddler in check with the other.

Ginny was an African American woman, 64 years old. She lived in a three-bedroom home in the predominantly impoverished inner city. She worked downtown in the packaging department of a factory, where she had worked since she was 18. She believed that her company valued her long-time work history and loyalty, although there was little tolerance for unexpected changes to her schedule. She complained that employees were held to a strict 8-to-5 schedule, Monday to Friday, clocking in and out. Ginny had never liked her job but stayed because it paid the bills.

Her primary care physician referred Ginny to our agency. Her blood pressure was up, and when I pressed for information, she reported rising stress due to the recent arrival of her three grandchildren on a full-time basis. Her physician thought she might benefit from talking about her situation. Overall, Ginny's health was good, although she was a regular smoker (1½ packs a day) and liked a nightly glass of wine or two to calm her nerves.

I was new at the clinic, working on my postdegree prelicense hours under supervision. I had earned my M.Ed. in community counseling but was still working on my Professional Counselor credential. I had an interest in working with family issues, and although the job was low-paying, it was the best I could find at the time. Ginny's preference for evening appointments fit perfectly into my schedule, so she was assigned to my caseload.

The agency was a nonprofit, and most of the clientele had little or no disposable income to spend on counseling. Typically, clients were billed through Medicaid if they had benefits for themselves or their children. Many of the children were in the foster care system or involved with Child Protective Services (CPS) and were seen for counseling as a condition of their treatment plans with those agencies. There was a sliding fee scale, but we hardly ever charged. Ginny firmly insisted on paying something for the sessions (which, based on her income, was $1/session). She had insurance but refused to allow our office to look into her counseling benefits.

Conceptualization

Ginny found herself caring for three children (10 months, three, and eight). Ginny's daughter was an addict, recently sentenced to prison for prostitution and drug dealing. One of the children's fathers was also in prison, while the other father was unknown. Ginny had been housing the children on and off while her daughter went in and out of rehabilitation programs, each time promising to "be a mom" and "do right by them."

Ginny was practicing second-generation parenting, and it had been many years since she had raised her own child. She wasn't sure what was appropriate anymore in terms of discipline. Once, in a Bob's Big Boy restaurant, she was given some stern looks when she spanked the 3-year-old for peeing in his pants. She said, "Back in my day, children knew their place. But these kids have been through so much, they don't know which way is up."

Ginny told me, "By this time in my life I thought things would be different. My girlfriends, they are playing Bingo at the church. Me, I can't even imagine leaving my grandbabies with someone else while I went out. I should be enjoying them; instead I'm worrying about money again." She was a single woman, and she still needed to hold down a job to make her mortgage and car loan. Ginny continued, "And then they get sick. Oh they get so sick all the time. You know the co-pays on the doctor and the medications add up, not to mention the extra time off work for me."

Her presenting problem was stress caused by full-time parenting but, in fact, there were many layers to Ginny's problems. Now she was setting a table for four, including a booster seat and a high chair. The children were acting out. I asked Ginny if she wanted a referral for them to be seen in individual and/or family counseling, but she declined.

Per my agency, my treatment plan was focused on Ginny, but I also had concerns about the children and wondered if some family sessions would be in order. I provided a diagnosis of adjustment disorder NOS (not otherwise specified). My goals for individual counseling were:

1. *Assist with parenting issues.* Ginny indicated that much, if not all, of her stress level was caused by her recent transition back to full-time parenting. She asked for help with practical parenting concerns (discipline, scheduling) as well as emotional support for herself.

2. *Build a support system.* Ginny indicated that she felt very lonely in her new role. Most of her friends "didn't want to be bothered" with her daily updates on kid issues, and she felt alienated from them. She also reported feeling like the oddball at the oldest grandchild's school, where most of the parents were her daughter's age. Part of the treatment plan would be to investigate resources for support for Ginny (parenting groups, grandparents raising grandchildren support groups, church activities, respite care) to help her with parenting.

3. *Investigate involving the family.* Ginny indicated that she did not want her grandchildren involved with the counseling sessions, mostly out of fear that someone (some system) would find out and take them from her. It was my ultimate goal to help her to feel comfortable enough to evaluate that decision honestly.

■ Process

Our initial treatment plan called for weekly session over a ninety-day period, after which time we would jointly reevaluate our goals. The following is an account of our sessions together.

Session 1. I saw Ginny for an initial intake/assessment. She was looking down, wringing her hands, and not making eye contact for most of the session. She shared her story with me, how the children came to live with her, and how she was feeling about these new changes in her life.

Ginny: I don't mean to complain . . . I love my grandbabies . . . but I am just so tired. I spend half the night awake with the baby, get up and get everyone off to daycare and school so I can make it to clock in at my job, work all day, pick everyone up, make dinner, give baths, try and get them to bed, and then fall down exhausted myself. The next day the whole thing starts again. Don't get me wrong, I love my grandbabies, I feel like I just need a break!

Ginny also worried about the system, the ever-present Child Protective Services organization just waiting to evaluate her parenting and her daughter's lack thereof.

Therapist: Sounds like a lot has changed for you. Who do you rely on for support?
Ginny: (laughs) Are you kidding? All my friends are off playing Bingo at the church or singing at choir practice or gardening or enjoying visits with their grandbabies. Most don't even work a steady job anymore! There's no one, it's just me. Most times I feel like I am the only one.

I asked her to check out a list of resources my agency had for older clients and report back next week.

      Session 2. Ginny was smiling as if she had a secret to share.

Ginny: Well, I thought a lot about what we talked about last time, about the support and looking for other people in my situation who I could talk to. I called one of the senior citizen agencies and found out that they have a group meeting of grandmothers raising their grandbabies every Tuesday night! I didn't actually go, but the lady on the phone said they had someone to watch the kids while the group was talking.
Therapist: So what kept you from going?
Ginny: Well, I'm worried that someone there might know me or the kids, or, worse yet, my daughter. I'm worried that they will keep a record of me going to the meeting and use it against me.

Several times during the past six years, CPS had removed the children from their mother's care and placed them with Ginny. Each time, when her daughter got sober or completed her time in jail, the children were given back to her, *carte blanche*. While Ginny appreciated the financial support from CPS during the times when she was caring for the children, she could not understand why they let her daughter have them back. Each episode seemed to end worse than the last. When the children were taken from her daughter, the caseworkers had used words such as "abandonment," "neglect," and "abuse."

Ginny: I never abused my kid. Parenting was different when she was little. I mean, gosh, you can't even swat them on the behind anymore

	without someone wanting to tell you what you're not doing right. Given how my own daughter turned out, I'm wondering if I was as good of a parent as I thought I was.
Therapist:	Tell me more.
Ginny:	Well, she has been on and off of drugs since she was a teenager. Then, she always has a different boyfriend; I can't keep up with her. She goes in these cycles where she gets her life on the right track and then something comes and knocks her back off. I'm wondering if I had something to do with that. Plain old wine and beer was good enough for me. I know that sometimes I went out and stayed out too long. Usually my mom or sister would come over and take care of my daughter while I got straightened out. We took care of our own. There was no need for CPS or anybody outside the family to be involved in our business.
Therapist:	It sounds like your own experience of raising your daughter was much different than it is now. Do you see any similarities between you and your daughter as parents?
Ginny:	Yes (begins to sob). I sure do. We both tried to run away when it got to be too much. Neither of us ever knew how to handle the stress. One time, when she was young, she had been a pistol all morning—hitting, being ornery, and fighting with me. By the afternoon, I couldn't take it anymore. When I finally got her down for a nap I went out on a walk and didn't come back. My sister lived down the street, and she came over around dinnertime to find my daughter screaming and crying in her bed, hungry, in a dirty diaper, just miserable. No one called CPS; she just took care of things. I came home later that evening, feeling a little bit better. I just needed a break.
Therapist:	Ginny, what brought the tears just now?
Ginny:	(sobbing again) I think I am sad because in some ways, my daughter has turned into another version of me.

Later, I asked about discipline with the kids.

Ginny:	I don't know how to discipline them, especially the 3-year-old. I get so frustrated with him, bless his heart. Sometimes my first choice is to swat his behind.
Therapist:	Have you ever tried a time-out? Sometimes, with that age, they just need a few minutes away from the situation to calm themselves down.
Ginny:	I'm willing to try anything!

I taught her about time-outs and role-played to practice. I also suggested that she plan for taking breaks away just for herself.

Session 3. Ginny was worried about her grandchildren. Ginny's sister had taken them to visit their mom in prison, and they had come home angry and unruly. She reported that the 8-year-old slammed his bedroom door and didn't come downstairs for dinner. The 3-year-old spent much of the evening whining, and he pushed his baby sister down when she was trying to sit up. Ginny didn't know what to do.

Ginny: Maybe they should come in here and meet with you. I'd like to hear what they would tell you about the situation, especially the oldest one. He's having such a hard time. Not only at home, but his grades are falling in school.

Therapist: Why don't we have them come in with you next week?

Ginny: All right.

Session 4. I was a bit surprised when Ginny showed up at our scheduled session alone.

Ginny: I was worried about how to pay for the session with my grandbabies. I told you before that I didn't want to use insurance benefits for them and have them connected with the system. I'm scared that their mom will hold it against me in the future if she tries to come back and take them. I'm also worried that if CPS finds out then they'll think the kids needed counseling or something was wrong with me or my parenting and try to get involved with our family.

Therapist: Are you worried that I will involve CPS?

Ginny: No, not really. You just never know who you can trust these days.

Ginny told me that a neighbor had called CPS the other day. I never saw Ginny after that. When she didn't show for our next session, I got worried and called her and was disappointed to learn that her phone had been disconnected. She didn't call and let me know what happened, even if only to say that she wouldn't be coming to counseling anymore.

Outcome

Overall, I am not sure if I think this case could be judged as a success or a failure. I think it was a little bit of both. Ginny and I were able to join together, and we did talk in depth about her family issues as well as parenting, her regrets about her own daughter, and her disillusionment with her phase in life. I think it took major trust for Ginny to open up to me, a much younger person.

Reflections

In retrospect, I think Ginny's fear of "the system" overshadowed almost all of the work we did together. She kept bringing it up while I wanted to focus on her coping skills, parenting, and rebuilding her support system. I wish that I had actively listened a bit more and maybe I would have really heard her concerns. At times, her words about the system have echoed in my head when I've heard other clients share the same thing.

When I was working with this client I was a relatively new counselor, and I was young (about 26) and had yet to have my own children. Perhaps my professor's words, "You don't have to have children to help a client with parenting issues," are valid. But now, after changing my share of diapers, disciplining my children even when it breaks my heart to do so, and learning that I could love someone more than anything and be willing to give my life for them have given me new perspective.

I think that I had some big "goals" for Ginny, including working on parenting issues and styles. I think that my slowing down would have been optimal. Perhaps this woman didn't need handouts on procedures for time-out and the appropriate amount of TV watching for a toddler, but instead needed someone to listen to her frustration with her grandchildren and affirm her resolve to care for them. Maybe that would have been more helpful.

I learned a tremendous amount from Ginny, the kind of stuff that you don't get from a classroom in your counseling program. I learned more about a particular type of nontraditional family. After some investigation, Ginny was able to locate quite a few other grandparents, particularly grandmothers, who were raising their grandchildren. It was an interesting phenomenon. To say the least, family dynamics were complicated— the parents of the children were somehow unavailable, most due to drugs or prison. Other parents were deceased. There seemed to be cycles of problems in some of these families, including poverty, addiction, and a lack of parenting skills.

Ginny always harbored the secret hope that her daughter would rehabilitate and somehow come back into the children's lives, even if she was not very willing to express this. Despite her love for her own daughter, Ginny had to put the welfare of her grandchildren first. Being caught in the middle of these two out-of-sync phases of parenting was very stressful. It caused such a burden on Ginny financially and with her health.

Finally, we are taught developmental models, such as those put forth by Erikson (1968), when those in middle adulthood face a period of "generativity vs. stagnation." Ginny, being 64, would seemingly find herself somewhere toward the end of this stage. She is an example of a conflict during this stage, one defined by the successful completion and accomplishments of parenting and career choices. Ginny is not feeling successful as a parent (for example, the numerous problems of her daughter), and she is struggling to accomplish the task of raising her grandchildren. She is also feeling at odds with her same-age peers and their ability to retire and enjoy the beginnings of the golden years. Developmentally, she may be years behind her peers, and this conflict—and the expectation that this stage of life should have been different— causes her much strain and stress.

In summary, Ginny was struggling with a life challenge that was not only more common than I thought, but also more difficult. When working with older adults, you can't stereotype their developmental phase of life. I can only wish the best for Ginny. She was dealt a rough blow, and although she took care of her grandchildren, I think she lacked the support, both financial and emotional, to deal with all of the challenges of encore parenting. The ever-present concern about her daughter coming back into the picture leaves me with a lingering question of what happened to this family.

Reference

Erikson, E. H. (1968). *Identity, youth, and crisis.* New York: W. W. Norton.

Suggested Readings

American Association of Retired Persons. (2007). *Help for grandparents raising grandchildren.* www.aarp.org/families/grandparents/raising_grandchild. Retrieved September 5, 2007.

Brown-Standridge, M. D., & Floyd, C. W. (2000). Healing bittersweet legacies: Revisiting contextual family therapy for grandparents raising grandchildren in crisis. *Journal of Marital and Family Therapy, 26,* 185–197.

Glass, C. J., & Huneycutt, T. L. (2002). Grandparents raising grandchildren: The court custody, and educational implications. *Educational Gerontologist, 28,* 237–251.

Hayslip, B. J., & Kaminski, P. L. (2005). Grandparents raising their grandchildren: A review of the literature and suggestions for practice. *Gerontologist, 45,* 262–269.

Kelch-Oliver, K. (2008). African American grandparent caregivers: Stresses and implications for counselors. *The Family Journal: Counseling and Therapy for Couples and Families, 16,* 43–50.

Lever, K., & Wilson, J. J. (2005) Encore parenting: When grandparents fill the role of primary caregiver. *The Family Journal, 13,* 167–171.

Biographical Statement

Heather Trepal, Ph.D., is an assistant professor in the Department of Counseling, Educational Psychology, and Adult and Higher Education at the University of Texas at San Antonio. She is a Licensed Professional Counselor. Heather is the author of articles on counseling with miscarriage and counseling with self-injury. You can reach Heather at heather.trepal@utsa.edu.

Existential Crisis and the Loss of a Spouse

Montserrat Casado-Kehoe

Carl, 65, came to counseling with a *complicated* grief. His wife of forty years had been murdered, and the perpetrator had not been caught. Of course, Carl was depressed, but he was also angry. There was also guilt as Carl acknowledged his failures as a husband. Profound existential fault lines surfaced that many of us will face when losing a spouse. How do I manage day by day? Who am I? What is my purpose on earth? Casado-Kehoe found Elisabeth Kübler-Ross's (1993) stages of grief to be a useful concept. She used an experiential approach that allows the client to fully experience feelings and gain insight.

C

arl was a 65-year-old Caucasian man who had been retired for two years. He suspected that his wife Debbie had been murdered at work. This had happened four months before coming to therapy. The murder was still being investigated, and there were suspicions that Debbie's boss or a client from work may have been involved. Carl wondered if Debbie had had some knowledge of illegal financial issues involving her boss. According to the police, Debbie had been shot, but it was unclear whether this was a homicide or a suicide.

Carl was clinically depressed. He was angry about the murder. He believed that Debbie's boss knew what had happened and was not telling the truth to the police. Debbie had never shared much with him about what went on at work, but Carl suspected that the boss was involved, directly or indirectly. He struggled with feelings of wanting revenge.

Carl had a small pension and was struggling financially because he did not have his Debbie's income any more. He had discovered that Debbie, who had handled the finances, had accumulated a substantial amount of debt. Carl had a conflicted relationship with his wife of forty years. Now he had many regrets about that. Carl lived by himself but had been spending some time with his only son, Mark, 36. Mark was engaged to be married. He dropped by to care for Carl on occasion, and he helped financially as well.

Mark called to schedule the appointment for his father. Carl had been diagnosed as depressed by his primary physician and was currently taking antidepressants. Carl reported that he was having problems sleeping and had lost his appetite. He was apathetic about life and his purpose in it. When asked how he spent his day, Carl said he found himself thinking about Debbie all the time and that he had a really hard time getting anything done. Mark was trying to get Carl involved with his church.

I was a Licensed Marriage and Family Therapist at the time, and I worked at a counseling center in a hospital. Carl was self-paying using a sliding scale. There were no limits to the number of sessions he could be seen.

Conceptualization

Carl was dealing with grief and with life without a partner. This was an existential crisis—who am I by myself, and what is my purpose?—and fears of his own death. He worried about his relationship with his son and his son's fiancé, coping with the possibility of his wife's homicide, and financial difficulties.

The treatment plan was to offer individual counseling with the goal of helping Carl move through the stages of grief and to reestablish himself in the world as a 65-year-old widower. Another goal was to help Carl feel less depressed.

I used an experiential approach that allows the client to experience feelings and gain insight from an experience and move toward growth. Some of the specific strategies I used were the empty-chair technique, letter writing, and psycho-education.

─────────────── ■ **Process**

There were a total of fifteen sessions over the course of five months. Here is dialogue from our first session.

Carl:	(sobbing) I can't stop thinking of Debbie and how she may have died. I wish I had a chance to talk to her before this happened. I am sorry for my tears.
Therapist:	It's normal for you to feel sad, and it's healthy that you allow yourself to cry.
Carl:	But I feel exhausted after I cry, and I have never cried this much. Men aren't supposed to cry.
Therapist:	It's healthy for men and women to cry when they lose a loved one. The tears are a way to express sadness and honor the individual. Tell me more about the relationship you had with Debbie.

I was normalizing the experience and giving him a chance for him to share his story. I wanted him to be able to release the intense emotions he was feeling and develop a counseling relationship with me.

Carl:	I don't do much during the day if I am at home. Everything in the house reminds me of Debbie. That's the reason I spend time at my son's, but I know that's not an ideal situation either. I feel like I am burden to Mark.
Therapist:	Tell me more about these feelings of being a burden to your son. Also, how often do you feel like life is not worthwhile anymore?
Carl:	I've always been the weak one. Debbie was always the strong one. I wonder why she had to die and not me.
Therapist:	When you feel weak, do you ever think of hurting yourself?
Carl:	No, I wouldn't hurt myself.
Therapist:	Tell me more about your depression and how much your medication is helping you. For how long have you been taking the antidepressants?

Older adults experience many crises that may lead to situational depression, such as the death of a spouse. They may also have less active lifestyles with less physical activity, which would also contribute to depression. Also, sleep disturbances are common, which only aggravates overall physical and mental health.

Therapist:	Have you noticed any change in your appetite and sleeping patterns?
Carl:	Yes, I've lost some weight because I don't feel like eating. The doctor gave me some sleeping pills, but they make me sleepy during the day. My son tells me that I'm very lethargic.
Therapist:	Tell me about your overall health.
Carl:	I have high blood pressure and high cholesterol and I take medication for both. The doctor was also concerned about my heart, and they're running some tests.
Therapist:	How much exercise do you do on a daily basis, even if it's small walks?

Families in later life experience changes in family status such as psychological decline, dealing with the loss of a spouse or peers, and preparation for one's own death, life review; and integration of one's life (Carter & McGoldrick, 1989). Carl was facing all of these. His health was declining, he had retired early, his wife was dead, and now he found himself doing a life review and questioning the meaning of what comes after death. As he was doing that, he also had to reevaluate his spiritual beliefs and determine what was his purpose on this earth.

Carl's son Mark was entertaining the idea of creating his own family, which would bring realignment of relationships, change in relationships, and renegotiation of roles. Mark was also facing the violent death of his mother.

Therapist:	Carl, I want you to think for a moment that Debbie was here with us in this room. Imagine she is seated in that chair. What would you have liked to tell her before her death?
Carl:	I don't know. . . . There's so much to say that I'm not sure I have the words.
Therapist:	Take your time. Close your eyes for a minute, and think of what you may want to tell her.
Carl:	I'm sorry. I wish I was a better husband. I wish I was stronger for you. (starts crying) I'm not even sure I was a good dad. I feel like I failed you and Mark. You two had a much stronger relationship. You understood him more than I did. I know he misses you a lot too.

We discussed the concept of forgiveness, what it would take for Carl to forgive himself.

Therapist:	Carl, I wonder what Debbie would say about you as a husband and father.
Carl:	I know she would say I encouraged Mark to follow his dreams, even at times when they didn't seem too rational. I always encouraged him to play sports, tennis in particular. I'd always been a good tennis player myself. But I know at times she wished I would have been stricter with him. She had to do a lot of that for me.
Therapist:	So, there is a part of you that feels like Debbie did appreciate you. Especially how you supported Mark with his dreams.
Carl:	Yeah. He seems to have turned into a successful young man, more than I ever imagined. For a while, I wasn't too sure.
Therapist:	You are proud of who Mark has become. I wonder what Debbie would tell you to do if she was to see how sad you feel about her passing. What do you think she would say?

In subsequent sessions, I used the empty-chair technique to help Carl express the inner dialogues he was having in his head anyway. Carl also came to understand that the voice of Debbie may also continue to live through him, that this part had not left him. That was a comfort to him. I also used letter-writing exercises between sessions, and he would then talk about these letters in sessions. Developing grieving rituals allowed Carl to acknowledge the loss and honor his wife. Carl and Mark visited the cemetery together, something Carl had not been able to do on his own.

I asked Carl if he would mind having Mark come to a session or two. He agreed, so I alternated between individual and conjoint sessions. I wanted to hear how Mark was coping and to learn more about the relationship with his father. Mark participated in the second session and in some of the final sessions.

Outcome

I used Elisabeth Kübler-Ross's (1993) five stages of grief to help Carl understand that his feelings toward his wife's death were normal, and particularly in this case, in which Debbie had not died a natural death. Carl had many feelings, including anger, and was struggling with sorting out all the feelings and allowing himself to experience them. Because of the suspected murder, the case remained open, and he was repeatedly having to revisit the idea of his wife's murder. This prevented him from moving toward closure. Every time the police called Carl for an interview, he would regress and we had to address these issues in therapy. Although death is always hard, it would have been much easier for Carl if Debbie had died of natural causes.

For me, the most meaningful part of therapy was seeing Carl learning about life development and how it affects people emotionally, physically, and socially. Therapy allowed Carl to do a life review, to honor his wife's unexpected passing, and to contemplate the idea of having a second chance to enjoy the later years of his life.

To my surprise, Carl was committed to therapy and as a result learned a lot about himself, his "failed marriage" as he described it, his feelings for his wife, and his new relationship with his son and future daughter-in-law. Once his medication was adjusted, the depression lifted noticeably. Toward the later part of therapy, Carl acknowledged that he was lucky to have had Debbie as long as he did. Carl also made changes in his lifestyle with the addition of mild physical activity and volunteer work in his church.

Reflections

When I reflect on this case, I realize how important it was for me to think of life development and changing family life cycles. Understanding Carl in the context of his age and the loss of his wife were crucial. Behind the loss of his wife, there were many existential questions for Carl. Who am I in the world now? How do I live day by day? What gives me meaning? What is my purpose on earth now that Debbie is gone? How do I forgive myself for what I did not give to Debbie as a husband? How do I forgive myself for not having been able to protect her? What is a good death? Who am I as a father today? Who is important in my life now? And how do I take care of myself, not just physically but emotionally and spiritually? Developmentally and socially, Carl had to face the meaning of death and dying.

Clients are resilient. My role is to help them connect with the inner strength that we all have as human beings, which sometimes seems to be lost in the midst of a crisis. As a therapist, I could not take away Carl's sadness, but I could comfort him and help him go back and open his wounds so time would heal them. As an experiential therapist, I wanted Carl to experience as much as possible and to be able to feel and verbalize feelings. I believed many of his depressive symptoms resulted from bottled-up emotions and that gender values played a role in this.

This case taught me some essential lessons about life and dying and how much we take for granted those we love. Carl helped me understand the meaning of existentialism, because so much of his work involved understanding life. Personally, I have experienced the loss of loved ones and know how hard it is to accept their passing, that grief is a process. As a therapist, I also know that losing a spouse is different if the person is in their 30s or 40s versus being in their 60s or 70s. This is why the integration of a developmental perspective can be so helpful in therapy.

References

Carter, B., & McGoldrick, M. (1989). *The changing family life cycle: A framework for family therapy* (2nd ed.). Boston: Allyn & Bacon.

Kübler-Ross, E. (1993). *On death and dying.* New York: Collier Books.

Suggested Readings

Felber, M. (2000). *Finding your way after your spouse dies.* Notre Dame, IN: Ave Maria Press.

Kübler-Ross, E. (1997). *On death and dying: What the dying have to teach doctors, nurses, clergy and their own families*. New York: Touchstone.

Loeschen, S. (1998). *Systematic training in the skills of Virginia Satir.* Pacific Grove, CA: Brooks/Cole.

Mabry, R. (2006). *The tender scar: Life after the death of a spouse.* Grand Rapids, MI: Kregel Publications.

Satir, V., Banmen, J., Gerber, J., & Gomori, M. (1991). *The Satir Model: Family therapy and beyond.* Palo Alto, CA: Science and Behavior Books.

Wegscheider-Cruse, S. (1987). *Learning to love yourself: Finding your self-worth.* Deerfield, FL: Health Communications.

Biographical Statement

Montserrat Casado-Kehoe, Ph.D., is an assistant professor of counselor education in the Department of Child, Family and Community Sciences at the University of Central Florida (UCF) in Orlando, Florida. Dr. Casado-Kehoe is a licensed marriage and family therapist and a registered play therapist. She is the play therapy coordinator at UCF. Her research has focused on family therapy, play therapy, supervision, and the integration of health-related issues in counseling. You can reach Montse at mcasado2@yahoo.com.

An Absence of Light: The Case of Marie

Catherine B. Roland

Sometimes a client presents an unforgettable metaphor that illuminates therapy, and that was the case with Marie. At 66, she was losing vision. It was also true that the lights of her life had gone out with the accumulation of losses of family members. Catherine Roland uses client-centered therapy to build a mutually rewarding relationship. The case of Marie took place ten years ago, and so we benefit by Roland's reflections with the benefit of hindsight. As editor of ADULTSPAN Journal, Roland brings extraordinary perspective to the meaning of aging.

T his client came to me, in the mid-Southern city in which I resided, through a grief and loss caseworker who knew that I specialized in counseling mid-life and older adult women. My part-time private practice of counseling families and adults allowed me, at that time, to choose clients who be might interested in working with me, and I with them. Based on the little referral information I had, this client would be an older woman, depressed, and suffering from deeply rooted grief, but I hadn't been told her exact age or how she might present. Imagine my surprise when Marie, an attractive, vibrant woman whose smile lit up the office, who appeared to be in good spirits and in excellent physical shape, stood to greet me.

As a relational therapist and someone who is always interested in the seating choice a client might make, I had furnished the office with two large couches facing one another and two chairs. The chair that I typically sat in was to the side. One of the chairs was an oversized, softer chair, and the other was a straight-backed chair with arms, closest to the French doors leading to the outside. Marie chose the straight-backed chair immediately. As I looked at my potential client, I noticed that her smile wavered slightly as she took a seat, her hands folded tightly in her lap as we completed introductions.

Marie was a 66-year-old professional with a B.A. in English literature and two master's degrees, including an M.B.A. from an Ivy League school. She held a high-level position at a pharmaceutical company, where she had been employed for the past eighteen years. Noticing that her regional accent did not sound Southern, Marie told me that she was originally from the Northeast and had relocated to the South many years earlier and raised her family here. She remarked that my own accent didn't sound Southern, either. I shared with her that I also had relocated to the South from the Northeast a number of years back. That interchange seemed to relax her a bit; her hands unclenched, she took two very deep breaths, and nervously laughed, "Goodness, I guess I was holding that in!"

Marie was the elder of two children and now the only surviving member of her family. Her sister had died of stomach cancer three years earlier, and her mother, who at age 96 had lived "happily alone" until her last year, had died five months earlier. Marie's father had died when Marie was 30 years old, and her mother had never remarried. Marie has two sons, Andrew, living in New York City, and Steven, living in a small town 100 miles from Marie. Steven, closest to her in both "spirit and distance," is married with three children, all of whom Marie sees regularly. Her youngert son, Andrew, is gay and lives with his life partner of twelve years. Marie does not see him as often, however during the past several years of family trauma, she has had good interactions with him and expressed hope that he would visit more often. Marie was divorced twenty years ago, and she said that she and her former husband are on cordial terms. Her sons keep in touch with their father, although during the past few years the contact had seemed to dwindle.

Marie lives alone in a house that she owns, which she proudly told me she completely redecorated a year ago. She loves to garden and raises prize-winning roses. Lately, she said that gardening was depressing her, she avoided it at all costs, and her roses were dying. Her sadness was palpable as she bowed her head, whispering that her mother had been the real gardener in the family, and she had taught Marie about raising roses when she was a child. Having never been in counseling prior to her meeting with me, she expressed concern that it would be "ok to just let down my guard, which is what I need to do." She seemed to close up after that statement, and I thought it best to alter direction.

I asked Marie what had brought her to counseling at this time, and she reported loss of physical energy and annoyance with herself for not being able to concentrate and do the physical things she had been able to do a short time ago. Marie had consistently worked out at a gym four and five days a week and swum in masters' competitions once a month for the past fifteen years. Suddenly her desire to work out and swim was gone. It felt "heavy and burdensome," which was a feeling she was unfamiliar with. Marie had always considered herself an athlete. She had been a semiprofessional tennis player after college and still plays with friends and colleagues.

Her concerns about concentration were mysterious. She complained of not being able to "see as well as before" and that the "dimness" was keeping her from reading all the materials she was assigned at the office. She had missed her last conference, where she was supposed to update a room full of people about what she had gleaned from the readings. Marie had visited her ophthalmologist two months ago but was told there was no evidence of loss of sight. The doctor prescribed reading glasses, but they weren't helping much. Marie said, "I feel like there just isn't enough light." She was a bit hesitant to drive long distances, and the typical household chores she did seemed dangerous. Her demeanor was quiet and sad. When I asked how she felt at the moment, Marie replied, "Not good, not good at all. I guess I feel really old." Marie shared that she felt her own mortality for the first time. She felt that the death of her mother had caused her to slow down in all aspects and now she worried, "I think I'm slowing down to die."

Conceptualization

I decided not to assign a DSM-IV-TR diagnosis. I could rethink that decision if Marie was self-harming or became more fundamentally depressed. Marie was experiencing the natural process of grief over the loss a parent, her last parent at that, and of part of herself. Marie's process of aging and staging as a professional woman who was active and fairly accepting of the developmental process had been changing in a short period of time. The death of her mother and her subsequent eyesight problems were becoming a focal point. Relationally and therapeutically, the situation with Marie seemed to center around three main areas: (1) her relationship with her mother, (2) multiple losses throughout her life, and (3) her sense of self as a strong capable woman was waning and growing dim as she grew older.

Gardening was a direct path to the grief she was experiencing about her mother's recent death. Marie's deep concern about "not seeing" could be a manifestation of fear of experiencing the grief, as well as coming to terms with her own mortality. Loss of financial independence also might have been a factor, because she "had to keep working to live."

It has been my experience that developmental issues must be addressed quickly once they are acknowledged. Marie was clearly ready to begin the process. Her fear of losing her sight, or her light as I saw it, was a manifestation of the losses she had experienced, a culmination of sorts that could lead, finally, to her own demise—if not in death, then through inactivity, depression, and isolation. If Marie couldn't see, then she couldn't "see" her papers for her job, her roses to tend, or her body as a tool and source of joy and strength, as she had regarded it for her whole life.

My approach was a blend of relational and client-centered therapy. The mutuality inherent in the relational approach to counseling is the aspect I feel is most rewarding for the client. The counselor demonstrates unconditional positive regard and there is empathy between counselor and client. It is indeed powerful, and I envisioned positive interactions between Marie and myself in future sessions. I thought that her strength was amazing and that one way to support her would be to share my thoughts with her about her demonstrated ability to evolve and proceed regardless of setbacks. I did, in fact, share that with her during our initial session.

I asked if she felt like we could work well together. In this first session, Marie acknowledged that she was still fearful but that she felt comfortable with my style and with my being a woman. One concern she expressed was that of the difference in our ages. At that time I was only 50 years old, a difference of sixteen years. Never much of a self-discloser to clients, I decided to disclose to her that I had lost my father a few years earlier. This act of giving of myself seemed, thankfully, to assuage her concern, and she asked how many times a week I wanted to work with her. I told Marie that short-term therapy was where we could begin and suggested that we meet twice a week for two weeks, then once a week for eight weeks, for a total of ten sessions. We would reevaluate after that time. Marie made it clear that the time frame seemed reasonable as long as it was short-term and not "forever." She did not require nor would she use her insurance.

During this first session, I observed Marie fighting an inner battle to remain composed, a battle that she won, momentarily. My perception was that the win cost her some energy that she did not have to give and might add to her depression in the short run. Our work together, through a relational/person-centered approach, would focus on Marie's strength, her proven ability to prevail, and her acceptance of loss as a natural aspect of aging.

Process

Session 2. My first goal with clients is to build a strong therapeutic alliance, one in which trust begins to be established, as well as mutual respect and regard. Marie arrived early and apologized for being early. She had been anxious all morning about this lunchtime appointment. She said she thought we'd better make the appointments in the late afternoon so she did not have to return to the office. I mentioned that she seemed anxious about how she might feel at the end of the session, and she agreed.

She told me that she was "happy to be here and annoyed I have to be here." We discussed her annoyance, and Marie reported that she felt weak and needy. I detected a sadness in her eyes, and we discussed this. She became observably more animated the more she talked. It occurred to me that Marie might not be talking to anyone else much these days, at least about anything personal. She revealed that she had indeed not spoken to friends or family about her feelings or about being in therapy. As far as she knew, they thought she was fine.

My goal for the session was to establish deeper rapport and a basic layer of trust on which to build. Marie was a willing storyteller, and the session passed quickly. Marie told me that she was looking forward to Thursday's appointment. Interestingly, when I offered to change it from lunchtime to later in the afternoon, she declined.

Session 3. I had planned to broach the topic of her mother and loss, but Marie had a different goal that would have a profound influence on the remaining sessions. She had brought a card from her son Andrew in New York, an invitation to a Holy Union ceremony for himself and his partner, Chris. There was a handwritten note enclosed, stating that it was very important to Andrew that she be present. He offered to send a ticket and also asked if she would encourage his brother, Steven, to attend. As I listened, Marie's face changed from puzzled, to sad, then to satisfied. When I asked about these feelings, she told me that she was surprised about the invitation, and excited about attending. But as she spoke, I could see doubt creep in. "Do you think I could handle the trip alone?" Marie was frightened about her eyesight—both that Andrew would find out it was becoming an issue and that she felt vulnerable traveling when she couldn't see well. I asked when her last trip had been and if she had been alone. I could literally see her weighing my prompt. It turned out that eighteen months earlier she had traveled alone to New York, then to England, then to France, and she had done just fine. Marie's smile ended the session.

Session 4. I was curious to see whether Marie would mention that this was the last twice-a-week session. Marie talked about her mother's death as soon as she got settled. I had previously suggested that she bring family pictures, and now she pulled out an envelope with several inside. The first was of her mother as a young woman holding a baby, Marie. She said she was going to have it enlarged and framed, because it showed a side of her mother she couldn't know. She held the picture and looked up to the ceiling and said, "I know she knows I love her, but I feel so alone because I can't see her anymore." She cried silently for a very short time. She told me that she had called her son Steven and asked him to dinner, at which they talked about her mother. Steven said that he missed his grandmother, and Marie was able express her great loss. During that dinner, Steven asked if she was planning on going to Andrew's wedding. Steven immediately said he would like to go too, and they made plans to travel together. Steven's wife was a teacher, and she couldn't take the time off to go.

Much had just occurred in the session, and I struggled with how or if I should pull it back to Marie's feelings about her mother's death. What I did reflect was that when Marie had been able to express that great sadness to me, allowed some tears of sorrow, she then didn't hesitate to share with me her success in connecting with her son and arranging the trip. Marie, so bright a woman, got it right away. Her take was, "So, I guess my pent-up sadness and confusion isn't allowing me to go on. I feel better right this minute anyway."

Sessions 5 and 6. In the third week of therapy, we began to look at relationships and losses throughout Marie's life. Her relationship with her ex-husband was a short topic, because Marie had dealt with it. It was a situation that needed to change, she changed it, and she remained comfortable with the outcome. Her only regret was that her sons hadn't had their father around much, both while she was married and now that she wasn't. Although it was a loss, it didn't seem to be a profound loss. We still had the deaths of her father and her sister to consider. Marie had brought a picture of her sister and herself to the last session and she brought it again. Her "little sister," Carol (four years younger), had suffered during the last six months of her life. Marie had been close to her and had spent much time with her during her illness, leaving her job for three weeks and caring for Carol. That was the loss that Marie had the most difficult time discussing, because she viewed it as "just bad timing and bad luck" that Carol had become ill. The two sisters, though not living very close to each other, managed to spend holidays together, especially after Marie's divorce. Carol's husband had passed away several years earlier, and they had had no children. Carol and Marie were supporters for one another and caretakers of their mother. Marie expressed that her greatest sadness was that Carol had not lived long enough for them to grow old together.

I conceptualized in my mind that while the loss of her mother had left a void, Marie's most devastating loss was her sister's death. Marie had lost confidence and acceptance of herself as an aging woman, feeling vulnerable in a way that was not conducive to graceful aging. The remainder of those sessions dealt with the loss of her sister and Marie's feelings of fear of not seeing, not feeling, and not doing as she always had in her life.

Sessions 7 and 8. Sometime earlier, Marie had told me offhandedly that she had tried going back to the health club. In the next session, Marie proudly pulled her key ring out and waved a white tag that had the name of her health club printed in red. She smiled, then nearly laughed, and told me she had been going at 5:30 AM for three days, "I am stiff, I ache, I'm not tired though, and I'm back there!" She told me her plan was to go to the club three days a week, not the four to five she had done in the past. She had started swimming again as well, but didn't think competing in the masters' swimming round was what she wanted to do. That seemed to unsettle her. She feared the chlorine in the pool might hurt her sight, so she used goggles, but she had never been able to race with them. Not long ago, though, she hadn't been setting foot in the club at all.

Marie had gone back to the ophthalmologist and had gotten new glasses. She was reading better but still didn't see well in the dark. She suspected she had cataracts, although her doctor disagreed. I suggested she seek a second opinion. We touched on the subject of her father and his death, but she seemed to have dealt with that to some degree. It was my opinion that although her father's death had been a loss, it was the two most recent losses that were causing the most pain.

Marie said that she had never told Andrew that she accepted his sexual orientation or his life partner, or that he had chosen to live so far away. As for his move to New York, instead of a snub, she reframed it as the place he loved and the best place for his law practice. She did accept Andrew and loved him very much, but she wanted him to know that, somehow, intuitively, without having to say it. We discussed ways she could tell him. Just attending the ceremony in New York was one way. When I presented to her that Andrew likely knew but might like to hear it, Marie teared up and said, "It's hard for me to admit I made a mistake." It turned out that her mother had not accepted Andrew, and perhaps now, Marie felt free to express her love and acceptance.

I pondered to myself after we ended the session that emotions could definitely take positive and negative turns, and losses combined many various feelings, even relief and sometimes guilt.

Sessions 9 and 10. The ninth session, at the beginning of the last week of our agreed-on therapy, went by quickly. Marie had made an appointment with another ophthalmologist for a second opinion. I offered what support I could.

She told me about exercises for bone health and posture her trainer at the health club had given her. Marie was taking control of her life, and I did not notice nearly as much sadness. Her reconnection with her son in New York was a positive for her, and it helped frame our last session together.

I had previously asked Marie to make a list, either in her head or on paper, of feelings, attitudes, perceptions, or actual happenings that she noticed were different. Our last session was spent discussing three photos she had brought—one of Andrew and his partner, one of herself and her two boys when they were teenagers, and one of herself and her sister Carol sitting on the beach under a stripped umbrella playing with two sand pails and shovels. Marie said she would also frame these three, along with the picture of her mother and herself as an infant, and put them where she could view them often.

One of the last topics we discussed was her gardening and her reticence even to discuss that in therapy. Marie said that she still could not go out into the garden and work; however, she had been able to walk in it a few times and pick a rose or two for the table. My instincts told me that Marie had done just about all she would or could do. When I asked whether she was comfortable with ending our sessions, she replied, "Oh yes, this is really good for now. But if I need to come again, may I?" Her question touched me. Typically I am the one suggesting that if some issue should arise, a call to me should be made. Marie beat me to it, and I, of course, let her know that I would be there for her.

▪ Outcome

Marie came back eight months later for a follow-up visit. She reported that her second medical opinion had proved very important. Cataracts were found to have begun in one eye, and the other eye had a full-blown cataract. Marie had the surgery on the more compromised eye and was seeing much better. The second surgery was scheduled for the following summer.

Marie's connection with her children seemed stronger. Steven and Andrew were now her "e-mail buddies." She showed me a picture of the ceremony with Andrew and Chris holding her hands in front of a beautiful wooden door to what was, I supposed, the church where the ceremony took place. Marie told me she was still having a very hard time getting over her sister's death. We worked on reframing the perception that she was, in some way, supposed to get over that or any other death.

Reflections

Reflection has always been a valuable self-training strategy for me. When I reflect on the case of Marie, the first thing that comes to mind is the actual length of time we worked together. I wonder whether, if I had not brought forth the brief therapy model, Marie would have consented to a longer-term relationship, for at least six months. I feel that if we had that time together, many more issues might have been discussed; the brief time we had together seems inadequate as I think back on it now. I respect that Marie did not seem open to working longer, but I won't ever know what her reaction might have been had I mentioned that I felt she should continue.

For the most part, I doubt I would have done much differently with Marie, but I do feel that the losses in her life, including that of her divorce, could have been explored more thoroughly. Often a client will relate that she has "worked through" a certain issue, but that shouldn't deter me from fully exploring those issues if it becomes clear they are still important.

I do feel that Marie's relationship with her sons was deeper and more satisfying, even after the brief time we spent together. I imagine Marie relating to both her sons, differently for sure, but gaining much pleasure from those connections in her later life.

When I reflect on Marie's case, ten years later, I am aware that my own life has changed. I am now nearing the age of 60, and I wonder, would I have a different view of Marie's issues now than I did ten years ago? I suspect that regarding the physical issues, including the issue of her sight, my reactions would have been closer to Marie's in that I can now relate more deeply to the physical losses associated with aging.

The lessons I am learning about the aging process on a personal level are allowing me to become a better therapist for the mid-life and older population, and Marie's case was one of the most poignant for me. The fears that people harbor about getting "old" are partly emotionally based, partly societal myths, and partly based in reality. They are also somewhat self-determined, and that is what I now try to teach my clients who are over the age of 45. For some, 45 seems to be the age at which physical changes begin. I have also learned that lifestyle, stress, vocation and/or avocation and love of career, and family bonding can influence the aging process greatly. Marie's case profoundly affected me and my work with clients of all ages in the areas of self-esteem and the power of the cognitive relational process. Marie was an example to me of a client who realized that the help she needed was available, took the difficult path of sharing what had never been shared before, and worked hard on her own to reframe her life. As I progress through the aging/staging process, I strive to continually reframe events and "losses" to include the natural process of aging with grace.

Suggested Readings

Beck, C. J. (1989). *Everyday Zen: Love and work*. New York: HarperCollins.

Degges-White, S., & Myers, J. (2006). Women at midlife: An exploration of chronological age, subjective age, wellness, and life satisfaction. *ADULTSPAN Journal, 5*, 67–80.

Duffy, M. (1999). *Handbook of counseling and psychotherapy with older adults*. New York: John Wiley & Sons.

Jordan, J., Kaplan, A., Miller, J. B., Stiver, I., & Surrey, J. (1991). *Women's growth in connection: Writings from the Stone Center*. New York: Guilford Press.

Knight, B. (2004). *Psychotherapy with older adults*. Thousand Oaks, CA: Sage.

Moustakas, C. E. (1961). *Loneliness*. Englewood Cliffs, NJ: Prentice Hall.

Muller, E., & Thompson, C. (2003). The experience of grief after bereavement: A phenomenological study with implications for mental health counseling. *Journal of Mental Health Counseling, 8*, 183–205.

Russell, L. (2003). Stopping by a cemetery on a snowy morning. *Journal of Grief and Loss, 8*, 221–227.

Walsh-Burke, K. (2005). *Grief and loss: Theories and skills for helping professionals*. New York: Allyn & Bacon.

Weil, A. (2007). *Healthy aging: A lifelong guide to your well being*. New York: Anchor Books.

Biographical Statement

Catherine B. Roland, Ed.D., is professor and chair of the Department of Counseling, Human Development and Educational Leadership at Montclair State University, Montclair, New Jersey. She is a Licensed Professional Counselor, Licensed Marriage and Family Therapist and supervisor, and a National Certified Counselor. Areas of clinical interest include women and depression in mid-life and beyond; treating survivors of abuse; and couples and family counseling across the life span. She is the editor of *ADULTSPAN Journal*, a publication of the American Counseling Association and the Association for Adult Development and Aging. Catherine may be reached at rolandc@mail.montclair.edu.

Living with Dying: Alcohol Is Not the Answer

Mary Ballard, Hunter Alessi, and June Williams

Seventy-year-old Lloyd was having trouble concentrating and was experiencing chest pains. His physician could find nothing physically wrong and referred Lloyd for counseling to address symptoms of depression and anxiety. Lloyd had been drinking heavily since the death of his wife of fifty-two years. Mary Ballard saw clearly that Lloyd was grieving. Operating from a strengths-based perspective, Ballard used a solution-focused approach to help get Lloyd back on track.

There was a thirty-year gap in ages between counselor and client that worried Ballard. She wanted to make sure she understood any countertransference that might occur. Wisely, she consulted with her colleagues, Hunter Alessi, who has expertise in substance abuse, and June Williams, who has expertise in grief and loss. Our bird's-eye view of this process is instructive.

Seventy-year-old Lloyd came to counseling at the urging of his two adult daughters, after being referred by his primary care physician. He had been "having trouble concentrating" since the sudden death of his wife of fifty-two years, and he went to his doctor a few weeks ago when he started experiencing chest pains. He was taking a beta-blocker for high blood pressure. After a series of tests, his doctor told him that he was fine and suggested he talk to me to address what appeared to be symptoms of depression and anxiety, probably related to the death of his wife.

Lloyd is a dairy farmer in a rural area of southeast Louisiana. He has lived alone for the past eight months, since Betty died. His daughters (Sue and Janice) and their families both live adjacent to his property, and his sons-in-law (Jack and Ed) work with him on the dairy farm. When Betty was alive, she would get up at 3:00 AM with Lloyd and make him coffee before he went out to supervise the milking. Now he was having trouble waking up before mid-morning.

At his initial visit, Lloyd seemed a bit uncomfortable with the idea of seeing a counselor. I learned that he really enjoyed spending time with his grandchildren, ages 12, 14, and 15. He really perked up when he told me of attending their ball games, ballets, and recitals. He also shared that he had few close friends outside of his family, and that his primary social outlet was his church. Most of his friends either farmed or worked in the large mill nearby. Like Lloyd, most had high school educations. Lloyd was a World War II veteran and occasionally participated in local VFW activities.

Lloyd seemed to have no prior history of substance use problems. The long hours on the dairy farm left little time to socialize during the week; however, both he and Betty liked to have a highball or two in the evenings before dinner. They would frequently have dinner on the weekends with friends and family. Both enjoyed having a few drinks on those occasions, but neither had a history of drinking to excess. Alcohol use had seemingly not been problematic for Lloyd up until now. Since Betty's death, Lloyd had been drinking more; the occasional highball or two after work had turned into three or more. His daughters noticed that he was having trouble remembering, experiencing difficulty getting up in the mornings, and often slurred his words in the evenings. This was disconcerting for the family.

Lloyd has both Medicare and a Medicare supplement, so his insurance paid for a large portion of his sessions, and he paid the balance himself. There was no limit to the number of sessions he could have; however, the nature of his problem lent itself to counseling of a fairly short-term duration.

Conceptualization

Lloyd is currently experiencing problems resulting from the coping mechanisms he has selected in an attempt to deal with the death of his wife of fifty-two years. His consumption of alcohol in the evenings after work has escalated to levels that leave him disoriented by bedtime and unable to wake for work in the mornings. When I first met with Lloyd, he denied drinking to excess, but he later confided that it "helped ease the loneliness and pass the time away." Lloyd was clearly grieving the loss of his wife and felt overwhelmed by the emptiness and sadness he felt.

Operating from a strengths-based perspective, I utilized a solution-focused approach in an attempt to help Lloyd see past his grief and into a brighter future. While acknowledging that Lloyd is desperately mourning the death of his wife, Betty, this approach does not believe that dwelling on the pain and sadness will be beneficial to solving his problems. Lloyd's family is a very good support system, and he has spent many hours sharing his memories of Betty and their life together. Lloyd's problem was his inability to see past his loss.

Because Lloyd's generation was typically skeptical of counseling, I felt that it was important to talk to him about my profession, including my theoretical approach. A strong and prideful man, he seemed to appreciate the fact that I fully recognized and admired his ability to choose for himself the remedy that best suited his needs. He also seemed grateful for my confidence in his ability to change in ways that only he could define. We built a relationship based on mutual respect.

By focusing on Lloyd's strengths and abilities, I assisted him in constructing meaningful goals for counseling. His overall goal was to return to "feeling and functioning" the way he was prior to Betty's death. More tangible goals included spending more time with his family and friends and ordering the memorial headstone for Betty's grave, something he had been avoiding. I used solution-focused therapy to help Lloyd imagine a meaningful life in the absence of his wife but in the presence of his memories. Once this picture was in place, I hoped that he would take steps to achieve his goals.

Process

Session 1: Establishing the Relationship, Exploring Goals. Lloyd seemed uneasy in the first few minutes of our first session. It was clear to me that he had no idea what to expect, or why his doctor and daughters thought that seeing me would be helpful. So, I spent much of our initial time together explaining to Lloyd what counseling is all about and my philosophy in approaching it. Lloyd signed my disclosure statement, and we proceeded to spend the rest of the session talking about the past eight months of his life.

Counselor:	Well, Lloyd, it's obvious that you miss your wife very much. I can't imagine how lonely you must feel after spending fifty-two years of your life together with Betty. So, tell me if you can, what are you hoping will be different as a result of your coming for counseling?
Lloyd:	Hmm. I don't know, really. I guess I was hoping that I could start feeling and functioning a little better.
Counselor:	Can you tell me how that would make your life different?
Lloyd:	(long, thoughtful pause) Well, for one thing, I'd be able to get myself up for work in the mornings. Seems like all I do here lately is sleep.
Counselor:	And, how would that make your life different, Lloyd?
Lloyd:	I just think I'd feel better to be back in my routine. I'm used to being up before the crack of dawn. And, goodness knows, I'd be more help

	with the dairy if I'd get back to doing my part. And, my kids might quit worrying about me so much. . . . I don't like that.
Counselor:	What is it that you'd like for your kids to notice about you as a result of counseling?
Lloyd:	That I'm my old self . . . that I'm not crazy.
Counselor:	And how would they recognize you as your "old self"?
Lloyd:	Well, our conversation wouldn't revolve around me and my problems. We'd go back to talking about the dairy and the grandkids!

Lloyd's first session was the beginning of a trusting relationship. By the end of the first session, his expressions had positively changed, and he was smiling at times. Because Lloyd did not mention his excessive use of alcohol in the evenings, neither did I.

Session 2: Asking the Miracle Question. In the second session I explained to Lloyd that one of the specific techniques of solution-focused counseling involved asking the "miracle question." I explained its purpose and he agreed to try it.

Counselor:	Lloyd, suppose you go to sleep tonight, and, while you're sleeping, a miracle happens and your problems are solved. But, because you are sleeping, you have no idea that this miracle has taken place when you get up in the morning. So, describe to me how you will know that this miracle actually happened.
Lloyd:	Well, my first clue would be that I woke up on time to supervise the milking! (laughing) Wouldn't Jack and Ed be surprised! Then, I guess I'd have enough energy to make it through the day.
Counselor:	What else?
Lloyd:	Well, I wouldn't feel so lonely . . . miss Betty so much. And, I wouldn't get real anxious in the evenings.
Counselor:	How would you know you weren't anxious in the evenings?
Lloyd:	For one thing, my chest wouldn't get so tight, and I wouldn't get so antsy.
Counselor:	So you would be relaxed.
Lloyd:	Yeah. And, if I were more relaxed, I wouldn't need those extra drinks to help me sleep.
Counselor:	So your miracle would involve drinking less.
Lloyd:	Yeah. And I think that's what's really got the kids worried. They think I'm drinking too much.
Counselor:	Can you tell me what your family would notice if your miracle happened?
Lloyd:	I think they'd say I was more available. Since Betty died, I haven't been as involved in their lives . . . guess I stay home more. I do miss the grandkids.
Counselor:	So your miracle would mean you'd spend more time with your family, especially your grandkids.
Lloyd:	Yeah.

Counselor:	And how would that make your life different?
Lloyd:	Guess I wouldn't be as lonely . . . probably wouldn't miss Betty as much. Guess I'd drink less . . . I don't like to drink too much around my grandkids . . . you know . . . want to set a good example.
Counselor:	So you think drinking less makes you a better grandpa.
Lloyd:	Yeah. If I skip those extra drinks, I'm more likely to walk over and visit with them. Of course, that gets my mind off my problems.
Counselor:	Your miracle day sounds like one in which you're back to your old self! You're back in your regular work routine, having energy and feeling relaxed, and visiting more with your family, which means you're spending less time alone missing Betty.
Lloyd:	Yeah . . . sounds good, doesn't it.

The "miracle question" helped Lloyd envision his life in the absence of his problems. It helped him realize that his excessive drinking was interfering with relationships and work. As the session ended, I asked Lloyd if he'd be willing to take steps to make his miracle a reality in the coming week. He agreed to try and seemed enthusiastic about the possibility of doing so. I really sensed that Lloyd felt some hope for the future when he left my office.

Consultation with Colleagues. Even though I felt comfortable working with Lloyd and his issues, after the second session, I decided to consult with two of my colleagues: Hunter Alessi, who has expertise in substance abuse; and June Williams, who has expertise in grief and loss issues. Part of my reason for seeking consultation was that Lloyd was around the same age as my father and shared many of his physical characteristics. I wanted to be sure I was not allowing my own countertransference to interfere.

Hunter observed that Lloyd's increase in drinking due to the circumstances of losing his wife of fifty-two years was not unusual. She cautioned that without help, he could slip into alcoholism. Social support is particularly important for older clients struggling with substance abuse.

Hunter also warned, "Another danger for older adults is that their tolerance for alcohol is not what it used to be. In the client's mind, he probably thinks he can handle the 'extra' drinks the same way he did when he was younger. But as the body's metabolism changes with age, so does one's ability to metabolize the alcohol, making the effects more pronounced."

That made a lot of sense to me. I think that many counselors may have focused exclusively on the drinking issue, immediately labeled Lloyd as an alcoholic, and referred him to AA meetings and treatment for his drinking problem. As we continued to process the case, Hunter pointed out that this would be the worst possible scenario. She also told me, "With older clients who are independent, have a lot of pride, and are somewhat skeptical of 'intervention,' traditional substance abuse treatment is often not effective." She encouraged me to continue to work with Lloyd using a strengths-based perspective.

I asked June for her insights into Lloyd's grief issues. Although I have seen clients working through grief issues, I valued her perspective and knowledge and wanted to get her thoughts. June validated my approach in working with Lloyd. After listening to my description of Lloyd and how he described his grief, she observed that he seemed to fit into the pattern of an "instrumental griever" (Martin & Doka, 2000), someone who is more comfortable in the cognitive-behavioral realm rather than the emotional realm in dealing with their grief. Instrumental grievers experience feelings but may not cry or even have the need to cry and, instead, focus on "doing."

I was not familiar with this conceptualization of grief, but so much of what June shared fit with my own experience of grief. So often counselors think that if clients are not crying or overtly sad, there is something wrong. Lloyd's way of grieving was to channel that energy into activity (e.g., taking care of his family, working in the dairy). However, now he had chosen a maladaptive activity, drinking. I brought up to June that Lloyd needs to buy the headstone for Betty's grave. We agreed that this would probably be a productive activity for Lloyd to help him work through some of his grief.

Session 3: Working Toward the Miracle.
Lloyd came to my office noticeably upbeat. He told me with great pride that he had "worked on that miracle" during the past week. We spent most of the session talking about the things he'd done differently and how much "better" he felt. Lloyd reportedly did not drink at all during two evenings but, instead, attended a meeting at his church one night and had dinner with Jack, Sue, and the grandkids on the other. I wanted to explore just how meaningful these small steps had been to Lloyd. During this process, I discovered another important goal.

Counselor:	Great, Lloyd! I'm really proud of you for having the courage to take these steps! So, on a scale of 1 to 10, with 10 being your miracle has become a reality, where do you feel you are today?
Lloyd:	I guess I'd say I'm at about a 4.
Counselor:	Excellent. Where would you like to be next week at this time?
Lloyd:	Oh, it'd be great to be at a 10! But, realistically, I don't think that will happen.
Counselor:	What steps would you need to take this week to increase that 4?
Lloyd:	Ahhhhh . . . (long, thoughtful pause) You know, I think I just need to take some time to finish this business with Betty's headstone. I think I mentioned to you that I'd been putting that off.
Counselor:	Can you tell me how your life would be different if you took care of this?
Lloyd:	Well, it's always in the back of my mind. I hate the thought of Betty's grave just sittin' there without a headstone . . . bothers me.
Counselor:	So, how would it be for you to have this taken care of?
Lloyd:	Oh, relieved . . . I'd be relieved. It would make me feel good to know that she had a nice headstone. Plus, I'd be finished worrying about it.
Counselor:	Sounds like you'd be more at peace with the headstone in place.
Lloyd:	Yeah . . . yeah, I really would. I need to quit avoiding it.

I felt that Lloyd's procrastination in taking care of Betty's headstone was symbolic of his need to hold on to her. The session ended with Lloyd explaining to me the process for ordering the headstone and his plans to tend to this next week.

<u>Session 4: Taking a Painful Step.</u> I sensed immediately that Lloyd had ordered the headstone when he came into my office. He had a bittersweet look on his face of having accomplished something that left him empty in the end. We talked extensively about how difficult it was to find the right words to engrave on her headstone, and how much he'd cried through the process. As he cried in my office, he admitted to me that this past week was the first time that he'd shed "real tears" since Betty's death. I sensed that Lloyd had reached a pivotal point in counseling. As the session ended, Lloyd thanked me for helping him "do what he wouldn't have done by himself."

<u>Session 5: Marching Toward the Future.</u> I wanted to assess where Lloyd was in relation to his other goals: spending more time with family and friends, and feeling and functioning better.

Counselor: You've come a long way in five weeks, Lloyd. Thinking back to that 1-to-10 scale, where are you today?

Lloyd: You know, it's hard to say. As tough as it was to talk to those funeral people about the headstone, I really do feel relieved. Sue and Janice even told me this week that I seemed more like my old self.

Counselor: Well, I know that was a goal of yours to have them say that!

Lloyd: Yes. Yes, it was.

Counselor: Well, that must make you feel good. What have you done differently to make them say that?

Lloyd: Guess the main thing is I've just been around more. I'd been sittin' at home most evenings since Betty died. But, now, I've tried to make it a habit to walk over and check on them or invite them over to eat supper with me. And, I guess the biggest difference they notice is that I'm not drinking so much at night.

Counselor: So you're drinking less and spending more time with your family.

Lloyd: Yeah . . . and friends. I had supper Friday night with Bob and Nancy. Betty and I used to see a lot of them before. . . . It was good to see them. I didn't realize they were worried about me too. (laughs)

The session ended early when Lloyd got a call from his daughter saying that he was needed to pick up his granddaughter from band practice. I thought this was another positive sign that Lloyd was regaining a sense of normalcy in his life.

<u>Session 6: Continuing the March.</u> After reviewing the goals he'd established in light of his answer to the "miracle question," I asked Lloyd to consider carefully where he'd fall today on the 1-to-10 scale. He assured me that he was a solid 7, maybe even an 8. I asked him to explain the difference between a 7 and an 8. He told me that some days he missed Betty more than others, and those were the days that dipped to 7 and sometimes below. With his perceptions defined, I wondered where his family would rate him.

Counselor: So, tell me then, on that scale from 1 to 10, where would your family say you are in achieving your miracle?

Lloyd: Oh, a solid 10!

Counselor: Really?! That's great! Describe to me their definition of a 10.

Lloyd: Sure. That's easy. I'm not drinking so much. I'm getting up early for work and helping the boys as much as I ever did. I don't mope and feel sorry for myself. The grandkids are seeing Papa at all their functions again. Want me to keep going?

Counselor: Only if you want to!

Lloyd: Guess the big change for me . . . (long pause) . . . is that I know Betty would want me to go on with my life. The last thing she'd want is for me to stop being a good dad and papa. I miss her . . . don't get me wrong. I miss her as much as I ever did. But, I know I can't crawl in a hole and die . . . that would be selfish.

Counselor: You've worked really hard, Lloyd. Sounds like your memories of Betty really motivate you and will continue to help you through those lonely times.

Lloyd: Yeah . . . that's right.

We both agreed that next week would be our last session.

Session 7: Termination. Saying goodbye to Lloyd was bittersweet. I assured him that I was available to meet with him in the future. As Lloyd left my office, I sensed that he would continue to live a full life, surrounded by friends and family and the fond memories of his fifty-two-year love affair with Betty.

Outcome

The solution-focused approach worked because it helped Lloyd focus on a life beyond grief. Lloyd did not need me to continue to process his sorrow for Betty. He had been doing this since her death with his family and friends. But he was stuck; he didn't know how to move beyond his depression and loneliness. My approach gave Lloyd an opportunity to push past his feelings and begin to experience life with a hopeful perspective once again.

Because Lloyd was from a rural area, it surprised me that he was so receptive to counseling. Pride and independence are ingrained in residents of this area, but I think being a native of this area and understanding the culture enabled me to establish a rapport with Lloyd rather quickly. And it was this rapport that kept Lloyd from terminating counseling prematurely, and doing the work that needed to be done.

I also thought Lloyd would be more resistant to discussing his alcohol consumption, but because I did not address it directly, he was able to deal with the issue on his own terms. It was gratifying to see how quickly Lloyd realized that extra drinks in the evening were contributing to his unhappiness.

Reflections

I enjoyed working with Lloyd. The thirty-year difference in our ages did not seem to matter to Lloyd. I felt that he respected me as a professional and never doubted my ability to help him. Having a father Lloyd's age made me examine my motives more than once. I learned that older adults are truly receptive to change, a fact that I had somehow doubted. Lloyd taught me that grief and loss are painful at any age, and that older adults value companionship just as much as younger couples. Lloyd's loss was deep, and no amount of counseling could erase that. However, counseling proved to be valuable in giving Lloyd back a sense of hope and a sense of purpose. Counseling reconnected him with all that was still alive in his life. I felt good about that.

Reference

Martin, T. L., & Doka, K. J. (2000). *Men don't cry, women do: Transcending gender stereotypes of grief*. Philadelphia: Taylor & Francis.

Suggested Readings

Barry, K. L., Oslin, D. W., & Blow, F. C. (2001). *Alcohol problems in older adults: Prevention and management*. New York: Springer Publishing.

Craig, R. J. (2004). *Counseling the alcohol and drug dependent client: A practical approach*. Boston: Pearson Education.

Miller, G. (2005). *Learning the language of addiction counseling*. Hoboken, NJ: John Wiley & Sons.

Pichot, T., & Dolan, Y. (2003). *Solution-focused brief therapy: Its effective use in agency settings*. New York: Haworth Press.

Van Wormer, K., & Davis, D. R. (2003). *Addiction treatment: A strengths perspective* (2nd ed.). Belmont, CA: Thomson Brooks/Cole.

Biographical Statement

Mary Ballard, Ph.D., is an associate professor of counseling in the Department of Counseling and Human Development at Southeastern Louisiana University. As a licensed professional counselor and a licensed marriage and family therapist, she has worked with addiction and families for over twenty years. She also teaches courses in substance abuse counseling in the counseling program at Southeastern and presents on this topic at conferences. You can reach Mary at Mary.Ballard@selu.edu.

Hunter Alessi, Ph.D., is a professor of counseling in the Department of Counseling and Human Development at Southeastern Louisiana University. She is a licensed professional counselor and a licensed marriage and family therapist. She has conducted research and presented nationally and internationally on the topic of substance abuse counseling. You can reach Hunter at halessi@selu.edu.

June Williams, Ph.D., is an assistant professor of counseling at Southeastern Louisiana University in the Department of Counseling and Human Development. She previously served as the assistant director of the University Counseling Center at Southeastern. She regularly teaches a course in grief and loss counseling and has presented on various grief-related topics. You can reach June at jwilliams@selu.edu.

I Don't Know if This Therapy Is Helping Me

Ana Blancarte

Dora, 72, was depressed after the death of her husband, but this wasn't a case of simple grieving. During Dora's childhood, her mother had been emotionally unavailable. An incident stood out in Dora's memory that had occurred when she was 5 years old. Dora heard music coming from somewhere, and something about the music moved her to tears. Seeing Dora's tears, her mother derided her in a loud, irritated voice. This is the kind of "loss" that could easily have been ignored in brief therapy. Anna Blancarte, a psychodynamic therapist, recognized the importance of exploring such in-depth issues. Dora grew up in a U.S./Mexico border town, and Blancarte's valuing of cultural issues adds still another dimension to our understanding of this client.

ora, a 72-year-old Mexican American woman, called cautiously for an appointment in mid-December, two years ago. She was referred to me for psychotherapy because of depressed mood and grief related to the death of her husband. He had died seven months ago. I knew something about this case because Dr. Martin, Dora's psychiatrist, had called me earlier in the week to discuss the referral. She told me that Dora's depression had intensified in the last two months. Dr. Martin had been seeing Dora for five years and gave Dora a diagnosis of bipolar disorder, predominantly depressed. Before seeing Dr. Martin, Dora had been treated for about thirty years by two different psychiatrists. About twenty-five years ago, Dora had one psychiatric hospitalization and electroconvulsive therapy (ECT) because of severe depression. There was no history of suicidal ideation.

Dr. Martin believed that sensitivity to cultural issues would be important. Dora grew up in a U.S./Mexico border town, and she spent summers in Mexico during her childhood. Dora was referred to my private practice because Dr. Martin knew of my training in geropsychology and my understanding and valuing of cultural issues.

When someone calls my office for an appointment, I talk with her or him before scheduling an appointment. I want to find out the caller's reason for seeking treatment; determine if this is a case I can treat; and give the caller an overview of how I work in psychotherapy. When Dora called, she stated clearly what she wanted from treatment. She clearly had good verbal skills. When I explained that I anticipated weekly sessions, Dora stated that "yes" she wanted counseling, "but" she was not sure how she could work out weekly sessions because she did not drive. She added that it would be inconvenient for her four adult children to bring her to sessions because they lived outside of the city (although within easy driving distance), and that she depended on someone else to drive her around. This was my introduction to Dora's "yes . . . but" approach to life. "Yes" she wanted to do something, "but" there were all these reasons why she could not.

I decided not to explore the transportation concern, or whether or not she really wanted treatment, or would keep appointments. That Dora had called fairly soon (five days) after the referral by her psychiatrist was to me motivation for treatment. I offered an appointment for the next week, and she took it without hesitation.

Dora lives alone in the five-bedroom house where she and her husband reared their four children. Her two sons and two daughters are married, and all have children. She talks with each of them by telephone at least once a week. One of her children visits every other week, two visit monthly, and one visits several times a year. Dora has a warm relationship with her grandchildren. Dr. Martin has met several of Dora's children and reports that they are supportive. In short, they are a nice family.

Dora is tall, mildly overweight, and wears glasses. She walks with a mild stoop and an awkward gait. Dora reports back pain when walking but will not go to the doctor for her back pain, or for anything else. Since her husband's last operation, Dora developed a fear of going to doctors, lest they give her "bad news" about her health. She reported some dental problems, and she does go to the dentist as needed.

Dora's source of financial support is savings and her husband's retirement fund. He was an engineer at a military base. She owns her home and is considered middle-class. She worries about money. In general, she worries about many things. A major stressor for Dora is deciding whether to stay in her house or to sell it and downsize. She refuses the idea of living with her children, although her two daughters have offered. She has considered moving to the town where one daughter lives, but she is unsure about all this. Dora would prefer to live in her current house until she dies, but maintaining a big house wears on her. When her depression worsens, even minor decisions about the house, such as when to trim the bushes, overwhelm her. For many years she has employed a gardener/handyman and a housekeeper. They work at her house once per week, and she trusts them. The housekeeper, Tina, also serves as Dora's driver, taking her to all her appointments. Dora pays Tina extra for each trip.

After the initial diagnostic interview, I decided on a diagnosis of bipolar disorder (most recently depressed). Dora is compliant with her medications for bipolar disorder, and this makes the mood fluctuations less pronounced, but they are obviously there.

When I asked what she wanted to get out of psychotherapy, Dora said, "I want peace of mind" and explained, "not to feel guilty, not to be depressed, not to worry so much about illnesses and being dependent." Since Frank died, she cries daily. Sometimes she thinks Frank is in the house, and when she realizes that he is not there, her sadness redoubles. She is anxious about driving, about going places alone, and about displeasing others. She is afraid "of having no one and of dying alone in a nursing home."

I am a licensed psychologist in private practice. Dora's treatment was covered by Medicare. A secondary insurance policy covered her co-payment and her deductible. As long as medical necessity for her treatment was clear, her psychotherapy sessions would be reimbursed.

Conceptualization

Dora's most obvious loss was that of her husband, but her history also showed significant losses early in life. Dora's mother was virtually unavailable. Dora grew up feeling isolated even though she lived in a house with an extended family of grandparents, parents, and unmarried aunts. Dora described her mother as having had "highs and lows—very emotional; hysterical." Almost daily, the mother would break into screaming and crying when minor things went wrong. The mother was irritable and did not show affection.

An incident stood out in Dora's memory. It occurred when she was about 5 years old. As was their custom, her family would take an evening walk. During one walk, Dora heard music coming from somewhere. Something about the music moved her to tears. Seeing Dora's tears, her mother derided her in a loud, irritated voice. Dora realized even at age 5 that her mother was not supposed to act like this with her. Her aunt comforted her, but Dora felt shamed and alone.

With her brother's birth when she was 5, Dora felt her mother become even more distant. She believed that her mother favored her brother. As an adolescent,

Dora became angry and "sassy" with her mother. Rather than deal with Dora's feelings, her mother gave Dora any material thing she requested. Dora openly resented her mother and adored her father. A form of this splitting surfaced in the course of psychotherapy.

Although Dora "adored" her father, he was not there for her. He was a businessman in Mexico and spent only a few days of the month at home. In the summer, the family would spend extended periods with him in Mexico. Although her parents argued and screamed constantly, Dora sensed more emotional stability in her father than in her mother. She felt safe with her father. For one, he was quite powerful in the business world; for another, he did not reject or humiliate Dora. The tall, blond absent father became the idealized parent for Dora. She pointed out that when she met Frank, her husband-to-be, she was immediately attracted by his tall, strong physique and blond hair, thinking, "He can protect me. I will be safe."

From a psychodynamic perspective, I viewed Dora's early losses in the form of emotional unavailability as central to her depression. When the mother or father is consistently available to help the child meet her or his needs and deal with the world, it helps the child contain anxiety and intense emotions. Disruptions in the availability of parents create anxiety, and there were many such disruptions for Dora.

Dora's father died when she was in her 40s. Her mother died when Dora was in her 50s. Her aunt died when Dora was in her 60s, and her husband died when she was 71. Dora first sought the help of a psychiatrist in her 40s.

The treatment goals were pretty clear: (1) decrease depression; (2) decrease anxiety; and (3) increase skills to cope with grief. Because Dora had so many fears, I focused on strengthening her sense of security. The fourth goal was to increase positive self-esteem.

Subgoals were to decrease tearfulness, increase positive cognitions, and increase assertive communication.

This would be a challenging, in-depth case, and I needed to work from the psychodynamic model with which I work best. I used cognitive and psycho-educational strategies, as well, but my guiding model was psychodynamic.

Process

This is an ongoing case. To date, Dora has had seventy-eight sessions. For the first eighteen months, sessions were on a weekly basis. At Dora's request, for the next three months, sessions were very other week, and then returned to weekly sessions in the fall.

Sessions were rarely missed and then because of health reasons, a transportation problem, or travel. With a psychodynamic approach, therapy sessions are kept as consistent as possible (same day of the week, same time of day for every appointment). This promotes a sense of trust and reliability and reinforces boundaries. On occasions that I will be away from the office for a week or longer, as much as possible I announce my absence weeks in advance The early notice allows us to address feelings that may be brought up for the patient. This processing minimizes the chances that unaddressed emotions will turn into problem behaviors during my absence. In the first six months of treatment, my absences created much anxiety for Dora. She was not sure if she would "make it" if we missed a session. Normalizing the anxiety and providing supportive interventions were helpful.

Sessions 1 and 2. Dora told me that after Frank's death, she enjoyed being alone in the house and liked creating (or not) her own schedule. Cooking was minimal, as she often ate toast and TV dinners. She spent time reading, watching favorite TV shows, and doing crossword puzzles. An avid reader, she consumed mysteries and suspense thrillers. However, something had changed in the last few months. Dora still liked living alone, but she was feeling overwhelmed, sad, and depressed in the house.

Dora summed up grimly: "I wake up in the morning and my first thought is . . . 'I hate my life.'" Evenings were better. With doors locked and curtains drawn, she felt safe and comfortable, as if she were in a cocoon.

Dora was afraid of displeasing others, being a burden, taking a shower, getting into an elevator alone, and going to doctors. Fear had been present for years but was now intensified. She compensated. For example, she took sponge baths instead of showers, and she arranged to be accompanied whenever she rode an elevator. She refused to try any desensitization technique for her fear of riding in elevators.

Dora reported persistent memory gaps following the ECT 25 years ago. She did not recall details about her psychiatric treatment (how long, when), but I did not observe any other memory problems in our sessions.

Sessions 3 and 4. Dora said, "I feel very alone. I miss Frank a lot." She was also anxious. Medication helped contain Dora's symptoms, but even minor aches and pains held the possibility for catastrophe. When she developed a mild foot ache, her first thought was, "What if I can't walk anymore?" She would not consult a doctor, and the pain went away after a few weeks.

Session 5. Dora was shrill and irritable: "I don't know if this therapy is working. I don't know if I want to keep coming." She went on to describe at length her depression and anxiety. Rather than focus on symptoms, I attempted to empathize with her ambivalence about treatment and about me, "Maybe you wonder if I really understand the way you feel. Maybe you wonder if it is safe to tell me that you want more than I am giving you in these sessions."

My empathy calmed Dora, and we were able to address her concerns about therapy further. I was aware that any kind of questioning by Dora as a child would have irritated and overwhelmed her mother. Dora concluded, "I think we made a breakthrough today. I'll come to the next appointment."

Session 6. Dora said, "I feel depressed and apathetic. Everything is an ordeal." She described a recurring theme of remorse and guilt. She added that for three days she had stayed in her pajamas all day. So much for breakthroughs!

Dora spontaneously told me about a dream in which she is in a packed elevator, feeling panic. I am there also, along with another doctor. Dora is comforted by my presence. When the elevator stops, we walk out of the elevator, and I help her calm down.

To Dora, the enclosed elevator space was related to her feeling of being enclosed by anxiety and fear. I asked if she had any other association to the elevator, and she had none. I thought there could be an association between the elevator's up-and-down and bipolar disorder, but I did not discuss this with her. An interpretation from me this early in the treatment could subdue her exploration of her dreams by placing me in the role of interpreter. I saw the dream as indicating that we had a therapeutic alliance.

Dora had difficulty understanding her diagnosis of bipolar disorder, although she could talk about the pain of her mood fluctuations. As in the dream, my task was to guide her in finding ways to cope with her depressive feelings and to help her find calm in her anxious state.

Sessions 7–16. Invariably, Dora opened sessions talking about depression and anxiety. "I've been up and down" was a common report. At times, she was introspective, noting, "I'm depressed because I'm anxious."

The one-year anniversary of Frank's death was coming up. Dora touched on disappointments in the marriage but did not elaborate on them. Frank's death was too recent, and the therapeutic alliance needed strengthening to address this difficult issue.

Given the intensity of her depression and anxiety, I introduced cognitive-behavioral interventions: deep breathing, negative thought stopping, and positive emotive imagery. She complained, "I can't do this! It makes me more anxious." I did not encourage her to try them at home.

Session 17. For the first time, Dora reported a positive mood: "One morning I woke up, and I wasn't anxious. I was just fine." Dora was beaming. Freedom from anxiety, even if it lasted only a few minutes, was remarkable. I reinforced this positive mood by processing it at length. At the end of the session, Dora mentioned, "Oh, I also got in the shower without being scared." Another big change! Yet she reported this offhandedly, almost indifferently.

Splitting surfaced, and in it I was the "nice" doctor who listened, and Dr. Martin was the "angry" doctor. "Dr. Martin gets angry with me if I tell her I'm depressed. I'm afraid to say anything to her." Again, I did not interpret this splitting to Dora. Such interpretation this early in the treatment can overly intellectualize the process and distance the patient.

Open communication with Dr. Martin was helpful in managing the split. We supported positive transference in order to strengthen Dora's self-image. I also worked to normalize both positive and negative feelings toward Dr. Martin and toward me.

Sessions 18–23. Hearing Dora's unceasing complaints of depression and anxiety brought on a sinking feeling in me. Acknowledging this feeling to myself helped me identify with Dora's pervasive depression and allowed me to maintain a therapeutic stance.

Dora was calmer in these sessions. When the anniversary of Frank's death came, she was sad, but felt less frightened and less disorganized than she (and her children) had anticipated. She noted how much she had relied on her husband for her own identity.

Dora casually mentioned that she was using the anxiety-reduction techniques I had taught her (the ones she said made her anxious): deep breathing, interrupting anxious thoughts, and shifting to a positive emotive imagery. I reinforced her efforts.

Telephone Call from Dora. Dora was quite energized as she related the following. A few weeks ago, Dora told her daughter that she wanted to die. Her daughter became alarmed and demanded to accompany Dora to our next therapy session. Dora did not want her daughter in the session, stating loudly, "It's an intrusion!" I recommend that we discuss her daughter's request at the next session and reassured her that the therapy would remain her individual treatment.

Dora's daughter also called Dr. Martin. I gave Dr. Martin a call. She supported my plan to talk with Dora individually. Neither of us saw Dora at risk of suicide.

Session 24. I reassured Dora that I did not see the need for her daughter to be part of Dora's therapy at this time. Of course, she appreciated this and also was impressed with the cooperative way that Dr. Martin and I handled the situation. As an aside, Dora had seen her parents argue often, but she did not see them solve problems together.

At the end of the session, Dora complained, yet again, about therapy.

Dora:	I don't know if this (therapy) is helping me at all.
Therapist:	(I was stunned, but I recovered quickly) How does it feel, not knowing if I am helping at all?
Dora:	(frowning, irritated high voice) I just don't know if this is helping me.
Therapist:	You might have some feelings about me as the therapist. (Dora shrugs and looks away, still frowning.) You've expressed positive feelings about me, but you could also have negative feelings.

One could say that my statements are suggesting feelings to the patient. However, I was guided by Dora's irritability and made an effort to normalize that Dora could have a wide range of feelings toward me as the therapist. I saw no use in Dora keeping me in an idealized position.

Dora:	I guess.
Therapist:	It's ok to have both positive and negative feelings about me and what I do.
Dora:	(hurriedly) I just said it because you said it first. Anyway, it's time to go. (She gets up and walks out the door.)

I wanted Dora to see that I would not react like her mother to Dora's expression of negative feelings. Notably, after this session, the negative comments about Dr. Martin gradually disappeared. Now that Dora could allow herself positive and negative feelings toward me, it was not necessary to split off her negative feelings toward a different person, Dr. Martin.

<u>Sessions 29–34.</u> Dora continued to express fear of sickness and aging. In spite of this, Dora reported, "Overall, I feel better." The intensity of her depression and anxiety had decreased! As her depression decreased, she began to address fear of abandonment and transference issues at a deeper level. Behavioral changes were also occurring. She began to undertake tasks at home, and to express a wish to have personal relationships.

<u>Sessions 35–45.</u> Even though Dora reported "extreme anxiety" about interacting with others, she was now initiating telephone calls to friends, making calls that she had previously avoided, and communicating assertively with her gardener. To reduce her anxiety, she would think of ways that we would address in the therapy, situations that triggered fear and anxiety.

Dora's cousin from out of state called. Dora had not seen this cousin for over ten years and felt that she could not decline when her cousin asked if she could visit. The thought of her cousin staying with her for a week made her very anxious. Dora decided to skip the session when her cousin would be in town.

<u>Telephone Call.</u> Tina (Dora's driver) was unavailable to bring Dora to her session the next day. Dora told me over the phone that her cousin's visit was worse than she could have imagined. Dora was having associations to anxious people in her childhood (mainly her mother and aunt), and many of her old anxieties had returned. She was even fearful about coming to her therapy appointment.

I reinforced Dora for calling when she was anxious. Reaching out to her mother to help her soothe Dora's anxiety had not been an option. I addressed strategies to decrease anxious thoughts and to increase activities that were pleasant for her. She reported feeling better and said she would keep her next appointment.

<u>Telephone Call from Dr. Martin.</u> Dora's eldest daughter called Dr. Martin out of concern that Dora had Alzheimer's disease because of Dora's alleged memory lapses. We discussed how to proceed and then decided that, with Dora's agreement, I would administer the Mini-Mental State Examination (Folstein, Folstein, & McHugh, 1975) and Draw-a-Clock (Nolan & Mohs, 1994). Dr. Martin would also do an evaluation the following week.

<u>Session 46.</u> Dora discussed the situation that had led to her daughter's call and agreed to take the MMSE and Draw-a-Clock. Results were within normal limits. Dora liked the way that her daughter's concerns were addressed.

<u>Sessions 47. + —- (Second Year of Therapy).</u> Dora continued to show improvement. She began to see her mood fluctuations in perspective. She was depressed and nervous when faced with problems, but her mood generally improved as the problem situations were resolved.

Dora's longtime family doctor was diagnosed with cancer, and Dora had to find a new doctor. She made it to the first appointment and liked the new doctor. Anxiety about going to the doctor was minimal.

The worry about whether to move to a different house or an unfamiliar community continued. A concern about moving away from San Antonio was leaving the Hispanic culture, which gave her a sense of security. Another concern about leaving San Antonio was leaving me and Dr. Martin. "Where will I find a therapist and psychiatrist who speak Spanish?" In sessions, Dora would occasionally interject an idiom or saying in Spanish, but otherwise spoke English. It was important to Dora that I knew Spanish, and that I understood her Mexican culture. It was important to her that I understood her parents and did not criticize them. Given that a child develops her sense of self based on her image of her parents, if she perceived me as critical of her parents, would she view me as critical of her? I assured Dora that if she were to move from San Antonio but stay in the region, we could continue therapy with some modifications, such as more time between sessions. I could also help her locate another therapist. She was not ready to think about changing therapists.

In early summer, for the first time Dora smilingly reported, "I feel happy." She especially enjoyed visits with children and grandchildren, and she felt more independent—the best she had felt in years.

Dora asked Dr. Martin if she could cut back her therapy sessions with me to once every other week. Dr. Martin encouraged Dora to talk with me about it. Dora assertively brought it up at the beginning of the session, and we changed to one session every other week. To me, Dora's request indicated an increased sense of security. Just as it was ok for Dora to get close to me; it was ok for her to move away from me. It had not been ok for Dora to move away from her mother, even though her mother was only marginally available. Dora's mother relied on Dora to allay her own anxiety. Notably, when Dora had a marriage proposal from Frank, Dora's mother gave her permission to the marriage, on condition that the couple not move away from town.

That summer, when I went on vacation, Dora felt much more secure than she had the previous summer.

Early Fall. Dora reported increased depression and strong anxiety again about going to the doctor. She connected her anxiety to Frank: "It's as if I am Frank when I go to the doctor, and I feel all the fear he must have felt when he had cancer."

A source of frustration for Dora was that Frank had not shown emotion. During his battle with cancer, he was matter-of-fact and emotionless, while Dora was frightened and overwhelmed. Her insight was positive but also painful, as it opened up issues of identity, of defining herself as separate from Frank, and ultimately as separate from her parents. Given this development, Dora asked that we return to weekly sessions. Our work continues.

■ Outcome

This is a case in which change and improvement does not appear in a clear-cut way. Neither Dora's depression nor anxiety has gone away, but she has clearly made progress. That she has the courage to address complex and painful issues is a challenge to those who may view the elderly as too set in their ways to make changes, or as unwilling to work with a psychodynamic model.

Interventions worked in ways that I did not anticipate! For example, I took Dora's rejection of my anxiety-reduction strategies at face value, and then she surprised me by trying them on her own. In the initial phase of treatment, with Dora's persistent complaints ("I don't know if this therapy is working; everything is the same"), I had to remind myself often that it is through the therapeutic relationship itself that the anxiety can be played out and worked out, if the therapist is attuned. Being attuned to my experience in session (frustration, bewilderment) helped me tune in to feelings Dora could be having.

When Dora's daughter called Dr. Martin, I became a little anxious and considered having family sessions. However, I was guided by Dora's preference for individual treatment and by her family-of-origin history. This was a woman who did not have a mother fully available for her. Dora's need to keep me attending to *her*, and not her daughter's needs, was the deciding factor.

Dora's experience of the mood fluctuations in her bipolar disorder has become more palpable. Over and over we review the fact that she has made it through a period of deep depression and has also had a period of feeling happy. Having such reference points gives her hope. The assertiveness and coping skills she has gained in therapy are serving her well. Above all, the experience of "feeling better" and "being happy" is no longer a foreign concept for Dora. She has seen change, is hopeful and is willing to continue working. To me, that is a success.

Reflections

Something I found particularly hard about this case was the diagnosis of bipolar disorder. Knowing that this disorder is chronic, and hearing the desperation in Dora's voice, "Nothing's changed; I'm still depressed," initially created some uncertainty for me. How much would treatment help? Getting in touch with this uncertainty helped me understand Dora's doubts about treatment. Another factor that was challenging was that I found myself wishing that Dora would not be saddled with bipolar disorder— a repeating struggle—all her life. I soon realized that this wish for the disorder to go away could interfere with my ability to truly be in touch with the desperation she felt about the disorder that was chronic. Her manic behaviors were well controlled, and had not been evident for years.

In the first half of treatment, Dora's approach–withdraw style would take me aback. Just when I thought we were doing well, she would complain, "I don't know if this [therapy] is working," or "Nothing's changed. I'm still the same." Especially the first year, I had to remind myself that I was dealing with her punitive, self-critical sense of self, and that my task was to show her an alternate (more adaptive, less critical) approach.

With the benefit of hindsight, there are two things I would do differently. Too early in the treatment, I did some interpretation of her relationship with her mother. I was frustrated with Dora's negativity, and I needed to keep in mind that my frustration could lead to an untimely interpretation. I wanted her to understand where her negativity was coming from, as if that would change her negativity. Fortunately, we had established enough of a therapeutic alliance so that when I did my interpretation, Dora did not hesitate to say, "I have no idea what you're talking about."

I did not affirm Dora as much as I could have in the beginning of treatment. I was aware of her anxiety and promptly provided strategies to decrease this. Although the strategies were useful, I missed (just as her mother did) that Dora needed more of an empathic, affirming, feeling response from me to relieve her anxiety. No wonder she said the cognitive anxiety-reduction interventions I gave her made her more anxious.

That Dr. Martin works with a psychodynamic perspective was most helpful in managing this case. Communicating openly about Dora's splitting helped us contain the split, avoiding a disruption of Dora's treatment—much as open communication and planning between parents can help prevent distress for a child. Dora's parents had great difficulty containing their differences, and this created much distress and disruption for her.

Several factors help me feel comfortable in working with the elderly. For a brief period in my early childhood, I had an extended-family experience, with my maternal grandmother and great-grandmother in the household. Later, my grandmother lived next door to us. Also, our neighborhood had quite a mix of age groups. It was not unusual to have grandparents living with a family or in a house very close by. Two of my playmates were being reared by their father and grandmother (their mother had died). In that community, the elderly were visible and part of my daily life.

Although having elderly people in the household was accepted as natural in my family, neither my siblings nor I have an elderly parent living with us. None of the siblings in my family live in the same town, and we all face the challenge of caring for elderly family members long-distance. Experience with geographic challenges helped me empathize with Dora's situation, and with her frustration that none of her children live near her.

Working with Dora reminded me of how I like to work with Hispanic elderly. With this case, I was particularly alert to the potential for countertransference. Dora is bright, verbal, well read, and witty—all traits that I like. I needed to make sure that my liking her and wanting her to get well did not cloud my ability to see what her experience actually was.

I take aging more seriously as I am well into middle age. Living alone, aging, and the loss of a partner are particularly difficult when there is no extended family close by. These points are salient in my work with Dora, and they are relevant to me on a personal level, because I have no extended family in San Antonio. The resilience of the elderly and their willingness to continue growing never ceases to impress me. I hope to have some of that courage and resilience as I age.

References

Folstein, M. F., Folstein, S. E., & McHugh, P. R. (1975). Mini-Mental State: A practical method for grading the cognitive state of patients for the clinician. *Journal of Psychiatric Research, 12*(3) 189–198.

Nolan, K. A., & Mohs, R. C. (1994). Screening for dementia in family practice. In R. W. Richter & J. P. Blass (Eds.), *Alzheimer's disease: A guide to practical management. Part II* (pp. 81–95). St. Louis, MO: Mosby-Year Book.

Suggested Readings

Guarnaccia, P. J., & Rodriguez, O. (1996). Concepts of culture and their role in the development of culturally competent mental health services. *Hispanic Journal of Behavioral Sciences, 18,* 419–443.

Kahana, R. (1979). Strategies of dynamic psychotherapy with the wide range of older individuals. *Journal of Geriatric Psychiatry, 12,* 71–100.

Meador, K., & Davis, C. (1996). Psychotherapy. In E. Busse & D. Blazer, (Eds.), *Textbook of geriatric psychiatry* (pp. 395–412). Washington, DC: American Psychiatric Press.

Morgan, A. (2003). Psychodynamic psychotherapy with older adults. *Psychiatric Services, 54*(12), 1592–1595.

Myers, W. A. (1986). Transference and countertransference issues in treatment involving older patients and younger psychiatrists. *Journal of Geriatric Psychiatry, 19,* 221–239.

Pollak, G. (1982). On ageing and psychotherapy. *International Journal of Psychoanalysis, 63,* 275–281.

Sue, D. (1998). In search of cultural competence in psychotherapy and counseling. *American Psychologist, 53,* 440–448.

Sue, D. W., & Torino, G. C. (2005). Racial-cultural competence: Awareness, knowledge, and skills. In R. T. Carter (Ed.), *Handbook of racial-cultural psychology and counseling* (vol. 2, pp. 3–18). Hoboken, NJ: John Wiley & Sons.

Biographical Statement

Ana L. Blancarte, Ph.D., is a psychologist in private practice. Both, her doctoral program (Texas A&M University) and a clinical internship (Bellevue/NYU Hospital Center) provided specific training in geropsychology. In addition to providing individual and group psychotherapy for adults, Ana provides consultation for families with aging parents on geropsychology issues. She can be reached at blancarte@satx.rr.com.

14

Catherine's Story: Challenges of Aging in a Rural Community

Dorothy Breen

Catherine, 77, had enjoyed vibrant good health, a loving marriage, and an idyllic lifestyle in rural New England. Now Catherine needed knee replacement surgery, and her husband, Joseph, had Parkinson's disease. Catherine wound up in the emergency room with chest pain. A heart attack was ruled out; stress and depression were the likely culprits. Dorothy Breen used cognitive behavioral therapy to help Catherine manage her stress and to set reasonable limits in her changing relationship with Joseph. Breen tells about the joys and challenges of a rural practice. For example, she and her client are both actively involved in the same small church, providing both a meaningful connection but also some awkwardness.

C atherine came to me in February, feeling unhappy. She was a 77-year-old woman, living with her husband, Joseph, their dog, Hickory, and their cat, Maple Syrup, in a rural town in New England. Catherine and Joseph were very much in love. Until recently, they had been in excellent health, living a very active life including biking, hiking, sailing, snowshoeing, and skiing. Now Catherine needed knee replacement surgery, and Joseph had Parkinson's disease.

Parkinson's disease was very difficult for Joseph to accept. He was an athlete, very active at that, and naturally, he resisted this diagnosis. Having been independent, he became dependent in his personality and manipulated Catherine by becoming more or less disabled. Stress mounted for Catherine as she watched Joseph change and felt responsible for his care.

Catherine and Joseph lived in a house they had built five years earlier. The house was tucked in the woods, and Catherine found solace in the quiet of the wilderness and the awesome moonlit nights. She fed the squirrels in the back yard, enjoyed the wildflowers, and watched for deer and moose. By design, Catherine did not have any near neighbors. Catherine did not have family close by, and her children lived in other states.

Catherine was active in her small, tight-knit community, and she had many loyal friends. She was involved in the local church, and her faith in God was a strong part of her life. She loved reading, and she served as a board member for the local library. For exercise, she swam at the health club three times each week.

Catherine was recovering from a recent bout with pneumonia. She found it difficult to get the sleep she needed to get well and, at the same time, be able to respond to Joseph's calls for help during the night. Her primary care physician recommended that she have counseling. Catherine asked me if I would work with her in counseling. She knew me and trusted me. We also went to the same church. Catherine paid for her sessions with Medicare and a supplement to Medicare.

Conceptualization

Catherine related a history of debilitating stress in changing life situations. She was previously married and divorced. After her divorce, she needed medical attention for chest pain. Catherine told me about what a doctor described as emotional hysteria following her divorce.

Now life had changed for Catherine once again. Health problems brought her active life with Joseph to a screeching halt. Catherine found herself in the role of caretaker rather than wife. She was experiencing sadness, anger, and guilt. She was not able to get out as often as she had before, and so she put her self-care on hold. She did not have as many opportunities to talk about these feelings with friends. She did not talk with Joseph about how she was feeling, either.

Catherine told me she had not been feeling happy since the summer before we began counseling. That summer, Catherine went to the emergency room with chest pain. Myocardial infarction was ruled out. She was diagnosed with hypertension, re-action and situational stress, possible depression, and sleep apnea. The emergency room doctor recommended rest and respite from care of her husband.

When Catherine started counseling with me, she was depressed, and my imme-diate goals were to help Catherine acknowledge her feelings and change some of her behaviors. I used cognitive behavioral therapy. My preference would have been to work with Catherine and Joseph together. However, Joseph did not feel ready to join us, so I worked with Catherine, trying to help her develop ways to communicate with Joseph. Catherine also wanted help with stress management and setting boundaries regarding Joseph's needs. She wanted help dealing with the guilt she was feeling when expecting Joseph to do things for himself, and she wanted coping skills for when she was feeling manipulated. Catherine was also preparing for knee replace-ment surgery. She was not only preparing herself, but making sure Joseph would be cared for.

I practice in a rural environment, and that presents a unique culture. Catherine did not have neighbors next door or within walking distance. Therefore, she did not have daily support from a nearby neighbor. She could telephone friends, but in rural areas like ours, many telephone calls are at costly long-distance rates. Catherine needed to drive an hour to get to her doctor, the hospital, and to buy prescription medicines. She had to drive half of an hour to buy groceries, do banking, and use the postal service. Fortunately, she was able to drive her car. However, during the winter months, snow, ice, and short daylight hours presented challenges. On the other hand, the community was very supportive. Catherine had friends who drove her where she needed to go and brought meals if needed, but accepting help was stressful for her.

As for me, rural life has a significant impact, and I need to live and conduct my professional practice accordingly. I spent most of my life in an urban environment, and the rural culture presents situations that catch me off-guard. I am aware that most people know that I am a psychologist. Making certain that I adhere to the ethical stan-dards is a constant test. I am challenged to honor confidentiality even when my clients may not care if others know that they are coming to me for counseling.

It is common for a client to approach me, even if I'm with family or friends. The client may simply want to let me know how he's doing, seemingly a friendly gesture to keep me updated with the positive things he's engaged in now. This presents an ethi-cal dilemma, though. My family members had no idea that I had worked with this client, and the client seemed to assume they knew. Even though I maintain confiden-tiality, the client did not. This can be an awkward situation.

I run into my clients in restaurants, church, at the gym, grocery shopping, or ski-ing. It can be particularly embarrassing when they see me skiing, by the way. In church it is not uncommon for the pastor during her sermons to make reference to me as a psychologist. The first time she did that, I was uncomfortable with the attention. I guess I was unrealistic in thinking I could hide from my profession.

Catherine and I are both active in our small church. Catherine will take private moments before or after the Sunday service to let me know how she's doing. She is not looking for counseling during those moments, but just keeping in touch. I am comfortable with this and see it as a nice way for me to be supportive.

▓ Process

Catherine and I met for seven sessions in February through April.

Session 1. Catherine complained about Joseph getting out of bed three to four times a night and needing Catherine to help him. At the same time, she had pneumonia. Joseph's doctor and his physical therapist assured Catherine that Joseph was able to take care of himself, yet he expected Catherine to do everything for him.

Catherine's doctor recommended that she sleep in the spare bedroom and take medication to help her sleep through the night. She was reluctant to do this, because if she took the medication she might not be able to hear Joseph's calls to her.

In this first session, I helped Catherine acknowledge her feelings. Catherine loved Joseph, yet she was feeling resentment toward him. Before she developed pneumonia, she went to the pool and that helped ease her stress, but she was not able to get to the pool now.

We practiced using "I" statements to communicate with Joseph:

"I will be happy to help you with the things you can't do for yourself."

"I'd like you to do the things you can do for yourself."

"I feel angry when you expect me to immediately drop what I'm doing to help you."

"Do you need my help right now? If not, I would like to help you and I will in a few minutes when I finish the task I'm working on."

We examined Catherine's thoughts. Much of her thinking was negative. And yet, when I asked her about the positives in her life, she said: "Oh, I have many blessings." Among them were her husband, her home in the mountains, her family, and her friends.

We talked about Catherine's expectation that she would like Joseph to do things for himself and to help out around the house the way he used to. She would jump in and do it for him rather than wait for him to get to it. You might say she enabled him not to do things. Catherine decided to ask Joseph to choose chores he could do. For example, Catherine thought he might agree to fill and empty the dishwasher. The challenge for Catherine would be to leave the dishes and allow Joseph the time to take care of them.

Catherine agreed to do some homework before her next session. She would (1) find time each day to acknowledge what she was feeling, (2) practice using "I" statements to communicate her feelings to Joseph, (3) remind herself each morning what her blessings were, and (4) discuss with Joseph a household task and allow Joseph to complete his task.

Session 2. Catherine told me that she tried some of the things we had talked about last week. She and Joseph discussed household tasks that he might want to take responsibility for. He decided that loading and unloading the dishwasher was something he wanted to do. Catherine told me that this was a test for her, because she had to give Joseph the chance to take this responsibility. She noticed that Joseph was beginning to feel more positive. They had a good day together, running errands and going out to lunch.

Catherine was worried about her upcoming knee surgery. Who would take care of Joseph, Hickory, and Maple Syrup while she was in the hospital for three days and then two weeks in a rehabilitation center? She seemed overwhelmed. Perhaps I was witnessing the emotional hysteria that her doctor described when she was divorced from her previous marriage.

We worked on reducing her worries. First, we talked about making lists, one for tasks she could do each day, and one for tasks to do over time. With these lists, she would be able to organize, and she would be able to experience the pleasure of crossing things off as she accomplished them. One of the things on the "today" list would be to find a suitable kennel to board the pets during her hospital stay. On the "over time" list, she would list the people who had offered to help with Joseph's care. She would begin contacting them to determine their tasks, and the days they would take responsibility. This seemed to be a tough assignment, since Catherine was very independent and used to helping others, not needing to rely on help from others.

Next we worked on changing thoughts. I asked her to practice stopping worries and say to herself, "Wait a minute, I don't need to worry, I have the kennel ready and I'm developing a list of people I can depend on."

Before the next session Catherine agreed to (1) visit a kennel and make plans for Hickory and Maple Syrup's care, (2) make a list of people who had offered to help and begin calling them, and (3) work on changing worries to positive thoughts.

Session 3. Catherine reported that she was feeling a bit less stressed. She made plans for Hickory and Maple Syrup with the local kennel. She practiced assertiveness with Joseph. For example, when Joseph called to her, she asked him if he would be able to wait five minutes so she could finish what she was doing.

It is noteworthy that Catherine and Joseph were both 77 years old. They were very loving and committed to one another, but communicating openly about their feelings had not been a not a normal pattern for them over their thirty-seven years together. Catherine was taking a risk in trying to change this pattern after all those years.

Session 4. Catherine reported that she had a tooth that needed emergency oral surgery, so her knee surgery had to be postponed to later in April. There were long drives to the dentist she had not anticipated. In rural areas there are many people who plan to help when needed. These people had taken on various roles to help Catherine and Joseph through the process of the surgery and rehabilitation. While this was a blessing, it seemed like an overwhelming organizational task to contact everyone and reorganize. Catherine said she had experienced a "mini crisis" for about a week in adjusting to this change, but with the assistance of her lists, and the use of cognitive restructuring, she was able to reschedule everything and see her way through this change in plans. Catherine was being assertive with Joseph as well, "I told Joseph I was not resigning as his wife, but I was resigning as his caregiver." She said he responded positively. He visited the doctor and began taking medication for his Parkinson's.

<u>Sessions 5 and 6.</u> Joseph had an unexpected health problem and required outpatient surgery. This meant almost daily drives to the emergency department at the hospital and to the doctor, each two hours in length round-trip. Catherine felt stress building. To relax, she read a book and played solitaire on the computer. She said thoughtfully, "You know, when you've worked all your life, it's hard to give yourself permission to read in the afternoon."

<u>Session 7.</u> This was the last session before Catherine's surgery. She was concerned because the doctor had ordered a stress test, and she was worried that something might appear that would postpone the surgery. She was also worried about how Joseph would be taking care of himself while she was recovering. We worked on cognitive restructuring to put the stress test in a positive preventive perspective. Catherine was ready to have the surgery. She was feeling less stress and depression, and she felt that she would not need to continue with counseling.

Outcome

In a rural setting, I often see my clients, or hear about them, after they terminate counseling. I see this as a blessing. Catherine's knee surgery was successful. Catherine asked if I would visit her in the hospital and I did that, just as any person in the rural community might, with no concern that I would be breaking confidentiality. She was healing faster than expected and was pleased with her progress.

I went down to the library to meet with Catherine so she could read this chapter before I submitted it for publication. It had been about seven months since our last counseling session. She smiled when she read it, saying that it was funny to look back and acknowledge the changes she has made. She said that she and Joseph are communicating much better now. When she comes home after running an errand in the morning, she acknowledges in an encouraging way to Joseph that he got dressed. He responds proudly that he also made the bed, took care of the dishes, and filled the jug with Hickory's food. Catherine has replaced enabling with encouraging. She said proudly, "I don't see the dishes anymore." "When there's a problem, I ask myself who owns this problem and who has to deal with it?"

Catherine has learned about herself in this aging process: "I think you prepare for the big thing, your own death and the death of your spouse. But you don't always prepare for these other things that happen before death." She smiled: "It's from here forward."

I continue to see Catherine in church and around the community. She feels that she can check in with me on an informal basis. She knows she can ask me for an appointment if she needs one.

Reflections

My preference would have been to have Catherine and Joseph participate in counseling together. I think this would have facilitated their communication more effectively. Even so, Catherine was successful in making some changes in the way she related to Joseph, which, in turn, seems to have affected the way Joseph related to Catherine.

Joseph was aware that Catherine was coming to counseling, and he respected and was supportive of that. Yet Catherine told me that Joseph seemed to want reassurance that we were not painting him as the bad guy: "I know you're not supposed to tell me about your sessions, but is Dorothy still my friend?"

While working with Catherine I was aware of the influence of my own family. About three years ago, I became a caregiver for my aging 84-year-old parents. They lived about 600 miles away but they moved closer to me, so I would be able to provide care for them when needed on a regular basis. They live independently, in their own home, yet my father has Parkinson's disease, and my mother has rheumatoid arthritis. Since I have been so closely involved with my parents' care, I am tuned in to the aging process and the effects on their relationship. They celebrated their sixty-first wedding anniversary this year. Their vows "in sickness and in health, for better or worse" are being tested especially now. We've found that a healthy sense of humor is helpful. But that's another book.

I learned so much in working with Catherine, the least of which is a deep respect for the older generation.

Suggested Readings

Bushy, A., & Carty, L. (1994). Rural practice? Considerations for counselors with clients who live there. *Guidance & Counseling, 9*(5), 16–25.

Erickson, S. H. (2001). Multiple relationships in rural counseling. *The Family Journal: Counseling and Therapy for Couples and Families, 9*(3), 302–304.

Hargrove, D. S. (1986). Ethical issues in rural mental health practice. *Professional Psychology: Research and Practice, 17*(1), 20–23.

Julia, M. (2000). *Constructing gender: Multicultural perspectives in working with women*. Belmont, CA: Wadsworth.

Schank, J. A. (1998). Ethical issues in rural counselling practice. *Canadian Journal of Counselling, 32*(4), 270–283.

Weigel, D. J., & Baker, B. G. (2002). Unique issues in rural couple and family counseling. *The Family Journal: Counseling and Therapy for Couples and Families, 10*(1), 61–69.

Weigel, D. J. (2003). Counseling in rural America. In R. L. Dingman & J. D. Weaver (Eds.), *Days in the lives of counselors* (pp. 1–6). Boston: Pearson Education.

Biographical Statement

Dorothy Breen, Ph.D., is an associate professor in the counseling program at the University of Maine. She is a licensed psychologist and has maintained a small private practice since 1992. Her research focuses on rural counseling. She is co-author of "Professional Counseling in Rural Settings: Raising Awareness Through Discussion and Self-Study with Implications for Training and Support," in *VISTAS 2005,* an American Counseling Association publication, and "The Professional School Counselor in the Rural Setting: Strategies for Meeting Challenges and Maximizing Rewards," a chapter in *Professional School Counseling: A Handbook of Theories, Programs & Practices,* edited by B. T. Erford (Austin, TX: PRO-Ed, 2004). You can reach Dorothy at dorothy.breen@umit.maine.edu.

15

Mama Del: A Case Study of Counseling in Post-Katrina New Orleans

Barbara Herlihy and Zarus E. Watson

After Hurricane Katrina, Barbara Herlihy returned to resume her career as a counselor educator at the University of New Orleans. Barbara volunteered at a community agency to help meet the enormous need for mental health services. Mama Del, an 82-year-old African American woman, was referred for depression and a suicide attempt. Her home in a public housing project had been destroyed, and her identity as a community leader had been blown away. Herlihy found Erikson's well-known developmental stages just didn't work for Mama Del. Following a consultation with Zarus Watson, she used a model for black racial identity development to conceptualize this case.

*O*n August 28, 2005, I fled my home along with thousands of other New Orleaneans, just as Hurricane Katrina slammed into the Gulf Coast. After living for two months as an evacuee in a neighboring state, I was among the fortunate few who returned to a fairly intact house in the city that had been my adopted home for eight years. As I resumed my work as a counselor educator in a local university, I was keenly aware of the critical need for qualified mental health professionals to serve the traumatized population of post-Katrina New Orleans. I began volunteering my services part-time at a community mental health agency that was severely understaffed and still in crisis mode. This agency was inundated with referrals from numerous sources, including the city's charity hospital.

Mrs. Odelle Parker, age 82, was admitted to the charity hospital after she ingested a large number of sleeping pills and pain pills. Dr. Adams, the admitting physician, noted that, in addition to the overdose, Mrs. Parker was suffering from dehydration and appeared to be clinically depressed. Dr. Adams requested that the staff psychiatrist evaluate Mrs. Parker, but when this had not occurred after four days, the doctor referred her to the mental health agency. In her referral, Dr. Adams requested that a counselor see Mrs. Parker right away, without waiting for the psychiatric evaluation, because the hospital's psychiatrist was overwhelmed and probably would not be able to see Mrs. Parker before she was discharged. At the agency, we knew that the doctor's concern was justified, as less than 15 percent of the city's psychiatrists had returned after the hurricane.

The agency assigned Mrs. Parker's case to me. When I arrived at the hospital the next day, the floor nurse provided me with some background information. Mrs. Parker had been found, unresponsive and semiconscious, by a member of the housekeeping staff at the senior citizens' residence where she lived. An ambulance had been summoned, and Mrs. Parker had been brought to the emergency room, where she was treated and then admitted to the floor. The nurse was concerned because, over the past few days, Mrs. Parker had refused to speak to anyone on staff and had refused to see any of the numerous visitors who had come to see her.

■ Conceptualization

I wish I could say that I came up with these ideas earlier in my work with Mama Del. In fact, I was not able to articulate my conceptualization until after the fifth session and, even then, only with the benefit of a consultation with Dr. Zarus Watson. This section may be a little confusing, because I'm going to mention some things here that readers won't know about until they've read well into my process notes. So it might be a good idea to jump ahead and read about the process through sessions 4 and 5, and then come back.

Reflecting on Mama Del's case, it seemed to me that, of all her losses, the one that was causing her the most psychic pain was the loss of her identity as her community's leader and spokesperson. When I thought of life stages and identity theory, my early training in Erikson's psychosocial development model came immediately to mind. According to Erikson, Mama Del at age 82 would be in the stage of "integrity versus despair." If she were able to look back on her life with few regrets and a feeling of accomplishment, she would be experiencing ego integrity. If she did not feel a sense of accomplishment and believed it was too late now, she would be experiencing despair, guilt, and hopelessness. This seemed to "fit," but I wasn't finding it particularly helpful. Where would this conceptualization take me, in my work with Mama Del? I could try to help her reframe her perceptions so that she could better appreciate the importance of her contributions to her community, and that might alleviate some of her guilt and sadness. But she would still be alone in that tiny apartment, isolated from the world in which she was once so engaged. Perhaps Erikson's theory, based on a white male model of psychosocial development and conceived in the 1960s, wasn't such a good fit after all.

I began to think, instead, of models that have guided me in my counseling relationships in recent years—my own feminist philosophy in conjunction with multicultural counseling theories had been working well for me in the richly diverse culture of New Orleans. I thought about feminist views on identity development. Although I doubted whether Mama Del would call herself a feminist, she was a strong, independent woman. I remembered my earlier questions about my cultural competence. Perhaps there would be something helpful to me in a theory of black racial development.

Both the feminist and the black racial identity development models conceptualize a five-phase process in which a person progresses from (1) a state of lack of awareness to (2) a transition catalyzed by a crisis or crises, resulting in self-questioning, anger, and guilt, to (3) an immersion into one's own cultural heritage followed by an emersion into a larger and more diverse world, to (4) the development of an authentic and positive identity, and finally to (5) a stage of active commitment to meaningful action for the benefit of the community. As I reflected on Mama Del's story, it seemed to me that she had lived her pre-Katrina life for many years in that final, active commitment stage. The crisis of the hurricane had propelled her back to the earlier, second stage of self-doubt and guilt. My question became: How could I assist her to move forward to live again in that final stage?

For readers who want to explore these ideas in more depth, please see the "Suggested Readings" at the end of the case study.

Process

Session 1. When I entered Mrs. Parker's room, I saw an older African American woman sitting up in her bed and staring at, but not really watching, the TV mounted on the wall. She glanced at me when I sat down in the chair next to her bed and then returned her gaze to the TV. Throughout our first meeting, she was polite but minimally responsive to my prompts. She continued to avoid sustained eye contact, although I could sense her studying me when she thought I wasn't looking. I asked her how she had come to be in the hospital, and she responded that "I feel all right now, I don't know why they're making me stay here." When I mentioned the notation on her admission chart about the overdose of pills, she said, "My arthritis, I was hurting real bad and I took too much medicine." I did glean some information about Mrs. Parker's history—she was educated through the ninth grade and had married young, while still a teenager, to a man who was more than a decade older than she. He had died thirty-four years ago from injuries suffered in a work-related accident. She had no children, although she had "helped raise a lot of children." Until Hurricane Katrina, she had resided all her adult life in a low-income housing development in an inner-city area. I recognized the name of the housing development as one that had been destroyed by the hurricane, declared uninhabitable, and slated for demolition.

Everyone in New Orleans has a "Katrina story," and I learned a bit about Mrs. Parker's ordeal. When the order to evacuate had been issued, she was unable to comply because she does not drive and does not own a car. Fortunately, some members of her church organized a caravan of cars to transport members of the congregation who lacked mobility, and Mrs. Parker was evacuated to Atlanta along with fifteen other church members. The entire group sheltered in a church there for two months. Because Mrs. Parker's home had been destroyed, a social services agency had placed her in the residence for low-income senior citizens where she now lived.

Session 2. My second meeting with Mrs. Parker, later in the same week, was much like the first. She was courteous and compliant in responding to my overtures in a minimal way. I realized that I was not making a connection with her. When I tried to take her perspective, I could understand her suspicion and reluctance to talk with me. I am very different from her—I am Caucasian, obviously (from my Yankee accent) not a native New Orleanean, and even though I am well into middle age I must have seemed young to her. Just as she may have been finding it difficult to relate to me, I was finding it difficult to relate to her. I began to question my cultural competence to work with her effectively.

Consultation 1. I decided to bring Mrs. Parker's case to the agency's weekly staffing the next day. At the meeting, when my turn came, I began to describe my client to my fellow mental health professionals. I had presented only some basic demographic information when one of my colleagues, Dr. Zarus Watson, sat forward in his chair and said, "That's Mama Del." Dr. Watson, like Mrs. Parker, is African American and has lived most of his life in New Orleans. He explained to the group that he recognized "Mama Del" from the description I was giving because his family knew her. He added that she was well known and highly respected in the African American community, particularly among the residents of the housing development where she had lived before the hurricane. He offered to meet with me after the staffing to help me understand the context of Mama Del's life, an offer that I gratefully accepted.

When I met with Dr. Watson, he began by describing Mama Del's pre-Katrina environment. She had lived in the city's oldest public housing development, which had existed for sixty-five years until it was destroyed by the hurricane. Traditionally, it had been inhabited mostly by African Americans, who in recent years had comprised all of its inhabitants. When Mama Del first moved into the development, it was a well-kept and tidy community of mostly blue-collar, working-class families. In recent years, however, the community had shown distinct signs of decline. With high rates of unemployment, teen pregnancy, and crime, the housing development had become an epicenter of hopelessness, depression, and fear.

As the oldest tenured resident, Mama Del helped raise most of the area's children, who now have children and grandchildren of their own. She was often sought out to resolve issues between residents, and she regularly represented the community when meetings were held with governmental or regulatory bodies. Educational and social service professionals who staffed the housing development's elementary school and community center knew that no initiative proposed for the development could get off the ground without the "blessing" of Mama Del.

Dr. Watson also pointed out that, in an area where the obligatory statues of Martin Luther King, Malcolm X, and other national historical figures could be found, there also existed a large outdoor wall mural, vibrantly painted, along the development's main thoroughfare. This twenty-year old mural of Mama Del, unlike most of the area's other memorials, had always been well maintained by the residents themselves. I left my meeting with Dr. Watson with a new appreciation for my client's strengths and for the magnitude of her losses.

Session 3. Over the weekend, Mrs. Parker was discharged from the hospital. I met with her on Tuesday in her apartment in the senior citizens' residence. Her apartment was very small, consisting of a living room with a kitchenette at one end, and a bedroom and bathroom. It was clean and tidy and seemed as impersonal as a hotel room. I felt a wave of sadness when I realized that she undoubtedly had lost all her personal possessions to the hurricane.

I began our session by telling her, "Mrs. Parker, I apologize. I had no idea that you are famous in your community." I reminded her of our first session when, during our discussion of confidentiality, I had told her that clients of my agency were often discussed during meetings of the agency counselors, when the counselors wanted help in being more effective in their work. I told her about my colleague, how he had recognized who she was because his family knew her, and how he had explained to me about the esteem in which she was held in her community. I shared with her that, on my way over to see her, I had driven down the boulevard in her old neighborhood and that the mural, which could be seen from the street, was still standing. I continued, "I can hardly imagine all the responsibilities you've had in your community. If you will, please help me to understand. Tell me, in your own words, what this community has meant to you and what you have meant to it." I realized, as I said this, that Mrs. Parker was looking squarely at me, and for the first time there was a hint of a smile on her face. She responded, "People call me Mama Del." And she began to tell her story.

Sessions 4 and 5. Throughout the next two sessions, Mama Del continued to talk about the neighborhood where she had lived for so many years before Katrina struck. A theme that ran through her stories about the people, the places, and the events was that it was once a nice neighborhood where "people looked out for each other, people cared for each other." Mama Del remembered the housing development as "mostly black, although we had a few whites and Choctaws, but we were all one group." The area's residents were mostly blue-collar workers, although Mama Del spoke with pride of the neighborhood's black school teacher, dentist, convenience store owner, butcher, and other entrepreneurs. She remembered that crime was almost unheard of, and consisted mostly of personal disputes that originated in the neighborhood bar.

Toward the middle of the fifth session, as Mama Del began to talk about the neighborhood's more recent history, her tone seemed to shift. Whereas she had once conveyed a sense of pride, she now seemed to be experiencing sadness and bewilderment. She stated:

> *In the old days, it was "live and let live." It seems like a long time ago, now. In fact, I can't even tell you when it changed. A lot of families started moving out, and others moved in. We didn't know who they were, but we welcomed them. I'd watch their children, give them advice. . . but I learned that some of them didn't want my advice. So I learned to wait to be asked. They were not bad people, just different. . . . I can't tell you when people stopped caring for each other. . . .*

As I listened, I realized that Mama Del was not only painting a picture of the neighborhood, but also seemed to be asking herself, "What happened?" The neighbors had been a cohesive group but had become fragmented, and Mama Del had tried to hold it together. I sensed an underlying tone of guilt that she had not been able to protect her "family" and her "children" from the disintegration of the housing development. I also realized that her story had become more personal and that she was allowing me to see her pain. I recognized that her reminiscences had real cathartic value, but found myself wondering, "Where do we go from here?" This seemed like a good time to get back in touch with my consultant, Dr. Watson.

Consultation 2. My second consultation provided me with some new and important insights. While Dr. Watson agreed that gender and racial identity development were useful conceptualizations, he also suggested that I consider age as one of the many-layered cultural variables salient to working with Mama Del. Whereas she had once been a "respected elder" with a considerable amount of informal power in her community, she was now just one of many residents in a complex filled with senior citizens who were being taken care of by others. This might be yet another element of loss for Mama Del.

Dr. Watson validated the utility of a systems approach and reminded me that Mama Del and I had also become a system. He raised a parallel process issue for me to reflect on. Just as Mama Del seemed to be feeling a sense of guilt that she had not been able to save her "family" and her "children" from the disintegration of her former neighborhood, I was experiencing some survivor guilt because I had sustained such minimal losses in the hurricane. I realized I needed to self-monitor and not allow myself to be driven by a guilt-laden sense of responsibility to rush in and try to "fix" things for Mama Del.

I raised a question with Dr. Watson about a statement that Mama Del had made to me during our last counseling session. Mama Del had told me that she had never had the chance to "go home" after she returned from Atlanta. Referring to her former home in the housing development, she had said, "I know there's nothing left, but. . . ." Her unfinished sentence had seemed to contain a yearning to see her one-time home before the entire development was razed. I shared with Dr. Watson my mixed feelings—my fear that seeing the devastation first-hand might precipitate a setback into depression for Mama Del, versus my desire to honor her need to "say goodbye" and perhaps achieve some closure. Dr. Watson and I agreed that I would take my cue from Mama Del in future sessions.

Sessions 6–8. Mama Del did not make me wait long to receive my cue. Midway through our next session, she expressed that she missed the old neighborhood and felt "stuck away" in the senior citizens' residence. She answered with a strong affirmative when I asked if she would like to visit her former neighborhood. We made plans to go there and "take a walk" at the beginning of our next session.

The next week, when I drove up to the senior citizens' residence to pick up Mama Del, she was already sitting on a bench beside the front door, waiting for me. Although she was wearing high-topped sneakers, a sensible choice for walking through rubble, she was otherwise dressed as if she were headed to church. She was wearing a silk dress and jewelry, and obviously had had her hair styled. She got in the car and we drove off.

As I parked on the boulevard adjacent to the housing development, I saw the mural and was glad I had remembered to bring my digital camera. I asked Mama Del if I could take a photo of her with the mural. She allowed as how she was "dressed all right for a picture, but don't show my sneakers!" I snapped a photo of her standing beside the mural, and then we began to carefully pick our way down the fragmented sidewalk and into the development. Many of the buildings were just piles of rubble, while others were still standing with boarded-up windows and entire sections of their roofs missing. I was surprised to see that, even several months after the hurricane, a few people were there, sorting through the debris for any possessions that might have survived.

As we approached the area where one family was working, a voice called out Mama Del's name and I soon found myself in the midst of a reunion between Mama Del and this family of former neighbors. After Mama Del introduced me as "a friend who is helping me," I moved aside and found a shady spot to sit and wait while they talked. After several minutes, Mama Del walked over to me and asked if we could postpone our counseling session until the next time we were scheduled to meet. It seemed that, not only was Mama Del visiting with these particular neighbors, but cell phone calls had been made and some other folks were on their way to see her. She seemed energized in a way I had never seen, and when she assured me that the neighbors would give her a ride home, I left.

Before our next session, I printed out the photo I had taken and placed it in a frame. I gave it to her when I arrived at her apartment for our session, and received a radiant smile in return. Mama Del placed the photo atop her television, next to a delicate bone china teacup that I had not noticed during my previous visits. When I remarked on its beauty, Mama Del told me that one of her old neighbors had found it while digging among the rubble, had recognized it as hers, and had saved it for her.

We both commented on the odd fact that so many people had found the seemingly most fragile items intact after the hurricane. When I remarked that "sometimes things are stronger than they seem," Mama Del replied, "people, too." Indeed.

Mama Del had a great deal to tell me, during the remainder of our session, about her visit with her old friends and neighbors. For the first time, I heard anger in her voice as she described the multitude of problems these friends were having—with finding adequate housing and schools for their children, with receiving their FEMA trailers, and in dealing with local, state, and federal bureaucracies. She had learned that an association had been formed through grassroots efforts of residents in the old housing development, and some friends had asked her to come with them to the next meeting. She seemed to want to go, but stated, "I don't know how I could help. I don't live in that part of town any more." She added with more emphasis, "I don't know how things work, now." I replied that no one seemed to understand how things work now, in our post-Katrina world; however, she did have quite a bit of experience in dealing successfully with bureaucrats. I suggested to her, "My hunch is that your successes have been due to *who* you are, not *where* you are." She gave me one of her long looks, then replied that "it wouldn't hurt" for her to go along to the meeting.

Outcome

When I called Mama Del to confirm our next scheduled meeting, she said that she was too busy to meet with me that week. When I inquired about the week after that, she wasn't sure she would have the time to meet, but she would call me. I didn't hear from her, and eventually I called her. I suggested that perhaps we could have another session or two to terminate our work together. She did schedule an appointment, but she called the agency and left a cancellation message that did not mention rescheduling.

One evening I was at home, settled in front of the television and channel-surfing when I came across a local channel that was airing one of the open-forum town meetings the mayor was holding. I watched for a while, left the room to get a cup of tea, and returned to see Mama Del standing at the microphone, chastising the mayor about the slowness of the city's recovery efforts. She spoke with a great deal of conviction and passion, and when she finished she received a hearty round of applause from the audience. It was at that time that I knew my work with Mama Del was done.

Mama Del and I never did have our termination session, although we talked briefly over the phone a couple of times. After one of the staffing meetings at my agency, Dr. Watson asked about Mama Del. As I was filling him in on what had transpired since our last consultation, I realized that I had wanted a formal termination session to meet my own needs, not Mama Del's. I thanked Dr. Watson for supporting and challenging me in my work with her.

Reflections

For Mama Del, being displaced geographically by the hurricane was only one contributing factor to her depression and suicide attempt. More significantly, she had lost her psychosocial "place." Although she had returned to the city that was her lifelong home, she had remained isolated and disconnected from the people who mattered to her and to whom she mattered. Once she was able to reconnect, she was able—on her own—to reclaim her identity as a spokesperson for her community and regain the sense of purpose that energized her. All I did was to facilitate that reconnection.

I learned a great deal from my work with Mama Del. I was reminded of the value of peer consultation, even for highly experienced counselors. Dr. Watson's insights had helped me to understand Mama Del and her world at a level I could not have reached by my own efforts.

My belief in the efficacy of a systems approach, particularly a feminist/multicultural perspective, was affirmed. Feminist therapists believe that clients are the experts on their lives. Mama Del was the expert who taught me about her community and its history, and in this process she began to reclaim her "voice." Multicultural theorists remind us that all counseling relationships are cross-cultural, and my work with Mama Del helped affirm for me that visible differences—such as differences in race, socioeconomic class, or generational status—need not be barriers to forming a therapeutic alliance. Multiculturalists also advise counselors to adopt nontraditional roles to serve diverse clients effectively. Restricting the boundaries of the counseling relationship to the traditional in-the-office encounter would not have worked for Mama Del. Rather than expect her to come to me at the counseling agency, I was better able to understand the context of her life by entering her world. Many of my insights originated in my visits to her apartment, such as the valuable cues I gained from seeing Mama Del's lack of personal possessions and later from noticing the china teacup. Taking a trip with her to her former neighborhood was hardly customary practice, and I shudder to think what a risk-management specialist would say about the fact that I transported an 82-year-old client in my personal vehicle and took her on a walking tour of an area that had been declared unsafe and uninhabitable. However, that venture provided a pivotal opportunity for Mama Del to reconnect with her friends and neighbors.

Finally, my work with Mama Del was personally as well as professionally meaningful for me. Through having known her, I gained a deeper appreciation for the lifelong resilience of the human spirit.

Suggested Readings

Helms, J. E. (1990). *Black and White racial identity: Theory, research, and practice.* New York: Greenwood Press.

Levinson, D. J. (1996). *The seasons of a woman's life.* New York: Ballantine Books.

McNamara, K., & Rickard, K. M. (1989). Feminist identity development: Implications for feminist therapy with women. *Journal of Counseling and Development, 68,* 184–193.

Sue, D. W., & Sue, D. (2003). Counseling African Americans. In D. W. Sue & D. Sue, *Counseling the culturally diverse* (4th ed., pp. 293–308). Hoboken, NJ: John Wiley & Sons.

Sue, D. W., & Sue, D. (2003). Counseling elderly clients. In D. W. Sue & D. Sue, *Counseling the culturally diverse* (4th ed., pp. 393–406). Hoboken, NJ: John Wiley & Sons.

Whalen, M., Fowler-Lese, K. P., Barber, J. S., Williams, E. N., Judge, A. B., Nilsson, J. E., & Shibazaki, K. (2004). Counseling practice with feminist-multicultural perspectives. *Journal of Multicultural Counseling and Development, 31,* 370–389.

Williams, E. N., & Barber, J. S. (2004). Power and responsibility in therapy: Integrating feminism and multiculturalism. *Journal of Multicultural Counseling and Development, 32,* 390–401.

Worell, J., & Remer, P. (2003). *Feminist perspectives in therapy: Empowering diverse women* (2nd ed.). Hoboken, NJ: John Wiley & Sons.

Biographical Statement

Barbara Herlihy, Ph.D., is a professor of counselor education at the University of New Orleans. She has been a Licensed Professional Counselor and National Certified Counselor for over twenty years and has counseled clients of all ages in a variety of settings including community agencies, schools, and private practice. You can reach Barbara at bherlihy@uno.edu.

Zarus E. Watson, Ph.D., is an associate professor of counselor education at the University of New Orleans. His areas of expertise in research and teaching include social systems theory, cultural competence in professional practice, and organizational counseling. Drs. Herlihy and Watson have co-authored a number of articles and book chapters on multicultural and ethical issues in counseling practice. You can reach Zarus at zwatson@uno.edu.

16

Dad Just Fell Again: Out of AA and into Grief

Peggy P. Whiting and Loretta J. Bradley

Peter, 84, falls, and the staff at the assisted-living facility realizes that he is drunk. In short order, Peter is enrolled in a substance abuse program. Peter's drinking is connected to grief over the loss of his wife of sixty years. Peggy Whiting uses narrative reconstruction, an approach that encourages a grieving individual to author a healing story about the past relationship, his new identity without the deceased, and the meaning of life as it unfolds in the future. Whiting relies on her mentor, Loretta Bradley, to sort out how her feelings toward her own father readily transfer to Peter. "My total lack of objectivity with my own father kept us apart from assisting each other in our grief. I discovered that I have a strong sense of protection toward others older than me."

T his is the case of an older male whose issue of grief might not have surfaced except for the curiosity of a professional who knew through experience that the presenting concern is rarely the whole picture. This client came to me after a precipitating event of a fall led the staff at a nursing care facility to seek an evaluation for drinking. This case, like most, had layers of issues to confront that had to be prioritized as his treatment evolved. Several professionals had seen this man before his grief came to the forefront as a concern for counseling. I was the grief therapist, and I consulted with my dear colleague and mentor, Loretta Bradley. Here is the story of Peter.

Peter Martin is an 84-year-old Caucasian man who has been living in an assisted-living facility for the past four years. Peter, a retired Episcopal clergy, has all the graces of a Southern gentleman. He has lived in small, rural communities in the South his whole life except for a few years right after college when he took a summer job as a police reporter near Boston. Peter speaks with great pride and affection about his heritage as a well-educated, middle-class family man. He talks with a pronounced cough every few sentences. He apologizes, while struggling to catch his breath, and explains that he has been diagnosed with cardiopulmonary disease with fluid buildup in his heart and a periodic need for oxygen. Peter is mobile with the aid of a walker. He immediately tells others, including me, that his walker was originally his beloved wife's and he uses it as a memorial to her. While this gentleman has some memory issues associated with his age, he has no cognitive impairment or diagnosed dementia.

Peter was married for sixty years to Mary Catherine, who died four years ago after a long illness during which Peter was her caregiver. He speaks of her with great admiration and love. His description of their partnership brings both a smile and a tear to his face. Peter is quick to recall how they met when he was working his first job as a police reporter in a small office where Mary Catherine was the office assistant. Peter corrects me if I call her "Mary" instead of "Mary Catherine." He liked her double name and says it is important I know her as the Southern beauty queen she was. Peter says, "Mary Catherine thought she was marrying a police reporter but stayed with me when I heard the call to minister . . . that was the kind of love we had." Peter and Mary Catherine had moved out of their home into a residential living environment that provides varying levels of care. They shared an apartment on the grounds of the same assisted-care building where Peter now resides alone.

Peter readily talks about his own parents as being the role models for his marriage with Mary Catherine. He speaks of their relationship as "remarkable" and "inspiring" and calls himself fortunate for growing up in a stable and nurturing home with no problems such as alcoholism. "My wife and I had that same kind of thing."

They had one daughter and two sons, all of whom live relatively close by. The daughter, Dianne, is the designated contact for Peter and has his legal power of attorney. Dianne handles all the business affairs and details of Peter's life—money, health care insurance policies, and routine necessities. Peter is grateful for her help yet doesn't call this a close relationship. Dianne worked quickly with the nursing facility after Peter's fall to arrange intervention related to his alcohol use. Dianne, however, did not provide any history to the addiction treatment team and seemed to just want the problem handled without need for her continued involvement.

Peter's middle child, Dave, is married and father to three young boys. These grandchildren are a source of delight for Peter. Peter is also close to his daughter-in-law. Dave brings various family members for weekly visits that are a highlight in Peter's week.

Peter describes his youngest son, Robert, as "irresponsible" and gives examples of how Robert has provided him with "an extra stash of booze" over the past few years. Robert has never married, and Peter has bailed him out many times when his son quit a job or mismanaged money. Peter has had very limited contact with Robert since his fall. None of Peter's children is reported as having a history of alcohol or other drug abuse.

<u>Alcohol History.</u> Peter was diagnosed some twenty years ago with alcoholism. It is difficult to get an accurate picture because Peter seems to "forget" the story. He reports that his drinking never adversely affected his job but was something his wife preferred him not to do. It is also difficult to know exactly when he started drinking again.

I do know that his assisted-living facility has a "social hour" each afternoon during which residents may have two drinks of alcohol of their choice. The nursing home had allowed Peter to participate, although it came to light later that they were aware of his previous diagnosis and treatment for alcoholism. His drinking became a concern about a year ago, when Peter fell and was found to be intoxicated. The staff, concerned about liability, reacted and called a local substance abuse program. Peter felt punished by the facility's social worker, who required that he must have a "companion" with him when he was outside his room. Peter describes these companions as the "police patrol."

Peter has stopped drinking for almost a year now and participates in an outpatient program for substance abuse with an addictions specialist, forty years his junior. The specialist noticed that the deaths of his wife and best friend occurred around the same time as Peter "remembers" his drinking starting again. Peter had not made this connection. The addiction specialist functions as Peter's advocate and educated the staff about setting realistic limits to protect Peter as he sustains sobriety.

As his recovery became solidified, the addiction specialist referred Peter to me for specialized counseling around his grief over the deaths of his best friend and his wife. I was identified as a counselor with expertise and credentials for grief education and counseling. Given that I hold a license as a professional counselor, I was an endorsed provider of care for Peter and was paid for service as a consultant to his addiction treatment. Medicare was billed as usual for the individual counseling sessions, and I was paid by the treatment center. This arrangement is an example of the collaboration that is possible between service care providers. Peter continued biweekly sessions with the addiction specialist and met with me for grief counseling on alternate weeks.

Conceptualization

My initial goal was to assess the grief experiences, first around his wife and then his friend. I wanted to hear the story of the relationships he had with individuals and how he has integrated their deaths. I wanted to "bear witness" to his construction of his own identity in relationship to them and now in life without them. I wanted to know if his family and friends and living setting were providing opportunities to grieve.

So often the grief of older persons is undervalued, unrecognized, and unsupported. Without a community that legitimizes grief and allows opportunities for sharing of grief, reconciliation is less likely and the bereaved are left with greater physical and psychological vulnerability. I wondered if drinking was triggered by grief as a means of coping. I am aware of the impact of unresolved grief on physical and emotional health. Especially in the elderly, grief can be fatal, and this particular individual already had serious health concerns. I was concerned about the toll of two significant losses so close to each other. The use of altering substances during grief usually signals that the individual is feeling a need to self-sooth by numbing. This pattern can lead to suppressed or prolonged grief, two categories of complications in the "normal" grieving process.

I chose a narrative reconstruction orientation to help Peter. This contemporary intervention has the theoretical premise that healing occurs as a grieving individual re-creates his personal narrative in an empowering way to design a resilient future. The client must author a story of meaning about the past relationship with the deceased, his present identity without the deceased, and the meaning of life as it unfolds in the future. Narrative practices use arts techniques such as writing, photography, and music to encourage expressions of grief. The counselor is an intuitive collaborator and listener who guides the narrative reconstruction process toward a story of survivorship. Narrative reconstruction of this sort can move an older client toward a review of life that is experienced as having integrity as opposed to despair.

Process

I met with Peter for grief counseling biweekly for six months, a total of twelve sessions, although we initially contracted for only eight sessions. Our sessions took place in a conference area in his assisted-living facility. This location was a bit unusual although helpful with the transportation issue, given he no longer drives, and it did provide for confidentiality. The social worker and other staff welcomed my visits. The tone of the caregivers surrounding Peter seemed to soften with his demonstrated sobriety. The addiction specialist advocated for more social opportunities with other residents and outside visitors. We all attended a treatment planning conference to coordinate our efforts.

<u>Session 1.</u> I began with the usual introductions. Peter was already familiar with counseling process and its limits of confidentiality. He seemed eager to work with me but a bit confused about how our role would be distinguished from that of the addiction specialist.

I was direct about the addiction specialist's hunch that his return to drinking might be linked to his losses. Peter had not himself made this connection, so I spent much of this session drawing out the time sequence of these events.

Therapist: I understand you lost both your beloved wife and your trusted best friend around the same time. I would like to hear about both of these important people. Let's start with Mary Catherine.

Peter: She was my love, my rock. I could not imagine my life being worth very much without her by my side. She had been sick for a while and I had been taking care of her. We sold our home and moved into assisted living because she couldn't get around very much any more and the house was too much for us to manage. We were in an apartment on the grounds here and pretty much did everything for ourselves. The kids helped out with errands, doctors' appointments, and house cleaning. I didn't expect her to die.

Therapist: So even through her illness, the two of you remained fairly independent and you thought you were settling into a new but longer-term living situation.

Peter: Yes. We hated to give up our home. I left my church that I had started and that was really hard. But we were together and the new place was comfortable and we had everything we needed. She just died one random day. Nobody expected it that day. I could tell she wasn't breathing and I called for help. They came right away but it was too late. I was shocked and don't remember a lot of the next few days.

Therapist: Tell me what you remember.

Peter: My daughter came in and kind of took over. I wasn't asked much about the plans for the funeral or anything. I don't know if I could have gotten it all together or not, but I sure wanted to be asked. I just tagged along and went where I was told.

Therapist: What would you have done differently if you had been asked?

Peter: I might have written something and had it read. You know I was a reporter for years and I like to write. Mary Catherine liked my writings, too.

Therapist: I wonder if you would be willing to write now what you might have written then. Could you have it ready the next time we meet? And maybe you could also write about what she meant to you. I would like to know this, too.

Sessions 2 and 3. Peter brought a folder of his writings from the years of his marriage. Some were in pristine condition, typed and printed on parchment paper. Other writings were worn, hand scribbled on scraps of paper and napkins stained with food. He proudly presented them: "Here is what she meant to me . . . take them all." I asked him to choose one to read that he thought captured her the most. I sat quietly as he rummaged to find his selection.

Peter: A Southern beauty says she will marry me. How could I be this blessed? I feel chosen and unworthy. I feel greater than I was before. I feel humble yet proud. I am not easy yet she finds me to be enough for her life.

Therapist:	This is very sacred . . . these memories and this marriage. Would you consider creating something with all these writings? Like putting them together in some way that you might keep and eventually pass on in your family?
Peter:	Who would care about this? About us?
Therapist:	Well, you tell me who might. Just think about it.

Peter had not written anything for the second session that he might have said at her funeral, but I prompted him and he had it for the third session. His eulogy was about her life, their marriage, and raising children. He wrote about her patience with his visits to spend time with his best friend. The two men spent time together without their families at a mountain cabin, where they fished and smoked cigars.

Therapist:	What, if anything, would you like to do with what you have written?
Peter:	Well . . . I could put it on the first page of that collection you wanted me to make . . . you know of the other writings.
Therapist:	So, can I take that as a decision to create a sort of memory book?
Peter:	Well, it feels like a silly thing for an old man to do, but if you think it might be good, I will.

Peter is very much a pleaser and usually complied. His voice was poetry and short stories. I wanted to use this creative outlet as a means of assisting Peter with reconstructing his narrative.

Sessions 4–6. Peter asked me to dispose of three empty, one-ounce bottles of vodka.

Peter:	Could you throw these away for me? They will put me on all kinds of restrictions if the staff sees these.
Therapist:	How long have you had these? What happened to the alcohol in them?
Peter:	Don't you panic, too. I drank these, of course, but a long time ago, right after Mary Catherine died. I kept them as my funeral bottles.
Therapist:	So these are memorabilia. What do they indicate to you?
Peter:	That I wasn't doing very well. I hadn't had anything to drink except for two times in twenty years. You know she was the one who got me to stop all my drinking before. I did it for her really. I loved her that much.
Therapist:	So when she died unexpectedly, you reached back to something you had stopped largely because of her influence. What were you feeling that you were trying to soothe by drinking?
Peter:	Emptiness. Heartache. I was lost and didn't know how to cope.

I did report this session and delivered the bottles to the addictions specialist after talking with Peter about the need for this. I decided with their consultation to let the treatment center staff handle any follow-up regarding the empty bottles. I did not see my role as one to check any possibility of current alcohol use. Neither did I want to generate suspicion with the staff at his residential center. They had grown to trust Peter and had responded by lifting his previous restrictions around outings and visitation.

I saw photos of their wedding, their children and grandchildren, their home, Peter's ordination into the ministry. I followed the prompts Peter gave us about the story of Mary Catherine's significance to him. I began to redirect our work around the issue of what Peter thought his life would be like now.

Therapist:	Peter, I feel honored to go inside your life with Mary Catherine. You have lived out a love story and you described some hard times of ill health, little money, and concern about your drinking. How is your life different since her death?
Peter:	Nothing is the same. I had to move from our apartment into this one room on this floor with all these strangers. I can't remember any of their names. Mary Catherine would have known all their names and everything about their families. She always did all that social stuff in my ministry. I'm not good at that. She was natural.
Therapist:	So everything seemed to get smaller . . . your living space and your social connections.
Peter:	Everything . . . I'm ready to go. The love story is over.
Therapist:	Well, it seems that particular part of the story is gone, but the bigger story doesn't end yet. That's why it might be important to create another part of the story that could go on even when you are gone. You seem close to your grandchildren and your story is a part of their story. Isn't that one of the reasons people write about their lives?

I believe narrative reconstruction is critical to grief reconciliation. In the sixth session, Peter told me about all the losses he experiences without Mary Catherine. My questions had elicited much reminiscence, and Peter seemed slower in his conversations and more resistant to my suggestion of an alternate ending to his love story. I slowed down our reconstruction work to accommodate his timing and to honor what had been true and important to him for sixty years. I used my best reflective skills to follow Peter's lead in communicating his myriad losses since her death.

Peter:	Maybe you are too young to get this but I spent my whole day around her . . . my eating, my sleeping, the chores, the conversations, my prayer life, our times with the family, our friends. When I was sick, she pampered me. When she was sick, I could feel useful when I took care of her. I knew what she liked without asking. I knew what subjects to stay away from in our conversation!

Session 7. This session had to be rescheduled on two occasions because Peter caught pneumonia and was in critical condition for several weeks, including a four-day hospitalization. I sent get-well cards and an anniversary card—Peter had told me how special occasions involving Mary Catherine were unrecognized since her death. As his health improved, we met for a short session to discuss whether we would continue our work. We had initially committed to eight sessions. Peter wanted to continue, and we extended our contract for five more sessions.

<u>Sessions 8–10.</u> Peter left urgent-sounding telephone messages for me, and yet when I contacted him there was no emergency. Peter said he was afraid I was not coming back. I reassured him that we would continue until we both agreed the work was done.

The goal of these three meetings was to continue the story beyond Mary Catherine's death. However, several issues arose that required my attention. Peter was labored in his speech because of difficulty breathing. The staff reported that he lacked the stamina to write very much. Additionally, his sleeping had increased and his social outlets had decreased. The social worker stated that his daughter thought it would be best to discontinue counseling. This was in conflict with Peter's wishes. I discussed this with him, and he stated emphatically that he wanted to continue. I asked if he would mind if I talked with his daughter, and he gave me permission.

I invited Dianne to join our next meeting. I spent much of our time describing what our counseling had been about in the preceding weeks. Dianne voiced concern that her father was "needlessly being dragged through the past," but Peter spoke up, insisting that this was not the case. I explained what I see as the benefits of telling one's story in grief. This seemed important to do, not only to gain Dianne's endorsement of her father's counseling but also because she has been living the loss of her mother. Peter showed Dianne his folder, and she was amazed that he had written so much about her mother over the years. She asked him if she could take the folder and he replied "Yes."

During the next few weeks, Dianne kept the writings and I continued to have sessions with Peter. He did not have the stamina to work actively on assignments outside of our sessions. He did say that he thought the residents would get a lot out of sharing the stories of their lives. I decided to follow through and the staff encouraged Peter to begin such a group. We talked about how he might lead the group. I saw an excitement in Peter that I had not previously seen. His functioning improved over the next few weeks.

<u>Sessions 11 and 12.</u> Peter came to these sessions with his folder of writings. He reported that Dianne encouraged him to put them together to pass on to his grandchildren. He wished that she had asked for them for herself. Peter said, "She learned avoidance from me." We outlined an advertisement for participation in a resident support group.

Peter: I guess I can still minister even though I don't have a church of my own and even though Mary Catherine isn't here to remind me of people's names.

Therapist: Yes . . . you are alive and you still have something to do. For our last session, would you be willing to write a story about what your years with Mary Catherine still mean? You could write about how her death has been important to your understanding of why grieving people need community.

Peter agreed to ask someone to help type as he dictated. Our closing session was spent listening to this writing. Here is an excerpt:

Mary Catherine gave me much of my life for most of it. Then, she suddenly died and all the lights went out. I forgot about my call to the ministry. I had already retired, so being away from the church responsibilities made it easy to forget this mission in my life. I knew people need others in times of great grief. Mary Catherine and I had been called a thousand times to sit with families in times of tragedy and loss. She just kept me focused. Now I realize I have been given a chance to keep this going. I didn't think it would be here. I certainly didn't want it to be without her. But it is and here I am.

Outcome

I felt mostly pleased about our work with Peter. I think he will stay sober and continue to reconcile his grief. Three indicators of grief reconciliation are Peter's investment in reconstructing new meaning while incorporating what is lost, his movement from isolation in his grief to reach out to others, and his self-report of feeling renewed interest in living beyond his loss. The addiction specialist confirmed Peter's commitment to sobriety.

I experienced some surprises throughout the therapy sessions that I processed with Loretta in peer consultation. I did not expect the interruptions associated with Peter's health. The empty bottles of vodka threw me for a loop. I hadn't planned to include any of his children, given their resistance to family counseling. I was pleasantly surprised when Peter started a support group for other residents. Maybe I should have foreseen these things. A look back makes the unfolding process seem much more obvious than it did during our counseling.

Reflections

In hindsight, I might have initiated more family involvement besides Dianne's session with us. Peter could probably have benefited from feeling my advocacy in his family. He repeatedly said that he felt neglected by his children. Family counseling in bereavement situations can provide safe opportunities for multiple narratives of meaning. Family interventions can bridge the separation that is common in grief. Also, I did not work with Peter on the death of his best friend. This was left largely unaddressed.

The most interesting learning for me as a therapist came from seeing Peter's strong attachment to me and subsequent dependency. My presence with him, the regularity and reliability of our visits, was more important to Peter than either of us realized. As a counselor some twenty-five years younger than Peter, I experienced some urges to take care of him in ways I might do with my own parents. Peter interacted with me in a fatherly way. I kept myself aware of how transference and countertransference might be affecting my work. I repeatedly discussed this with Loretta, and she helped a lot with this.

I am in mid-life, with the predictable evaluation of my own relationships and life events. My own father was a minister who lost his beloved wife early in life. I observed how my personal response to him after the death of my mother was so much different from the professional response I offered to Peter. My total lack of objectivity with my own father kept us from assisting each other in our grief. I caught a glimpse of my own family through Peter and Dianne. Somehow I was able to offer more grace as I looked inward at the meaning of my father's death a few years ago. I discovered that I have a strong sense of protection toward others who are older than I am. I'm also having to confront my own vulnerability about aging and death.

Suggested Readings

Balk, D. E. (Ed.). (2007). *Handbook of thanatology*. Northbrook, IL: Association for Death Education and Counseling, The Thanatology Association.

Doka, K. J. (Ed.). (2002). *Living with grief: Loss in later life*. Washington, DC: Hospice Foundation of America.

Gibson, F. (2006). *Reminiscence and recall* (3rd ed.). London, England: Age Concern.

Hospice Foundation of America. (2001). *A guide for recalling and telling your life story*. Washington, DC: author.

Neimeyer, R. (2000). *Lessons of loss: A guide to coping*. Memphis, TN: Center for the Study of Loss and Transition.

Neimeyer, R. (Ed.). (2001). *Meaning reconstruction and the experience of loss*. Washington, DC: American Psychological Association.

Neimeyer, R. A., Prigerson, H. G., & Davies, B. (2002). Mourning and meaning. *American Behavioral Scientist, 46,* 235–251.

Thompson, B. (2003). The expressive arts and the experience of loss. *The Forum, 29*(2).

Whiting, P., & Bradley, L. J. (2007). Artful witnessing of the story: Loss in older adults. *Adultspan Journal, 6,* 119–128.

Whiting, P., & James, E. (2005). Bearing witness to the story: Responses to shadow grief in diverse family contexts. *Journal of Healing Ministry, 12*(1), 31–34.

Biographical Statement

Peggy P. Whiting, Ed.D., is a professor in the Department of Counselor Education at North Carolina Central University. She is a licensed professional counselor and a nationally certified thanatologist with specializations in grief education and grief counseling. Peggy has maintained a private practice for twenty years while teaching in counseling programs at both Vanderbilt and Winthrop Universities. She is the author or co-author of more than 100 articles, presentations, videotapes, and manuals focused on loss. She is the 1998 recipient of the Distinguished Service Award given by the South Carolina Counseling Association for prolonged accomplishment to counseling. You can reach Peggy at pwhiting@nccu.edu.

Loretta J. Bradley, Ph.D., is Paul Whitfield Horn Professor and Coordinator of Counselor Education at Texas Tech University. She is a licensed professional counselor supervisor and a licensed marriage and family therapist and supervisor. Loretta is past president of both the American Counseling Association and the Association for Counselor Education and Supervision. She has authored or co-authored seven books and more than 150 articles and presentations. Loretta is featured in the book, *Legends and Legacies,* edited by J. West, C. J. Osborn, and D. L. Bubenzer (Philadelphia: Brunner-Routledge, 2003), as one of the top twenty-five counselors who have made significant contributions to the counseling profession from 1952 to 2001. You can reach Loretta at loretta.bradley@ttu.edu.

17

"Tired of Living" or "All Packed and Ready to Go"?

Suzanne Degges-White

Jane, 87-year-old widow, mother, grandmother, and great grandmother several times over, had enjoyed exceptional health throughout her life. Only during the past decade had she had to deal with arthritis and heart problems. Jane now lived with her newly divorced oldest grandchild, Penny, and it was Penny who made the referral. She was worried that her grandmother was becoming reclusive and disinterested in conversation and outside activities. For Suzanne Degges-White, depression, the obvious diagnosis, just didn't fit. She found it more helpful to think of Jane's behavior changes within the paradigm of *gerotranscendence*. In this paradigm, Jane was in a life stage marked by "closing in" and selectivity in activities. It is a healthy withdrawal that allows the old person to spend time preparing for the end of life.

My first meeting with Jane Hannah was on a chilly winter's day in the home in which she had lived for over sixty years in a city in the Triad region of North Carolina. Jane was an 87-year-old widow, mother, grandmother, and great grandmother several times over. Jane's husband had died some twenty years earlier, and after Jane had adjusted to being alone, she was able to continue living a busy and vibrant life. It was only eighteen months ago that her newly divorced oldest grandchild, Penny, needed a place to stay and had moved into Jane's home. Penny was a 27-year-old middle school teacher, and she and Jane had a comfortable relationship. Penny attributed the success of her move to her grandmother's strong, independent spirit and her awareness of the value of privacy and respect for others.

It was Penny who contacted me about changes in her grandmother's demeanor, mood, and behaviors. Penny was referred by a former client. I was a licensed professional counselor in my state, and I saw a small number of private practice clients in addition to my part-time position offering adjunctive counseling services at a medical center. Penny said she would foot the cost of the counseling, and so insurance reimbursement was not a factor.

When I was able to connect with Penny on the telephone after a few rounds of telephone tag, she provided a brief biography of her grandmother. Penny told me that Jane was very fortunate financially, as her husband had been a successful attorney and investor. They had been frugal throughout their lives and the family home had been paid off long ago. They had comfortably met the needs of their three children and now were able to assist with college tuition for their four grandchildren. As both Jane and her husband had graduated from college, and in fact had met at the state university, they very much valued education. Two of the Hannahs' children had left the immediate area but were still close to their mother. A third child, Andrew, and his wife lived only a half-hour away in a suburb of the larger city.

Jane had been exceptionally healthy throughout her life, and only during the past decade had she begun to deal with arthritis and heart problems. Jane's life since entering her 60s had been one of regular involvement in church, closeness with her family, and volunteer work with community organizations in the area. According to Penny, Jane was one of those women who modeled strength and spirit and was known by family and friends as living the type of life they all hoped they would be able to do themselves as they aged.

The description Penny provided of Jane's current status, however, was quite different. Penny shared with me that in the past couple of months, Jane was becoming reclusive, less interested in engaging in conversation and outings, likely to let the phone ring without answering. Jane complained about being short of breath and was reluctant to leave the house, stating "I'd just rather stay in and think a bit." These changes led Penny to contact Jane's physician and to seek mental health care. I made an appointment for my first visit with Jane a couple of weeks before her next scheduled appointment with her doctor.

Conceptualization

The changes in Jane's behavior, as described by Penny, at first led me to consider depression as a diagnosis. Penny saw her grandmother withdrawing from friends and family, avoiding the activities that had always brought her pleasure, and just not "doing as much as she used to." Although these observations of Jane seemed to match some of the diagnostic requirements for depression, I had heard nothing to indicate that her mental state supported such a diagnosis. Penny denied that her grandmother was in any way verbalizing thoughts of suicidal ideation, worthlessness, or hopelessness.

I began reflecting on the possibility that depression was off-target and started viewing Jane's behavioral changes within the paradigm of gerotranscendence. Gerotranscendence is a process in which older adults shift focus from the "here and now" to a more universal and transcendent perspective. This transition is marked by a "closing in" and increased selectivity in choices of interests, activities, and social interactions. Building on the eighth stage of Erikson's psychosocial model, gerotranscendence is typified by a desire to cultivate a sense of integrity and personal acceptance of one's life choices as the end of life approaches. I refer readers who wish to learn more about the concept of gerotranscendence to my article, "Understanding Gerotranscendence in Older Adults: A New Perspective for Counselors," in *Adultspan Journal* (Spring 2005).

After my first session with Jane on that chilly winter day, I became convinced that depression was not the preferred diagnosis. A more natural, nonpathological, turning-inward was occurring. She acknowledged that she had less tolerance for activities she felt were unnecessary; she now preferred the company of herself to others, for the most part; and she affirmed that these changes had been a bit surprising early on, but they now seemed to be the "right way to be."

Thus, we began our counseling work together within the unique paradigm of gerotranscendence, which would allow us to focus on the three dimensions encompassed by this process: *social and individual relationships, the self,* and *the cosmic.* I decided that it would be beneficial to include Penny in at least one of our sessions to help her better understand the changes in their relationship. I viewed the upcoming process to be an opportunity for unmatched personal growth for all of us.

Process

Feeling that it was important to help Penny cope with her grandmother's behavioral changes, I decided that with Jane's permission, I would include Penny in our next counseling session. I also believed that the work done with Jane would be brief in duration, as her current state-of-mind was quite healthy, when dying was viewed as a natural transition. Therefore, I proposed evaluating our progress after three additional counseling sessions with an open invitation to continue or recommence at a later date, if Jane felt it necessary.

Session 2. *Social and Individual Relationships.* This session with Jane also included Penny. I felt that helping Penny gain a better understanding of Jane's feelings and beliefs was important to helping Penny handle the impending transition her grandmother would complete. During this session, I discussed briefly the awareness many older adults gain as they recognize their mortality and the need to prepare themselves emotionally and spiritually for their passage from their earthly life. As is often the case, this open discussion of a loved one's death brought out Penny's own fears of death and dying.

Penny: I just can't stand the thought of you talking about dying, Gramma J. You've always a mover and shaker! You'd never let anyone else talk about slowing down, so I just can't understand what's changed with you. I'm scared. . . . I don't want to think about you dying, and I don't like hearing you talk about "The End" like you've been doing.

Jane: No, Penny, I've never easily tolerated others' laziness or procrastination or poor attitudes, for that matter. But there comes a time, Penny, when a body knows it's time to slow down and think about where they've been, what they've accomplished, the people they've loved, and even the people they've wronged. And it's time for that for me, Penny. I've done a lot of living in my eighty-seven years, and I've also done a lot of loving—of your grandfather, your father and his siblings, you grandchildren, my friends, my own parents and family. Relationships matter, Penny, and they matter to us throughout our lives, and sometimes it's at the very end before we can really look at how we've treated others and be honest with ourselves. And that's part of what I'm doing, now, Penny. Looking back at all the people I've known and cared about, and even hurt. It's time for me to take stock, Penny, and this requires time alone for me—time and space for me to look at the good—and the harm—I may have done to those I've loved. It's right, Penny, for me to do this, and I need to do some accounting to myself for my choices.

Penny: But I worry when you are sitting by yourself, when you don't want to go out and do things. I feel like you're slipping away or lost in your own world or something.

Jane: Penny, I am doing a little of what you call "slipping away to my own little world" now. It's time for this—I'm not scared, I'm not wanting to hurt you or anyone else, it's just time for me to think about moving on to another place. I love you, Penny.

Counselor: Penny, your grandmother is doing some important work as she prepares to leave this world.

As the session continued, Penny shared some of her favorite memories of Jane with us; she talked about the stories Jane had told the grandchildren of her own youth, and of their father and his siblings. Penny had learned many important lessons about life and family from her grandmother, and Penny took this opportunity to share these with Jane, as well as to let Jane know just how much she appreciated having such an extraordinary grandmother as a role model. After the session, as Penny and I were going down the porch steps, she teared up a bit and told me that while she was angry at having to talk about her grandmother's eventual death, she was glad that she'd been given a "formal opportunity" to begin the process of letting go.

Penny also decided to ask family members and friends of her grandmother to write down a favorite memory and send a photo to her so that she could create a "memory book" of her grandmother's life. Penny said that she realized that this was very selfish on her part and was really a legacy she wanted for herself, rather than being something "for" her grandmother. This is a good example of the discrepancy in perspectives that can occur regarding the passage from life into death between older adults and those who feel they are being "left behind." Jane had made it clear to Penny that she was accepting the upcoming passage from life, and this offered comfort to Penny, but Penny was just now facing the beginning of her own grief at the impending loss.

Session 3. *The Self.* During this session, which occurred two weeks later, only Jane and I met. Jane shared that she felt so much easier about things with Penny after our last session. Jane said it was harder, by far, to see the hurt others felt when someone was leaving this world than it was to prepare to leave it oneself. She went on to say that at 87, "you're too old to settle scores," but that allowing herself time to make sense of all the relationships she'd had brought peace with herself.

This level of self-acceptance is always a welcome step in the counseling process. Consonant with Erikson's theory of psychosocial development, the framework of gerotranscendence addresses the need to attain a sense of integrity about one's life path. This can be accomplished via the type of life review in which Jane was engaged.

Jane continued to open up about her "private scores" with life. She talked about the pride she felt in how she'd raised her family, how she'd been, overall, a good daughter herself, and the joy she had taken in her world. She also acknowledged that she was very grateful that she and her husband, whom she described as a man as perfect as the world would allow, had found each other early in their lives and been "selfish" about their relationship at times. Jane revealed that although she had lost many people in her life, she felt joy.

Jane acknowledged that physical aging was more bother than she'd expected, but she felt blessed in that her mind was still sharp. I encouraged Jane to share with me a description of herself that avoided mention of limitations or physical challenges. The words she used included "honest to a fault," "never shirk my duties," "a Good Samaritan," "faithful and loyal," "spiritual and God-loving," "tough as nails," and "love a good joke—whether it's pulled on me or I'm doing the pulling." Jane said that the good she'd done in this world far outweighed any harm. She chuckled as she made this comment. Jane joked that "I hope I'm called home soon, because I'm sure God could use another good'un like me up there these days."

As I was leaving Jane's home, Penny walked me to my car and said that she had just received a phone call from Jane's physician. Jane's heart was weakening and she was being admitted to the hospital the next day. Penny asked if I thought I should schedule a session in the hospital. I asked her to check with Jane. A day later, Jane phoned and asked me if I'd be willing to hold our session in her hospital room.

Session 4. *The Cosmic.* I entered Jane's hospital room, full of the requisite stainless steel and monitors, and was surprised to see how content Jane looked as her eyes and smile beamed at me across the room. She was sitting up in bed and there was a chair pulled up to the side to which she motioned me to sit. Before I could barely get a greeting out, Jane began speaking.

Jane: Well, I've been hooked up to all these monitors since yesterday, and I have to admit that I don't like being tethered to anything. I understand that a doctor's job is to heal the sick and prolong life, but I have to tell you, that I know it's not what's in *my* best interest, nowadays. I have been watching everyone here hustle around, responding to beeps and drips and whatnot, but for me, it's just not what I want. I want these tests finished and to be back in my own home. I guess my belief in the hereafter makes it easier for me now. Death isn't about the end for the person who's dying, but it feels that way for the living, doesn't it?

Counselor: Yes, it does. Please tell me more about your beliefs about death.

Jane: Well, to me, dying is just a way of moving on to another, better place. I feel like God puts us here to learn lessons, to raise our families, to do our best to show Him our love. I believe that by dying, God is giving us the chance to join Him in His world. I'm not sure what heaven is gonna' look like—it may be streets of gold or it may be just a beautiful meadow, but I do know I'll never want for anything there, that I'll be surrounded by people who love me and care about me—much as I was in this life. And I'm expecting that I'll still be able to be close to those I leave behind, that I'll be able to watch over them, if they need that. I can't imagine heaven being a place where that doesn't happen.

Counselor: So, it sounds as if you feel confident about your next "adventure."

Jane: Yes, Suzanne, I am confident. I'm eager to see what God has in store for me next.

Hospital staff interrupted our visit to let Jane know that she was going to the lab in a few minutes for another test. I then reminded Jane that this was the last session we had scheduled and invited her to share with me her feelings about the work we'd done. Jane said that it was surprising how ready she felt to die and how joyful she felt as she looked back over her life. She laughed as she affirmed that this was truly the way to "go out in style." She thought that Penny felt some relief now. Jane hoped that this experience might be a foundation for Penny when she had to cope with the loss of her own mother and father.

■ Outcome

It was barely a week later that Penny called and told me that Jane had slipped away the night before at her home. Her heart had given out. I felt a surprising sense of loss. I reminded myself that Jane was indeed ready for this, that she had done important work up to her final days, and that it was with integrity and dignity that she passed from this life. I made the decision to attend Jane's funeral and was gratified to see that with Penny's direction, the service was a celebration of Jane's life. Penny displayed the memory book that she had begun creating for her Gramma J, and it was with relief that I overheard Penny sharing with attendees that "Gramma J was such an extraordinary woman—she took care of all those she loved here on earth and when it came time for her to pass on, she took care of herself so that she'd be ready for her first face-to-face meeting with God."

■ Reflections

I think sometimes younger people are surprised at the strength of spirit and temperament displayed by older adults. Sadly, within our society, older adults are treated as if they were all the same—an invisible population, lumped together for ease of care. Working with Jane, I had a delightful opportunity to witness a strong woman face the final life transition in such a way as to serve as a model. Jane was luckier than some older adults, who must live out their final days in a residential care setting. The case of Jane underscores the importance of providing individualized care and treatment for older adults. It is important that the needs of older adults are assessed for each unique individual and that we listen carefully to what older adults share with us. With Jane, we used life review as a way of allowing her to make sense of her story, and this is important in arriving at a sense of integrity, purpose, and meaning of life. By acknowledging the fact of death, older adults are given the opportunity to prepare themselves for this final life transition, whereas avoiding the topic can fuel fear and foster false hopes. Finding time for solitude may be an important need for older adults, whereas pushing them to "join in" with group activities may deprive them of the chance to spend needed time reflecting and mentally preparing for the end of life. Rather than asking someone "How do you feel today?" it might be more beneficial to encourage him or her to "Tell me about your life."

Suggested Readings

Gamliel, T. (2001). A social version of gerotranscendence: Case study. *Journal of Aging and Identity, 6,* 105–114.

Jonson, H., & Magnusson, J. A. (2001). A new age of old age? Gerotranscendence and the re-enchantment of aging. *Journal of Aging Studies, 15,* 318–332.

Tornstam, L. (2005). *Gerotranscendence: A developmental theory of positive aging.* New York: Springer.

Wadensten, B. (2005). Introducing older people to the theory of gerotranscendence. *Journal of Advanced Nursing, 52,* 381–388.

Wadensten, B., & Carlsson, M. (2001). A qualitative study of nursing staff members' interpretations of signs of gerotranscendence. *Journal of Advanced Nursing, 36,* 635–642.

Wadensten, B., & Carlsson, M. (2003). Theory-driven guidelines for practical care of older people based on the theory of gerotranscendence. *Journal of Advanced Nursing, 41,* 462–470.

Biographical Statement

Suzanne Degges-White, Ph.D., is an assistant professor in the department of Counseling and Development at Purdue University Calumet. She is a licensed mental health counselor and has practiced since 2001. She has worked with clients of all ages, from children to older adults. She also has extensive experience working with clients coping with chronic illness. She has completed extensive research on women and their midlife transitions and has published articles related to aging, women's development across the life span, and identity development. You can reach Suzanne at dwhites@calumet.purdue.edu.

The Music of Memory

Bret Hendricks and Loretta J. Bradley

Bret Hendricks was under contract to counsel residents of a nursing home. Brenda, 87, was referred when staff complained about her "agitated depression" and wreaking havoc. Despite mild strokes, Hendricks concluded that Brenda's mental function wasn't impaired. He used cognitive therapy to clear up the distortions that triggered her depression. He played music to help Brenda remember past events. Hendricks was also a strong advocate for his client. In Reflections, Hendricks shares his personal experience in getting help for his own mother in a nursing home.

Brenda Wallace, 87, had been a resident of a nursing home for six months. As a counselor in private practice, I met Brenda when I contracted with nursing homes to provide professional counseling services. Brenda was referred to me for counseling by Paula, a social worker. My co-author, Loretta Bradley, also consulted at this facility. We have often consulted with each other about cases such as this.

Brenda, who had experienced two mild strokes, one of which precipitated her admission to the nursing home, was wreaking havoc. "I think that she has agitated depression," Paula said. "We have gotten to the point where we just don't know what to do with her. She walks the halls. She goes into other residents' rooms and goes through drawers. She becomes very belligerent when we tell her to go back to her room. She forgets little things, but overall she knows exactly what she is doing. She says that she has nightmares and cannot sleep, and she cries all the time."

In spite of this behavior, which immediately led me to suspect cognitive deficits due to the strokes, Paula reported that Brenda had few cognitive deficiencies. She had some short-term memory loss but otherwise strong recall. She could easily play games such as dominoes and bingo. Indeed, she was the bingo champion for the last month.

The nursing home is located at the edge of a small rural town in West Texas. Almost all of the residents depend on farming for a living. It is a ninety-bed facility that has been in operation for about twenty years and is the town's only facility of this type. It is part of the regional culture, and townspeople conduct church services, singings, arts and crafts, and story reading at "the home."

Conceptualization

In the first interview, I noted that Brenda was oriented to person, place, and time. She successfully completed a mini mental status exam. She was forgetful but fully able to process information that was presented in a logical fashion.

At the second interview, I administered the Beck Depression Inventory, and this supported my opinion that Brenda was depressed. For example, on one item she answered that she did not get satisfaction from the things that she used to enjoy. She told me that she felt guilty and believed that she was being punished; further, she was more irritated by things than usual.

Brenda told me that she had never received treatment for depression. In the written referral to me for counseling, the medical director stated, "If counseling does not alleviate depressive symptoms to a significant degree, then meds will be assigned."

I thought that Brenda needed an approach that addressed her cognitive distortions and anchored her firmly in the present. I decided on Aaron T. Beck's cognitive therapy (CT).

Brenda was presenting classic cognitive distortions as described by Beck (Beck, Rush, Shaw, & Emery, 1979). Beck believes that these systematic errors in reasoning must be reframed. Here are examples of Brenda's cognitive distortions.

Arbitrary inference. Brenda was told that her money was being held in trust so that her daughter could access it for her. Brenda immediately thought that her daughter had "stolen" her money.

Selective abstraction. Brenda said a nurse told her she would have to wait "a few minutes" to use the phone. Brenda assumed that this nurse thought Brenda would forget in "a few minutes"; therefore, Brenda assumed the nurse believed Brenda to be "crazy."

Overgeneralization. Brenda walked into the dining room and saw the nurse whom Brenda believed thought she was "crazy." Brenda sat at a dining table and became more and more agitated as dinner progressed. She finally became so frustrated that she picked up a piece of bread and threw it at the nurse.

Magnification and minimization. Brenda said that she overheard a conversation between the nursing aides in which one of the aides said that state auditors were coming to the nursing home for an annual accreditation visit. After some consideration, Brenda now believes the auditors are coming because there are major problems at the nursing home. Her fear is that the officials will close it, and thus she will no longer have a place to live.

Personalization. When a physician came to visit Brenda one time and did not return, Brenda believed that he did not return because he did not like her. When he did see her, he told her that he would only see her one time because he was moving, and yet Brenda concluded, "He did not come back because he did not like me." She was extremely distraught about his not liking her. She cried for days, believing that she no longer had medical care and that she could get sick and no one would know what to do to help her.

Labeling and mislabeling. Brenda stated that she should have forced her son to stay home the night that he was killed; thus she believed that she should not have allowed him to go to a party that she knew he should not go to because the party was with "wild kids." Her assertion is that she was a total failure as a parent because she made this perceived mistake in the past.

Polarized thinking. Brenda stated that she would not find friends at the nursing home; thus, she would always be lonely and die alone.

In addition to CT, I decided to use music therapy. Music therapy techniques combined with CT help clients express thoughts and feelings (Hanser & Thompson, 1994). Music has been used as a form of therapy in a variety of residential and adult day care centers to elevate mood and decrease depressive symptoms (Hanser, 1988; Hanser & Thompson, 1994). Hanser and Thompson (1994) reported that music therapy reduced depression for older adults. I have used music therapy techniques successfully with depressed adolescents. In Brenda's case, I hoped that music would facilitate remembrance of past events.

Finally, advocacy is almost always an important intervention for therapists working with nursing home residents, even when the home is of high quality, as is the case here.

■ Process

Following two introductory visits, I saw Brenda weekly for twelve weeks, after which we met biweekly for eight weeks and then once a month for three months.

Introductory Visits. I noticed a group of eight residents in the lobby listening to a story being read by a girl about 12 years old. Across from this group were two elderly women watching a basketball game on television. As I proceeded down the hall, Paula greeted me. "We are so glad you are here."

That very morning Brenda had told staff that she would walk out the front door to visit her daughter, Sophie, and "No one is going to stop me." Apparently, no one did, and Brenda walked two blocks in thirty-degree weather before anyone noticed. She wasn't even wearing a coat. The staff found her and escorted her back. Brenda told them that the town had changed and she did not remember where she was. This scared the staff, because runaway behavior is a major safety risk. The staff had to consider placing her in a locked unit, reserved for clients with major dementia.

The door to Brenda's room was open. It was a sunny room with a private bathroom. There were photos going back to the 1940s. There were pictures of two women, one about 45 and the other about 25. The bed was covered with an intricate quilt. The nightstand held a stack of paperbacks, a clock radio, and a lamp. There was a slightly worn recliner facing a small television, which was off.

Brenda was sitting in the recliner. She was a small woman with perfectly coifed white hair. She was wearing a purple pantsuit with wide lapels, and a white blouse. Bright orange earrings and red plastic bracelets completed the ensemble. She had large blue eyes, which were now peering at both Paula and me.

"Brenda, you have a visitor," Paula announced.

"No one told me that I was having company," Brenda replied as she held her hand out to me. She spoke with effort, and her words were a bit slurred. Other than this, I didn't see any stroke symptoms. She had a firm handshake. When Paula told her that I was a counselor, Brenda smiled and looked directly at Paula. "I would prefer to meet visitors in the lobby." Brenda slowly reached for the walker next to her chair. Paula made a resigned gesture and told Brenda we would wait in the lobby.

I told Paula that it might be better if I met Brenda alone. It took Brenda only minutes to walk up the hall. Brenda informed me that she had made her beaded purse herself. "Isn't it pretty?" I complimented her on her work, and I asked her if we could meet in the small family room adjoining the lobby. As we sat down, I told her that I was a counselor, and I was there to give her assistance. She smiled, patted my hand, and said, "I sure do need assistance." I explained about informed consent. I checked with her frequently to ascertain understanding. Brenda asked appropriate questions and clearly understood that she was giving her consent for me to speak to medical staff, nursing home staff, and her family.

Brenda told me that she was a lifelong resident of the town and that since the early 1940s, she and her husband had owned a farm implement company. While she described herself as a homemaker, she said that she also worked part-time at their business as a bookkeeper. Brenda's husband, John, died ten years ago of pancreatic cancer. Their daughter, Sophie, still lived in town. Their son, Adam, was killed in a car wreck in 1966 at age 16.

Brenda had voluntarily agreed to go the nursing home because of "not being able to take of myself." She had been driving prior to her moving to the nursing home, and she reported having two accidents. "In the first wreck, the policeman said I was going the wrong way down the street. In the second wreck, I just didn't see the other car and hit the back end. No one was hurt."

Brenda told me that she dislikes the nursing home and misses her home and neighbors. "I am so sad all the time. I cry every day, and I don't sleep. I have nightmares. I can't eat very much." Then, sighing heavily, "I don't know anyone here except for some ladies with whom I used to attend church. When I talk to them, they just look at me like they don't know who I am. I guess they just don't like me now that I am here."

I asked Brenda about her leaving the facility this morning. "I left to find my daughter; you know she lives just up the street. I know that the nurses don't like me because they are always complaining about not getting any time off. If I wasn't here, they would not have to work all the time. Anyway, when I went to see Sophie, I guess I took the wrong street because I couldn't find her house. It sure was cold out there. I'm afraid I'm going to get sick now." Brenda further explained, "I have a problem with my daughter. You know, she took all my money. Now that I don't have any money, I don't know what to do. I've asked Sophie about this, and she tells me that I don't need to worry about a thing. Well, I am worried. I don't know why Sophie would lie to me about this, but I know that I don't have any money and she can sign on my bank account." Of course, this raised a red flag, and I made inquiries. As per the social worker's investigation, there was no substance to Brenda's accusations against Sophie.

Brenda was very willing to share concrete historical details of her past. However, she would not discuss her relationship with John in any terms other than the dates of their marriage and some details of his funeral. Likewise, she would not discuss Adam's death other than relating that she felt she was a failure as a parent because she did not prevent him from going out the night he was killed. It was obvious to me that Brenda felt that she had no control of her life.

While Brenda seemed to enjoy some aspects of nursing home life, she refused to acknowledge this. She complained about the church service. "I don't like the music or the pastor. I miss my old church." Although she regularly played bingo and won, she lamented, "Bingo is boring." She liked the food, though she was rarely hungry enough to enjoy it. It was difficult to find people with whom to have a conversation. She did enjoy letter writing to friends. She shook my hand, smiled, and said, "I enjoy talking to you. Come back anytime." I gave her my card and told her that I would be back.

It was during a second introductory visit that I administered the Beck Depression Inventory that I discussed above in the Conceptualization section.

Session 3. Here begins an account of some of our formal sessions. Brenda questioned me about how often we were going to meet. I threw the question back at her, and she asked for two sessions per week. We wrote the schedule on her calendar. I told her that I use music in counseling, and I played a CD, "I'll Be Seeing You" by

Sammy Fain. Brenda's expression softened and her eyes watered. I asked her to talk about memories that she associated with the song. She remembered dancing with her husband to this song. At the end of the session, I reminded her that she had earlier told me she did not think she was a good wife. I said to her that after hearing descriptions of the enjoyment she and her husband shared, she was presenting a different picture of her marriage. She said, "I guess that you mostly remember the hard times." Brenda began the process of reframing memories of her marriage. "I want to write this down," she said as she reached for a piece of paper. I was impressed that she remembered to bring paper and pen to our sessions. She wrote constantly. I noticed that her writing, which was abnormally deliberate because of the strokes, became more proficient as time progressed.

Session 4. I asked Brenda how long it had been since someone gave her homework. "Seventy years! And I hated homework," she replied. I asked her to write about good memories of her husband so that we could look at these at our next counseling session. She responded, "That doesn't sound too bad."

Session 5. Brenda exclaimed, "I had so much fun remembering some old times with John and our friends." I noticed that she had written something almost every day. She shared, "It was so hard when I lost him, I just have not wanted to think about it, I guess."

Sessions 6 and 7. We listened to "A Ghost of a Chance" by Victor Young. Brenda said that the song made her feel uneasy and a little scared. I asked her about a time in the past when she had been scared. She told me about when she and her husband had a disagreement about household finances, "It got so bad that we called each other names. It was the only time that he ever left the house because of an argument. I knew sure as certain that he would come back and tell me to pack my bags. He didn't, though. He came back and sat down to look at television and did not say another word about the fight. The next day he apologized for calling me names." We talked about how fear can be overwhelming. She said that she had felt that way recently about the nursing home being closed by state auditors, ". . . and then where will I be?" Her fear was based on a conversation she overheard between the nurses' aides. I told her that the audit was routine and that she was overgeneralizing. Brenda concluded, "I guess that I am speaking too soon, for it is kind of like that argument with John." In both cases, she was afraid of having to leave her home. "So, if I'm afraid, I should ask rather than just worrying."

I asked Brenda to name some songs she enjoyed when she was younger. She named several titles, trying to sing some of the melodies when she could not remember the title. Although I went home and searched my compact disc collection, which was definitely lacking in some of the titles that she suggested, I did have a Benny Goodman collection, and he was one of her favorites. I played a Goodman CD for her, and she loved it. We developed a pattern in ensuing sessions. We first listened to Benny Goodman's music and then talked about the memories and feelings the song elicited. Next, we talked about recent times that she had these feelings. "When have you felt any of these feelings lately?" would be the question that I posed to Brenda.

Initially, Brenda resisted and talked only about negative emotions; with some redirection, she began to relate more positive emotions.

When counseling began, Brenda emphatically stated that Sophie moved her to the nursing home because "she thinks I am crazy." "She doesn't like me anymore." In an attempt to reframe these cognitive distortions, I asked Brenda to tell me song titles that reminded her of her daughter. She smiled and said "Little Susie." We listened to "Little Suzie" at the next session. Brenda remembered when she was not able to attend a spelling bee that Sophie won. I quickly asked her to "freeze the frame" and think about other situations in which she had attended Sophie's functions. Brenda recalled many band concerts, including one held when there was much snow on the ground. "Lord, I thought that I was going to have a wreck getting there. I almost fell going into the school. When I did get in, there were hardly any parents. She was so proud that I was there and I was glad I went."

Paula told me that Brenda was less tearful. Additionally, Paula said that Brenda was not asking staff to call her daughter as frequently. But Paula was worried about Brenda's lack of appetite, "Brenda has lost another five pounds, and we cannot get her to eat." Paula had consulted with the medical director, who said that he would look into it. Soon after our seventh session, medical tests showed an irritation in her digestive tract. She was prescribed medication, and it helped.

Session 8. After another Benny Goodman song, Brenda abruptly said she wanted to tell me about her son. She took a deep breath and, with great clarity, told me about her son, who was killed in a car accident at age 16. "Adam was a handsome boy. He could play football better than any of the other boys." Brenda stated that Adam had "decent" grades, although he was not good at reading. She wondered if he had dyslexia, "Adam just had problems. He started going out with these wild boys who drank." "I tried everything to get him to come in early. I grounded him, and he went right on." "I felt so helpless." Brenda told me that in the previous week she had remembered things about her son that she had not thought of in years, "It was like I was back there with him." She told me about a wonderful fishing trip with the entire family. "He knew that we loved him, but he sure could be a handful."

I reminded her that she had told me earlier that she thought she was a failure as a mother because she had not prevented her son from leaving the house on the night that he was killed. I said, "From what you have told me, he was a strong-willed young man. There was probably nothing you could do to stop him from going out that night."

"You are right. If we had tried to stop him, he would have gone right out the window like he always did." She said that it was God's will for her to have him for a little while and then to let him go. She reiterated, "It just makes me so sad to talk about him." In an attempt to reframe, I talked to her about the differences between being sad and being self-blaming. Brenda said, "I guess that I always blamed myself because I wanted things to be different. I see that I did all I knew to do with him. I really could not have changed things, could I?"

Sessions 9 and 10. During the tenth session, Brenda said, "I don't have much money, but could I buy that Benny Goodman music from you?" I was happy to give it to her. I talked to Paula about getting Brenda a tape player/CD, and she found a way to make it happen.

Brenda was showing fewer symptoms of depression. I administered another Beck Depression Inventory, and she came out normal. She was more receptive to feedback from nursing home staff and no longer viewed staff as the enemy. I saw fewer cognitive distortions. Overall, Brenda was doing much better, and I suggested that we see each other every other week. Brenda looked at me and said, "That would be fine. There is a new lady who cries all the time. I think she needs to see you." In what I considered to be a therapeutic milestone, Brenda reluctantly admitted that she needed to be in care at the nursing home.

Thus, I began to see Brenda every two weeks. Eventually, we began to see each other once a month. Once, I stopped by Brenda's room and she was listening to Benny Goodman. She smiled, "They just don't have music like that anymore, do they?"

Outcome

I continued working with Brenda and saw her depression decrease. Three months after counseling was terminated, Paula told me that Brenda was eating with a large group in the dining room and taking part in activities. Sophie brought more music for Brenda to listen to.

Six months after we stopped counseling, I found out that she longer needed medication for depression. At about that time, I ran into her in the hall. She shook my hand and said, "I am keeping company with a gentleman. My daughter is about to throw a fit." I told her that I was very happy for her. She said, "Well, I get along pretty good to be 81 years old." I did not remind her that she was really 87 years old.

Although I have not seen Brenda for more than four years and neither has Loretta, my co-author and colleague, I often remember the work that we did together. Music served as a catalyst for Brenda's recall. Further, when Brenda started listening to music, other residents were attracted to her room, and she made some friends. Brenda took pride in learning to operate the tape player. All for the good.

Reflections

For Loretta and me, Brenda's case is a reminder to check ourselves regarding stereotypical beliefs about older adults in nursing homes. First, Brenda taught me that not all persons in nursing homes are in frail health, nor are they experiencing major cognitive deficits. Indeed, Brenda's physical health was remarkably good, and her hearing and eyesight were good. Cognitively, she was sometimes forgetful; however, once the depressive symptoms were addressed, this tended to dissipate. I would sometimes overhear a staff person saying that a resident was "having the usual problems adjusting to nursing home life." I have not found any usual or predictable pattern to a resident's "adjustment."

Some new residents of a nursing home, whose cognitions are less intact, may need very concrete statements about their new surroundings so that they are physically oriented. These persons do not need to process their move extensively, because this would create more confusion for them. In other words, some residents need to look back and process the reasons for the placement, while others may need to be very present-oriented.

I was learning about nursing home care first-hand during this time. During the first week that I was working with Brenda, my own mother, who had been diagnosed with Parkinson's disease, was admitted to a skilled nursing facility as a result of a fractured hip. Her admission to the nursing home and subsequent absence from her home where she had lived with my father for forty-eight years was a huge adjustment for my family. My mother had always been an active individual and very self-sufficient. While I was grateful that mother had a caring social worker, I was also disappointed to find that the facility had no counseling services. Mother's options were restricted by funding sources; therefore, we had little choice as to which facility she was "allowed" to go to. There were many times I wished mother could have counseling, and many times I thought of her when I visited Brenda. I thought often of how beneficial counseling would have been for my father also. This was the first time that he and my mother had been separated in forty-eight years of marriage. I became vociferous in my quest to make counseling available to the residents of this home. Each time I asked about counseling, I was told by administrators, "We really should look into that sometime." I am proud to say that I persisted in my quest, and six months after my mother was admitted, a counselor (not me) began contract work, providing much-needed services for residents and their families. The counselor also became a valuable consultant to the staff, who grew to depend on the counselor for assistance in developing treatment protocols and positive behavioral supports. As I am writing this, I realize how much I wish my mother had known her influence in implementing counseling services at "her" nursing home, which she referred to as "the hotel." She was a strong advocate of counseling, and although she died before counseling was available at "the hotel," she often told other residents about her son, who "helped people like us."

References

Beck, A T., Rush, A., Shaw, B., & Emery, G. (1979). *Cognitive therapy of depression.* New York: Guilford Press.

Hanser, S. (1988). Controversy in music listening stress reduction research. *The Arts in Psychotherapy, 15*, 211–217.

Hanser, S. B., & Thompson, L. W. (1994). Effects of music therapy strategies on depressed older adults. *Journal of Gerontology, 49*(6), 265–269.

Suggested Readings

Berger, B. (1992). Counseling the elderly in a therapeutic recreation setting: An overview. *Activities, Adaptation & Aging, 17*, 57–63.

Crose, R. (1990). Establishing and maintaining intimate relationships among nursing home residents. *Journal of Mental Health Counseling, 12*, 102–106.

Duffy, M. (1992). A multimethod model for practicum and clinical supervision in nursing homes. *Counselor Education and Supervision, 32*, 61–69.

Faber A. J. (2003). Therapy with the elderly: A collaborative approach. *Journal of Family Psychotherapy, 14*, 1–14.

Giordano, J. A. (2000). Effective communication and counseling with older adults. *International Journal of Aging & Human Development, 51*, 315–324.

Harris, H. L. (1998). Ethnic minority elders: Issues and interventions. *Educational Gerontology, 24,* 309–323.

Hern, B. G., & Weis, D. M. (1991). A group counseling experience with the very old. *Journal for Specialists in Group Work, 16*, 143–151.

Hill, A., & Brettle, A. (2006). Counselling older people: What can we learn from research evidence? *Journal of Social Work Practice, 20*, 281–297.

Kawamura, N., Niyama, M., & Niyama, H. (2007). Long-term evaluation of animal-assisted therapy for institutionalized elderly people: A preliminary result. *Psychogeriatrics, 7*, 8–13.

Lewis, M. M. (2001). Spirituality, counseling, and elderly: An introduction to the spiritual life review. *Journal of Adult Development, 8*, 231–240.

Mosher-Ashley, P. M. (1995). Attendance patterns of elders who accepted counseling following referral to a mental health center. *Clinical Gerontologist, 16*, 3–19.

Norris, M. P., Molinari, V., & Ogland-Hand, S. (Eds.). (2003). *Emerging trends in psychological practice in long-term care*. New York: Haworth Press.

Norton, E. D. (1998). Counseling substance-abusing older clients. *Educational Gerontology, 24,* 373–389.

Qualls, S. H., & Knight, B. G. (Eds.). (2006). *Psychotherapy for depression in older adults*. Hoboken, NJ: John Wiley & Sons.

Westburg, N. G. (2003). Hope, laughter and humor in residents and staff at an assisted living facility. *Journal of Mental Health Counseling, 25*, 16–32.

Biographical Statement

Bret Hendricks, Ed.D., is an assistant professor of counselor education at Texas Tech University. He is a Licensed Professional Counselor and a Licensed Professional Counselor Supervisor. His major areas of research include adolescent studies, at-risk adolescents, treatment of depression for older adults, substance abuse treatment, and the use of music therapy techniques in counseling. Prior to his employment at Texas Tech, Bret was Clinical Coordinator for Children and Adolescent Programs at the Lubbock Regional Mental Health Mental Retardation Center. Bret is president of the International Association of Marriage and Family Counselors and on the board of directors of the Texas Association for Adult Aging and Development. You can reach Bret at bret.hendricks@ttu.edu.

Loretta J. Bradley, Ph.D., is Paul Whitfield Horn Professor and Coordinator of Counselor Education at Texas Tech University. She is a licensed professional counselor supervisor and a licensed marriage and family therapist and supervisor. Loretta is past president of both the American Counseling Association and the Association for Counselor Education and Supervision. She has authored or co-authored seven books and more than 150 articles and presentations. Loretta is featured in the book, *Legends and Legacies,* edited by J. West, C. J. Osborn, and D. L. Bubenzer (Philadelphia: Brunner-Routledge, 2003), as one of the top twenty-five counselors who have made significant contributions to the counseling profession from 1952 to 2001. You can reach Loretta at loretta.bradley@ttu.edu.

Index